LONDON · PAR AVION · FAST POST · AIR MAIL

Love, Loss, and Moving On

Lorie Kleiner Eckert

RoseWK
Publishing

Cover and book design by Mark Sullivan

ISBN (paperback): 978-0-578-21571-6
ISBN (e-book): 978-0-578-21570-9

Printed in the United States of America

Published by RoseWK Publishing
Cincinnati, Ohio

TABLE OF CONTENTS

Prologue

I wrote Bill Nighy a fan letter and he wrote back. And thus began the love story of all time—if only in my mind.

This letter-writing thing started with my friend, Vera, and my desire to make her laugh. And it started with my propensity in life to Google anything and everything. And it started with the fact that I was recently bereaved, having lost Big Irv—my good friend, my boyfriend, my buddy—to cancer almost two years prior to these events.

Vera and I are new-ish friends. I met her in a cancer caregivers' support group. Her husband, Bill, is alive and well, though together they have been through hell with his multiple myeloma. She was a longtime member of the support group when I joined, and she liked me even though I was possibly the worst caregiver ever, *enraged* with Big Irv for not "doing" cancer the way I wanted him to. In spite of all that, Vera and I started having lunches together monthly. After Big Irv's death, our monthly dates turned into weekly get-togethers with lunch, a movie, and ice cream after.

And so it was that Vera and I went to see *The Second Best Exotic Marigold Hotel* on April 2, 2015. (Hold onto this date. It is cosmically significant.) I came out of the theater charmed by Bill Nighy's performance. In the movie, Bill Nighy plays Douglas Ainslie, who in retirement in India works as a tour guide. The only problem is that Douglas has memory issues and cannot remember his spiel. He is dependent, therefore, on a young friend to follow the tour group around and to read the script to Douglas through a microphone and earphone setup. For an old codger such as myself—age sixty-three—I well understand these memory issues.

Over ice cream, Vera and I discussed the movie. "I am feeling rather smitten with Bill Nighy," I told her.

"Oh, really? He is kind of cute," was her reply.

"Actually, I think that's it. The way he looks. He reminds me of Jimmy Jet, the guy I dated for ten years, before Big Irv, my first serious relationship post-divorce."

"Reminds you of him how?"

"I think they're doppelgangers. They look a lot alike. Tall and thin. Lanky. Maybe even scrawny. Blond. Gorgeous skin. Light eyes."

"You never gave me a physical description of Jimmy Jet in the past. I only know he had post-traumatic stress disorder and refused to be medicated."

"Oh God, yes, he received disability benefits for his PTSD. And yes, he was opposed to drug intervention. So, while he was completely adorable, his pendulum could easily swing in two different directions. He was either in wise-Buddhist mode trying to follow in the footsteps of Thomas Merton or he was back in Vietnam searching for the enemy in the night."

"Well, to give him the benefit of the doubt, isn't it true to say that many men have two sides? You know, 'When he's good, he's very, very good, but when he's bad, he's awful?' Take Bill for instance…"

"Are we talking about my Bill or your Bill?" I asked her. At which time we looked up at each other and laughed out loud.

"He's your Bill now, is he, this Bill Nighy?" she asked, laughing at me.

"Yes! I love him! Please let the world know. I call dibs on the man!" We laughed. We ate ice cream. We went home.

But I have to say I love making Vera laugh, so when I got home, I decided to continue the "loving Bill Nighy" gig and play it for further laughs.

I have mentioned that I love to Google things. As a straight-A kid in school back in the 1960s and 1970s, I often wondered why teachers wanted me to memorize historical dates, the order of the American presidencies, the capitols of the United States, the Prologue to the Canterbury Tales, and so forth. Why clog my brain with all that stuff when I—a very capable researcher—could look up any needed information in the library?

Having this mindset, the advents of the smartphone, the Internet, and Google have been amazing for me. Like Douglas Ainslie having an associate whisper forgotten facts to him via an earpiece, Google recalls all sorts of things my old brain has forgotten. Recently, for instance, Vera and I saw the movie *Tomorrowland.* Though Rotten Tomatoes had only given it a "Tomatometer" of 50 percent, it was created by Disney and it starred George Clooney, so we figured, how bad could it be? In answer to that question, our friends Judy and Sue joined us at the movie that day and walked out halfway through. Vera and I stuck it out until the end but gave it only two stars out of five. In our postmortem, we said there was just one movie we have liked less than *Tomorrowland,* but of course we could not remember its title, though I remembered it featured two old men in Iceland. So I Googled "movie two old men Iceland" and came up with *Land Ho!* starring Earl Lynn Nelson and Paul Eenhoorn. When Vera took exception to my calling the men *old,* I Googled "DOB" followed by each actor's name, which turned up a *Los Angeles Times* article dated July 11, 2014. It said Earl Lynn Nelson was at that time seventy-two to Paul Eenhoorn's sixty-five. (It also said Earl Lynn Nelson is an eye surgeon, not an actor—I love little tidbits like that!) Given that Vera and I are sixty-eight and sixty-three respectively, I apologize most sincerely for calling them old.

Forgive me for digressing. Long ago, I started to say that I went home to Google Bill Nighy in order to make Vera laugh at my over-the-top-ness. I seem to recall hearing he had some sort of medical condition with his hands, so I Googled "Bill Nighy's hands" and indeed was reminded that he has Dupuytren's contracture, a condition Wikipedia says "causes the ring and little finger of each hand to be permanently bent inwards towards the palm." This is very interesting to be sure, but it does nothing to alter the fact that Bill Nighy is adorable.

As I scrolled down the list of things my Google search pulled up, though, I noticed that Bill Nighy had rave reviews for a play he had starred in in London. The play was *Skylight* and it ran from June 6, 2014, through August 23, 2014. *The Telegraph* said the play was a "knockout." *The Guardian* said it was a "moving mixture of politics and love." Quentin Letts at *The Daily Mail* said, "Bill Nighy at full belt on stage is astonishing, unbalancing, unforgettable." I was thrilled for my guy to have such great reviews! As I scrolled through even more links, I was amazed and shocked to learn he was currently starring in this very same play on Broadway! Indeed, the play had previewed starting March 13, 2015, with opening night on April 2. Yes, April 2, the very day I was Googling it, the very day Vera and I saw *The Second Best Exotic Marigold Hotel*. Was it a coincidence or a cosmic zinger trying to catch my attention?

I immediately texted Vera, "My beloved is opening on Broadway tonight!!" And of course I attached the link for her to see. She wrote back immediately, "You must go see him!" Quite frankly, as an inveterate homebody, I never would have had the idea, but it was a good one, so I made plans to do just that.

My friend Roberta lives in Philadelphia but longs to live in New York City, so she is always up for a trip there. She and I have been friends since elementary school. In her younger days, she aspired to sing on Broadway but turned her voice skills into a profession as a speech pathologist instead. She is the one who sang at my wedding and who helped me learn to hum again after my divorce. Beyond her voice skills, she is an accomplished procurer of Broadway tickets and she got us a couple for the Saturday matinee on June 6!

I had tunnel vision as I traveled to New York, 100 percent focused on being in Orchestra seat H5 at the John Golden Theatre at 2 p.m. on June 6. Air travel these days can be difficult, so I booked an early flight on Friday, June 5, on an airline that had many flights to LaGuardia. I figured that should my flight get canceled, another one was not far behind. Luckily, my flight took off without delay or incident and I made it to New York. When I arrived, I posted this on Facebook: "Just landed at LaGuardia. Hot date with Bill Nighy tomorrow. (Tickets to see him on Broadway.) Woo hoo!!" Twenty-five friends liked my posting and six posted comments, including my dear Vera who said, "So exciting!"

Roberta and I had a lovely Friday afternoon and evening in New York. And we had a relaxing breakfast there Saturday. But then, Roberta wanted to take a walk on the High Line. (I Googled it and here is how Wikipedia describes it: "The High Line—also known as the High Line Park—is a 1.45-mile-long New York City linear park built in Manhattan on an elevated section of a disused New York Central Railroad spur called the West Side Line.") Of course I was gracious and went along with her plan, but my innards were screaming, *What if we get lost? What if we get hit by a car walking there or walking back? What if we come down with heat prostration? I just want to go get in line at the John Golden Theatre! Two o'clock will soon be upon us and I don't want to risk missing my man!* But I didn't say any of that. I just walked and walked and walked, and thank God we managed to walk our way back to the theater in plenty of time for Bill Nighy.

Being in line to get into the theater was exciting unto itself. The billboard above the marquee announced SKYLIGHT with photos of Carey Mulligan and Bill Nighy and mention of David Hare as the playwright and Stephen Daldry as the director. The marquee itself quoted *The New York Times* and read, "Laser-sharp and Nigh Perfect." And then there was another placard hanging from the marquee. It boasted, "7 Tony Award Nominations Including Best Revival of a Play." I had already Googled all of those Tony nominations, so I knew my guy was up for Best Leading Actor in a Play. (Ultimately, my beloved did not win the award. What were those people in New York thinking? Of course he was the best—he was laser-sharp and nigh perfect.)

When Roberta and I made it to our seats, I followed the lead of *The New York Times* blurb and posted on Facebook, "Bill Nighy is nigh! Eighteen minutes until curtain." Twenty-six of my friends were thrilled for me but not as thrilled as was I!

Here's an interesting note—not to mention an anatomy lesson: The John Golden Theatre does not have an adequate number of restrooms, so to accommodate all in need in those eighteen minutes before the opening curtain, the men's room became open to men and women alike, with the men at the urinals and the women in the stalls. Back at my seat after that exciting experience, I pointed out a fellow across the theater and announced to Roberta, "Oh! I saw him in the restroom." And I meant it quite literally and graphically.

So this is what I thought about the play: I loved it! But I would have loved seeing Bill Nighy on stage even if he were just the stage manager helping pick up props after the show. That said, I went into the play with some concern that I would not understand it. Of course, I had researched the play extensively before arriving in New York, and its subject matter gave me pause. In the play, Kyra Hollis

(Carey Mulligan) is teaching underprivileged children and living in a self-imposed exile in a poor part of town. Tom Sergeant (Bill Nighy) is her wealthy ex-lover, ex-boss, happily enjoying the comforts of his class. He pays her a visit wanting to rekindle their affair, but their differing politics get in the way. The fighting over ideologies is not something I understand. I have my politics, you have yours, and I see no need to even discuss them, much less fight over them. Instead the lyrics from "Get Together" by the Youngbloods play in my head, encouraging all people to come together, to smile at each other, and to love one another. The words instruct us to do all of this right now, and I love that concept! Feeling this way, I just ignored the politics being discussed in the play and focused on the parts where Kyra and Tom were trying to love one another, and like in all love stories, that's a hard thing for people to do.

In trying to figure out their love, I am thinking about the title of the play and wondering why David Hare chose it for his work. The most direct use of the word "skylight" in the play came as Tom Sergeant described the home he built for his wife, Alice, after she received the one-two punch of learning that Tom and Kyra were involved in a long-term affair and that she was dying of cancer. In the new home, Alice's sick room had a magnificent skylight. To my thinking, Tom built it so Alice could swap one image in her mind's eye for another. Poof! Out goes the image of Tom and Kyra fooling around together for six years. Presto change-o! Here is a lovely image of nature instead. But human nature being what it is, Alice didn't fall for Tom's trick and she died without forgiving him. I am thinking, therefore, that the skylight is synonymous with Tom's guilt and that guilt of such magnitude would make it hard for him to reconcile with Kyra. Perhaps all the politics are there in the play to give the characters an easy explanation for their breakup instead of this more painful reality.

Though the character of Alice was not a physical presence in the play, there is more we are told about her. Specifically, we learn how Tom convinced Alice to love him at the start—he wooed her with red roses, dozens of them, daily, for a month until she finally allowed him into her life. Doesn't this show that Tom was strongly drawn to Alice too? And doesn't the putting aside of this love for the much younger Kyra add to his guilt?

So that is what was happening inside of my head as I watched the play. I was completely taken by these characters and the relationship they shared. I saw Tom Sergeant up there on the stage and not Bill Nighy at all. What a testament to his acting.

As Roberta and I left the theater, we stopped to snap a photo of me "with" Bill Nighy, or at least the poster of him that advertised the show outside the theater. Roberta asked me if I wanted to wait by the stage door to see HIM after the show and of course I did, but it was just too embarrassing to feel that way. And so I said no and we went on our merry way, but as we did, I felt as bereft as a new mom going home from the hospital without her baby.

Roberta and I proceeded to have a lovely evening, meeting up with Ed, a theater friend of hers, who regaled us with stories of his long career. Closing in on retirement, he has a very full list of acting credits, though most people would be hard-pressed to know his name. Still, he told us of the couple of fans who had found their way to his website and written him lovely notes. His delight at receiving such missives was charming to see.

And thus, the idea to write Bill Nighy a fan letter was born.

June

June 9, 2015

Dear Bill Nighy,

I loved you in *Love Actually*. I loved you in *About Time*. I loved you in all three Johnny Worricker films, and in both Marigold Hotels. It was upon leaving the movie theater when I saw *The Second Best Exotic Marigold Hotel* that I found myself giggling over and Googling you. How odd to be a sixty-three-year-old woman—with a crush on a famous actor! At any rate, in my Google research, I learned that you were appearing on Broadway in the revival of *Skylight*. Completely out of character for me, I made plans to schlep from Cincinnati, Ohio, to New York to see the play. Thus, I was in your audience Saturday, June 6, at 2 p.m., and your wonderful performance—and adorable demeanor—did nothing to quell my crush.

I thought of waiting outside the stage door after the final curtain, but that idea made me cringe with embarrassment. Being a writer, though, I thought I could write you a note, so here it is. Thank you for your wonderful work. Your performances make me bubble with happiness. I better close now...I need to go track down more of your films!

Best regards,
Lorie Kleiner Eckert

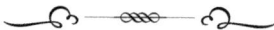

<u>TUESDAY, JUNE 9, 2015</u>

Dear Diary,

Oy! What have I done? I just put a fan letter in the mail to Bill Nighy. I have never written such a letter before, but he is a man whose work I greatly admire. To a large extent, I think I am sending this letter to flatter and delight him just as Ed had been flattered and delighted by the couple of fans who wrote to him. At the same time, though, Bill Nighy is also a man who I find to be adorable and so to some extent— this is so embarrassing to say—I am sending this letter to woo him.

There are 206 words in my letter, but in those few words I tried to tell him a variety of things about myself: that I am sixty-three, that I live in Ohio, that I am a writer, and that I am Jewish (the Yiddish word "schlep" being the giveaway). I also hope I have planted a couple of seeds: namely, that he should Google my name to learn about the column I write, the books I have written, and the motivational talks I used to give. Of course, he would also see some photos of me online. In this manner, he could see that I am tall and thin, that I have shoulder-length dark hair, that I have a propensity for gold earrings and for tailored clothing, and that on the continuum from God-awful to gorgeous, I am strongly somewhere in the middle. I hope he also will realize that I am no slouch in the real world, that I have accomplishments of my own, and I hope he will put my sixty-three next to his sixty-five and figure out how compatible we are, at least according to age. And then borrowing from Tom Sergeant's method of wooing Alice, I added a red rose sticker next to my signature and put three more rose stickers on the envelope. My fingers are crossed that he picks up on some of these hints.

Like many women, I have read countless articles in women's magazines that warn women *not* to try subtle messages with men. For instance, one said not to leave a magazine open to a significant article with the hopes of him picking it up, reading it, and getting the hint. Most likely, he would never notice the magazine in the first place, but even if he did and even if he read it, he would surely think the article referred to someone else and not to him. Oh well, whether my subtlety will work or not, I sent the letter to Bill Nighy using the address of the John Golden Theatre in New York City. I mailed the letter today, June 9, knowing the play continues until June 21, so really, there's a good chance he will get it, right?

Now that I have mailed the letter, I feel embarrassed. What was I thinking? I would never come on to anyone in my acquaintance in Cincinnati. How do I fathom coming on to a star? What will Bill Nighy think of such a letter? Will he be humiliated to even have the stage manager hand it to him? Will someone tease him about having a besotted fan? Or is teasing something only we commoners do? I comfort myself with the knowledge that at least I resisted the temptation to spray the letter with rose-scented perfume. Embarrassed as I feel, the envelope is already in the mail, so I have no other choice but to put these worries—and the fantasy of true love with Bill Nighy— out of my mind and get busy with real life. My monthly column is due to editors on Friday. I better get cracking.

A Slice of Life: A Monthly Column
NO COMPLAINING ON THE YACHT

I am a very fortunate person. I have a lovely home. I have friends and family who seem to like me. I have good health. I have sufficient money to do what I want in retirement. I am intelligent and creative. I have a variety of hobbies—walking, reading, quilting, writing, and travel. And yet I often feel that something is missing. My friend Kim tells me that when she has similar feelings—in her similar circumstances—her husband reminds her that there is no complaining on the yacht. I don't know Kim's problem, but I think mine is loneliness.

People look at me like I'm crazy when I mention that I suffer from Empty Nest Syndrome. After all, my children are thirty-eight, thirty-six, and thirty-two, so it is a L-O-N-G time ago that they left for college. I remember how oppressively quiet the house was without them. The quiet seemed to have weight, and it pressed down on me, squeezing out the life I had known. In the intervening years since college, the noise level in the house has picked up again as the kids have come back to Cincinnati, first with spouses and then with their own children. But even as the head count increases, this old nest of mine will never be the same. At one time, I was very important in the life of each of my children. The arrival of a spouse for each of them bumped me down a notch on the list of people important to them. The same happened with the birth of each grandchild. Of course, this is what I expected to happen and what needed to happen, but it still creates my own brand of loneliness even in the middle of all the hubbub that this mass of loved ones creates.

I am confident that when the day comes that my health fails and I need help, the kids will take care of my needs. But I also know that if they think about me at all at this moment, they are hoping and praying I stay well and independent because they simply cannot handle one more obligation in their lives. Thus, I try not to impose on them, but in so doing, my yacht and I feel a bit adrift.

As an antidote to this problem, I try to keep busy. This was easier in recent years when I was in a relationship with Big Irv. In his healthy years, we were on the go constantly. In his years of illness, I took him to dozens of doctors, I spent time worrying about him, I helped out with his needs, and I talked to him on the phone daily. And then, after his death, I was his executrix so I shuffled his papers, sold his assets, fought his financial battles, and just recently closed out his estate. When all was said and done, though, all was said and done. Now there is nothing left to keep me busy. As Big Irv would say, I have too much time on my hands.

Being a person who recognizes the analgesic properties of having a routine, I am trying to find one. Here is my week:

- Monday—My eight grandkids are ages one and a half to nine. They call me Marmel, and on Mondays we have Marmel School from 9:30 until 4. Whoever is not in school full-time attends. It's summer now, so I get all eight kids. We have free play, we eat a morning snack, we have circle time where we sing songs and read stories, we have craft time, we have lunch, we have naps for the little ones and quiet TV time for the bigger ones, everyone gets a turn on the iPad, and then we close out the day with water play.
- Tuesdays—I recover from Marmel School.
- Wednesdays—I continue the recovery, plus I shop for and prep dinner for Thursday.

- Thursdays—I work out with a personal trainer from 9 until 10. I go to lunch, see a movie, and have ice cream with a friend from 11:30 until 3. I have all the kids and grandkids—as many as fifteen people—to dinner at 5.
- Friday—I recover from family dinner and I go to evening Shabbat services at Temple.
- Saturday—I try to figure out something to do. (But it's hard!)
- Sunday—I read the paper, do the laundry, and prep food and crafts for Marmel School.

I am an early riser, so I get up at six on weekdays to exercise, and then I am out the door at seven for an hourlong walk with a friend. Coffee and the newspaper come next, along with the daily Jumble and Sudoku, and then as a hedge against depression I make sure I do my hair and makeup and actually get dressed daily even if I have nowhere to go. I am not a TV watcher, so if nothing else fills the day, there is always a book to read or a game or two—or ten—of Sudoku or FreeCell to play.

Basically then, besides a little exercise and a pinch of God and friends, my life consists of this: I am either getting ready to be with my kids or recovering from the experience. Though my friends whose kids and grandkids live out of town are very envious of me, I still find myself a little bored, a little lonely, and a tad depressed. Yes indeed, I find myself complaining on the yacht.

I remember the day when my son was a teenager and I wanted to be too much a part of his life. He told me, "Get a life, Mom!" And so I am at a similar juncture today. I have reinvented myself before and I will do it again! I just am not exactly sure how. Stay tuned…

THURSDAY, JUNE 18, 2015

Dear Diary,

Here it is, short and sweet and shocking: When I opened my mailbox today, I discovered a letter there. My walking buddy, Robin Newland, has an adult son in New York named Ben, so when I pulled the letter from the box and saw that it was from BN in NYC, I wondered why Ben Newland was writing me. When I actually got around to opening it, which was not an immediate thing, I was floored to see that it was not from that BN at all, but instead from Bill Nighy—yes, from my Bill! It's not Pearl Harbor day, yet it seems as if a bomb has dropped, because after signing his name, he added an X! I am thinking he loves me in return.

After the three families arrived for dinner tonight, I handed the letter to my daughters and daughter-in-law, to Cheryl first and then to Lisa and Shana. "What is it?" each asked in turn. Containing my glee, I just shook my head and said, "Open it." And in turn, they each did. I watched their eyes run across his unusual and darling handwriting until they reached the end and saw his signature and began shrieking in delight, "Oh my God!"

Oh my God indeed!

And he wrote:

LORIE ECKERT
THANK YOU FOR YOUR LOVELY CARD.
I THINK IT'S ONE OF THE NICEST
THINGS I'VE RECEIVED.
I'M SO PLEASED YOU ENJOYED 'SKYLIGHT'
AND OTHER STUFF.
THANK YOU.
BILL NIGHY.
X

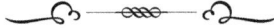

Thursday, June 18, 2015 – Continued

Dear Diary,

It's me again. That very last element of his letter, that X, gives me pause. Well no, it doesn't give me pause; it gives me heart palpitations followed by screaming fits. Bill Nighy is sending me a kiss? And then when I looked over his note card, I discovered two more X's on the front of the card. Surely there is some confusion here. He's British; an X must not mean the same thing to him that it means to me. And so I Googled it, asking: "Is an x a universal sign for a kiss?" Up popped mashable.com with the answer: "The Oxford English Dictionary's earliest written reference of the X used as a kiss dates back to 1763." Mashable.com also said that in 1894, Winston Churchill sent kisses in a letter—three of them—just like Bill Nighy sent to me. Kiss confirmed. The man must love me. Right? Something in my letter resonated in him. Right? What else could that X mean? These thoughts set me off on a Googling frenzy to find out more about him. And so now I know:

- His full name is William Francis Nighy.
- He was born December 12, 1949, in Caterham, United Kingdom.
- His parents are Catherine Josephine Whittaker Nighy, a psychiatric nurse from Glasgow, and Alfred Martin Nighy, who managed a garage and who was born in England.
- He has two older siblings, Martin and Anna.
- He was brought up in the Roman Catholic faith and served as an altar boy.
- He is six feet, one inch tall.
- He has blond hair.
- He has blue eyes.
- Interesting tidbit—he loves Bob Dylan!
- And the Rolling Stones!

- His listing on the Internet Movie Database, IMDb, shows 127 acting credits between 1976 and the present, which include roles in film and television.
- Many articles express the opinion that the character of Billy Mack in the 2003 film *Love Actually* was a breakout role for my man. He says repeatedly in interviews that after Billy Mack, he no longer needed to audition for parts. Casting crews begged him to accept a role instead of the other way around.
- Many other articles mention his self-deprecating personality, such as the one from *The Telegraph* dated September 4, 2013, and written by Gaby Wood, which carries the headline: "Sharp-suited, scene-stealing and charmingly self-deprecating: no wonder Bill Nighy is one of our most beloved performers."
- And like Gaby Wood's story, every third article about him— at least it seems that way—mentions his bespoke navy suits. *Be-what*, I wondered? As it turns out, the word is more prevalent in British English while American English tends to use the term "custom-made" instead. While print articles and interviews with Bill Nighy abound about these bespoke suits (does he get sick of talking about them?), what I really want to know is this: Is the man bespoken for?
- So I checked out his marital status only to learn that he is single, though he had been in a long-term relationship with actress Diana Quick, whom he met in 1981 and with whom he was linked until their separation in 2008. According to an article in the *Daily Mail* that is dated August 2008, she playfully called him her POOSSLQ: person of opposite sex sharing living quarters. The article reports his attitude toward her as being a bit more loving—or maybe just more serious—saying that when he spoke of her, he "had developed the superstition of touching wood as if

to stress just how lucky he was to have her." The article explains the couple's demise by saying, "It is Nighy's recent success that is blamed by many for the collapse of his relationship with Miss Quick...By his own admission, he has become obsessed with work to the exclusion of almost everything else."

- Though the couple is no longer together, I note that in their twenty-seven-year relationship, they had one child, Mary Bing Jamie Alfreda Leonora Quick Kit Nighy (huh?). She was born July 17, 1984, and she follows in her parents' footsteps in the acting profession. As I have found out in my own life, when there is a divorce with children involved, even adult children, the divorcing couple can never really be 100 percent apart. As the Eagles song "Hotel California" explains, "You can check out anytime you like, but you can never leave." It is not odd to me to read, therefore, that the never-married and therefore not-exactly-divorced couple remains close friends.

Well, dear Diary, it is getting rather late and my brain is in knots over all this information, not to mention the fact that the batteries on my iPhone and iPad are wearing down. (I can research two things at once!) But wait a minute; I just thought of something. Grandson Josh taught me that beyond articles and film clips, it is possible to search for images online! Back in a flash...

Oh my God! There are hundreds of photographic images of my man! He is serious. He is silly. He is smiling, then pouting, then scowling. He is sexy—lounging on a sofa, then lounging on a bed. He is dancing or playing the air guitar. He is his younger self and then his current self. He is wearing no glasses or adjusting his glasses or wearing them cockeyed. He is wearing sunglasses and sometimes a hat. He is giving a two-finger salute—repeatedly. He is out and about and dressed to the nines. He is on the red carpet, then accepting awards. He is decked out in every manner of costume representing his many acting roles. It's a Bill Nighy lover's jackpot!

I go off to bed a happy woman. Sleep since Big Irv's death has been difficult. This won't help matters.

A Bit of Fantasy — The Mail

I see Bill Nighy gorgeously dressed in his bespoke blue suit over his open-collared, pale blue, Margaret Howell classic shirt with his dark blue Pantherella socks and his lovely Oxfords from Church's. Of course, his slacks are perfectly hemmed and there are no puddles of excess fabric on his shoes. (I have done my research.*)

He comes into the John Golden Theatre through the stage door and enters his dressing room. There, propped up by his mirror is a white envelope, hand-addressed to him from someone named Lorie Kleiner Eckert in Ohio. Huh, it has three rose stickers on the back of the envelope. He wonders what that's all about. He reaches into his pocket and takes out the small pocket knife he carries and uses the blade to neatly slice open the envelope. Taking out the letter, he reads it and a smile crosses his face. *Nice letter! She seems like a pleasant lady and she has a way with words,* he thinks. He tosses the letter into the trash can after reading it and carries on with preparing for his performance, but once out on stage he finds he is feeling extra fond of his co-star tonight. It's as if the compliments in this Lorie Kleiner Eckert's letter need to be paid forward to someone else, and so Carey Mulligan's character of Kyra Hollis is especially cherished in tonight's performance. The applause after the show is off the charts. Bill Nighy, Carey Mulligan, and Matthew Beard can't stop bowing to the adoring crowd. After the play, aglow in all that adulation, Bill Nighy looks into that trash can and pulls out the fan letter. Huh! Here he is in a city that never sleeps. Here he is wound up from all of the applause. Sleep will be difficult; he might as well go find a note card and a postage stamp and write this dear woman a letter! And while he's at it, he's going to hold onto to her missive, one of the nicest things he's ever received. Meanwhile, the rose stickers continue to tickle his consciousness. This Lorie person just saw the play and she knows the significance of red roses, he thinks. Maybe in Tom Sergeant fashion he should send her roses as well…

* Note to self: Googling "Bill Nighy's clothes" brings up many articles with many brand names listed, not to mention many fabulous photos of him dressed in those clothes. I loved the article called "The Look: Mr. Bill Nighy," dated November 11, 2011, in *The Journal.* Another great one was called "Style Icon: Bill Nighy," which appeared in *St. James Style: Men's Style and Lifestyle Blog* dated Friday, August 23, 2013.

SUNDAY, JUNE 21, 2015

Dear Diary,

I am losing my mind, not to mention lots of sleep. My game or two or ten of FreeCell and/or Sudoku has been replaced by Google searches, dozens of them. Maybe a dozen dozen, which is literally gross! Every spare minute in my day is spent online. I want to scream. My house is built upon a lake and I want to throw my various devices into it. But even feeling this way, I cannot stop the Googling. As they say, enquiring minds want to know.

Beyond the Internet searches, I am spending time watching the various Bill Nighy movies I have checked out from the public library. And let's not forget time spent opening my front door to see if anyone has delivered roses. With confidence that the roses will soon appear, I think of a relationship with Bill Nighy and ask myself with conviction, "Well, why can't this happen?" And then the air goes out of me as I explain to myself exactly why it can't.

While insanity may be defined as not only talking to myself but also answering back, here I go again. "Why can't this happen?" said the Pie in the Sky person.

"What do you even mean by *this*?" said the Voice of Reason, having flashbacks to Bill Clinton and his issues with the equally innocuous word *is*.

"I mean, why can't I have a relationship with Bill Nighy?"

"Uh, maybe because you are a mere mortal and he is a *star*," replied VOR.

"But there are all sorts of precedents for such a relationship," argued PITS. "There is big movie idol Julia Roberts falling in love with lowly book shop owner Hugh Grant in *Notting Hill*. And there is Hugh Grant again, this time as the prime minister, for God's sake, falling in love with one of his secretaries in *Love Actually*. And let's not forget aviation officer candidate and then ensign Richard Gere dramatically carrying factory worker Debra Winger right off the assembly line into a life of assumed bliss in *An Officer and a Gentleman*. And what about billionaire tycoon Richard Gere who falls in love with Julia Roberts, now a hooker, in *Pretty Woman*? And, while we are on the topic of high and mighty men loving lesser beings, there is my man himself, my Bill, in *Skylight*, falling for one of his employees, Carey Mulligan!"

"I have three words for you," replied a very unimpressed VOR, "far-fetched fiction! But let's go back and discuss *this*, this relationship you want with him. You're looking for a relationship? I thought you were done with all of that post-Big Irv. Surely you remember how difficult it was to be a girlfriend and a Marmel all in the same breath? Certainly you can't have forgotten the little jealousies the one person felt when you paid too much attention to those others and vice versa? And what about dealing with a man again? Don't you remember that gift shop with Vera and how you guys chuckled over the parlor pillow that said, 'Mr. Right, Mr. Always Right'? You want to do all that again?"

As a Marmel, I know that one is never supposed to say, "Shut up!" but what else is there to say to VOR than that?

On to other topics, I spoke to Roberta tonight, my Sunday evening habit. I told her about the letter! And about the three X's! And I told her I was feeling a little déjà vu in that we had done this together before, this letter-writing thing with a famous person. She wrote a letter to her musical theater hero, Stephen Sondheim, and he wrote her back and they repeated that process a few more times. Roberta reminded me that it happened more than a decade ago and that each wrote five letters to the other. She was the one who ended the correspondence because she wrote him letters while he responded with notes. After a while, that felt demeaning to her. Roberta asked me what return address my man used, and I reported that it was the address of the John Golden Theatre. We marveled over the fact that Stephen Sondheim used his home address on the back flap of his envelope, making that experience seem from another era entirely.

"Do you plan to write another letter?" she asked.

"I did that already, twice. The first letter was so embarrassing, I tossed it. The second attempt is in an envelope waiting to go to in the mailbox tomorrow. I'm rushing this because *Skylight* closes its run today, but I'm hoping he will hang around New York a bit and the theater will be able to get the letter to him."

"And what did you say this time?"

"Oh my, that's embarrassing too. You remember that Cate Blanchett recently filmed a movie, *Carol*, in Cincinnati and that a friend of mine was an extra in it?

"Sure…"

"Well, that put the idea in my head that famous people might actually choose to spend time in Ohio, so I invited him here and told him I'd be delighted to show him the sights." She didn't choke or laugh at me, which is a testimony to the kind of friend she is. And so I went on. "I also included a photo of myself with my business card so he has all my contact information." Again, she didn't laugh—whew! But my courage stopped there, so I didn't tell Roberta how completely consumed I have been with thoughts of Bill Nighy. I didn't tell her of my fantasy about him or about watching out the door for the florist's delivery truck. Even if I had, Roberta wouldn't have chided me about it. She would have been willing to enter the fantasy with me and wish me well.

Ultimately she said, "If anyone is capable of getting Bill Nighy's attention, you're the one. You wrote your first book, endured countless rejections, and then managed to find a publisher. You said you were going to syndicate a column, and then suddenly you have it appear in newspapers across the country. So what are you hoping for here, to be pen pals as I was with Stephen Sondheim?"

"Oh. No. That's not what I want. I want more."

"Well, again, knowing you, if you want more, you'll get it. But whenever I have a girlfriend in the throes of falling madly in love with a man she barely knows—which is such a typical thing for us girls to do—I always tell her about this terrific short story from long ago written by this author I know named Lorie Kleiner Eckert."

"Oh God! I hate it when someone quotes me to me," I moaned.

"No, you don't, you love it!"

"Yes, you're right, I do. And I'll read that story again and I'll slow down a bit even though I think the three X's in his letter mean he loves me back."

"What's not to love, Lor?" she asked, and I loved her for saying that instead of pointing out exactly what there was not to love—my cringe-worthy letter to Bill Nighy. So here's the new game plan: Instead of putting it in the mail tomorrow, I will put it through the paper shredder tonight lest anyone ever see it. Inviting him to visit me in Cincinnati and sending my business card—was I insane?

I am done with the fantasy I have been spinning for all these days. I am exhausted and sick of it and done. (In my mind, I hear Big Irv reminding me that turkeys are done while people are finished. So that too—I'm finished!)

Signed: Lorie Kleiner Eckert!

P.S. Dear Diary, if it is true that those three miserable X's mean the man loves me, he has my address and can initiate a correspondence. Ha!

MONDAY, JUNE 22, 2015

Dear Diary,

I searched my computer after Marmel School today and located the original manuscript for the short story Roberta mentioned. I have printed it out here. She's right to remind me that falling in love with love is easy—it's factoring an actual man into the equation that is so difficult. I know I'm not the only woman to be such a fool for love, but I am mortified by the story just the same. And yet, here I go again with Bill Nighy. What is my problem? As I try to figure that out, I also printed out copies of the two aborted letters to BN. Perhaps they will give me a clue.

The Short Story –

THE VIEW FROM FEBRUARY 19, 1999

This is either a very romantic or an entirely insane thing to do. If things work out, it will make a wonderful tale. If not, I hope to laugh and learn from the experience.

I've been fixed up exactly twice in the five years since my divorce, both times by my daughter. The first man was one of her professors at the college she attends forty-five miles away from home. He was marvelous in many ways except for that other woman he confessed to living with several weeks into our torrid relationship. My daughter felt bad and somewhat responsible for the pain I suffered and thus was compelled to make it up to me. She therefore kept an open eye on campus for another prospect—a man of the right age and bearing, a man who would appeal to me—and found him living in the house next door to the one she rented.

It took several months of watching him walk his dog to find the courage to approach him, and when she did, she had a girlfriend in tow. "We want to ask you out on a date," they said, to which his response was a horrified and wide-eyed silence. Having failed to mention a forty-seven-year-old mother, they could see thoughts of a ménage à trois with two easy pieces of jailbait explode in his mind. After managing to define terms and calm him down, they had a little chat with the man and did indeed come away with a date on the calendar, February 19, some three weeks into the future. He said he would meet me at a YMCA on the campus of a nearby but different college, as he knew of a dance there that we could attend.

My daughter called me excited with the news. "You have a date on February 19!" she shouted.

"I do? With who?"

"Kevin!"

"Kevin who?"

"Kevin. The man next door. With the dog. Remember? I've told you about him."

"Oh, OK, Kevin. But Kevin who?"

"Kevin…um…O'Connor," she said haltingly, seeming to pick a name from thin air.

"His name is Kevin O'Connor?" I said with doubt.

"Well, he looks like he might be an O'Connor…but I'm not sure."

"So you just kinda made up his last name?"

"Kinda."

"But his first name is Kevin?"

"Yeh, I'm pretty sure…and you have a date with him on the nineteenth!"

It's difficult to explain why I accepted this date. Perhaps it will help if I relate a recent experience. I was home, alone, and the phone rang. I answered it only to have a man's voice say in a baffled manner, "Oh…sorry…wrong number." I wrote in my journal that night that I wanted to shout, "Wait! Don't hang up! Talk to me!" and I gave that short journal entry a title, "Eleanor Rigby." So, there you have it: Like Ms. Rigby of Beatles fame, I am a lonely person, and being a lonely person, I accepted the date.

My daughter has had several short conversations with Kevin in the weeks between their first encounter and now. In each case, she immediately called me and relayed the new information and/or misinformation to me. So now I "know" the following:

- He is forty-five to fifty years old.
- He's *probably* taller than I am.
- He wears his long, dark hair in a ponytail and he has gray frizzies.

- He's attractive and he looks like…me?
- He really likes his great big dog.
- He *probably* teaches college—either at my daughter's school or at the one near the Y.
- Most likely he teaches art or computer art.
- He is divorced.
- And has been for two years.
- Or maybe three.
- It might be four.
- He hasn't dated in all that time.
- He's rather shy.
- He's kinda excited about our plans.
- The dance is a waltz.
- Everyone at the dance will know him, so all I have to do is ask for Kevin.

Having gotten such "solid information" from my daughter, I must confess to doing some detective work. It turns out there are actually two YMCAs in the area of that college. After a few phone calls, I found the one with a dance on the nineteenth. The party is from 8:30 until midnight and costs $18 per person. It is sponsored by a dance club and is a costume ball with a theme, The Great Stock Market Crash of 1929. I am instructed to come in black tie, no tie, in rags, or in riches, and I am told we will do the waltz, the foxtrot, the Charleston, and the Lindy. Short of the Hokey Pokey, I am not a dancer at all. So I am more than a bit intimidated by these dance steps and with this step I am taking in life, but take it I will though I still have questions. And so I wonder: *Why didn't he ask for my phone number and call even if just to give me the party specifics? Is he a hermit disinterested in people? Does he lack social skills? Is he an ax murderer trying to stay away from women as he swears off more victims? Or is he just a nice guy who is a little leery of love after experiencing divorce and who is ever so slowly getting back into the dance of life?* It is my hope he is the romantic type and that he is waiting for love to drop into his lap. It is my hope he is sitting *alone* at his house right now singing old show tunes and wondering if some enchanted evening—February 19 to be precise—he might meet a stranger across a crowded room.

As for me, I have more than just wondered; I have consulted an astrologer. Before I even mentioned the date circled on my calendar, she asked me what was happening February 19 and told me there was the great possibility of a karmic meeting, a meeting with someone from a past life, that night. And so I am less than forty-eight hours away from my date with Kevin, and I am excited. I wonder if the outcome of the evening will be determined by my mindset and expectations. Hoping this is the case, I choose to go into this date with a positive frame of mind and a willingness to show Kevin exactly who I am. Thus, I won't be dressed as a flapper, though I will wear a vintage dress: a sexy little black number from the back of my closet that is ten years old. I will also polish my black shoes with the high heels, having faith that he will either be taller than I or that we will be able to handle the differential. And as I prepare to go, I will continuously sing my rendition of "Some Enchanted Evening." And with my slightly off-key alto, I will hope to find perfect harmony with his tenor or bass. For I am what I am, a romantic at heart, and I choose to accept this date because I am willing to consider all the possibilities and, like beautiful fireworks, let them explode in my mind.

THE VIEW FROM FEBRUARY 20, 1999

Clearly I was blinded by those fireworks. Clearly I did not consider all the possibilities, just the ax murderer nightmare and then the dream come true while there are so many scenarios between those poles, such as Kevin himself. He is a perfectly attractive, tall, intelligent, outgoing and conversant man, not to mention that he is an accomplished dancer. When he divorced, he lost not only his wife but his fabulous dance partner, and it is only the dance partner he seeks to replace. Kevin thought it funny that I had sung show tunes before our date because he did too—he sang "I Could Have Danced all Night" from *My Fair Lady* as he sought to "spread [his] wings and [do] a thousand things..." on the dance floor. Unfortunately, "Twinkle Toes" is not my middle name, so I could not help him out in that regard.

Even though things did not work out for Kevin and me, this still makes for a wonderful story—a cautionary tale—with a very succinct lesson that is ever so easy to remember, though I probably won't. But here it is just the same: Next time around, I should meet the man first and fall in love with him second.

Aborted Letter Number One

June 19, 2015

Oh my God, Bill Nighy, you replied to my fan letter! I'm shocked! I'm thrilled! I'm swooning! I'm writing again! So here goes:

> **F** emale in
> **A** merica
> **N** eeds
> **M** an to
> **A** lleviate
> **I** ntense
> **L** oneliness

To tell you a smidge about myself, I am a happy person, yet some bit of joy has been missing in my life as of late. Could it be this new thing called retirement? Could it be the recent loss of my significant other? I don't know. All I do know is that I have enjoyed feeling giddy over you these last many weeks. And, I must confess that your response to my letter lights my fire, which feels great after being lukewarm for so long. I hope something in my letters likewise resonates with you and that you will be in touch.

Best regards,

Lorie Kleiner Eckert

Aborted Letter Number Two

June 21, 2015

Dear Bill,

I have written exactly one fan letter in my life, to you, in early June. Thus, I am totally inexperienced in the protocol of such missives. It is only in my imagination that I would have hoped for a letter in return, but then I got one! Which was thrilling! And confusing!

If you wrote back just because you are a nice person, it would be unkind of me to write again with its implication that I am hoping for more. Indeed you could feel put-out, having proved to yourself that "no good deed goes unpunished." If, on the other hand, you wrote back because something I said touched a nerve, then it behooves me to reach out again.

While I have no idea what a friendship would look like between a mere mortal and someone of your stature, please know that my hand is extended to you in that regard. Therefore—hold on to your hat—I cordially invite you to visit me in Cincinnati, Ohio! While it may seem odd to visit Middle America, please know that your friend, Cate Blanchett, did so recently to film *Carol*, and evidently she survived the experience. While here, I'd love to introduce you to the city's many charms, including Skyline Chili, Graeter's Ice Cream, and of course…me.

Very sincerely yours,

Lorie Kleiner Eckert

TUESDAY, JUNE 23, 2015

Dear Diary,

I own a television and pay DirecTV $52.02 per month so that I can record *Sid the Science Kid, Doc McStuffins, Dora the Explorer,* and other such shows for the grandboys and girls to watch at Marmel School on Mondays. The TV is almost never in use beyond that, yet in the past week I watched four—count them, four!—Bill Nighy movies on that very TV screen. If the television was an animate object, I think it would suggest a game of Twenty Questions by now, seeking to figure out, *What's wrong with this picture?*

A Report on the Film Festival

Speaking of questions, if you are a woman who is newly turned on to an actor with more than 100 film credits to his name, how do you choose which movie(s) to watch first as you get to know your man? IMDb is a good starting point to get a listing of said films. IMDb lists each actor's movies in reverse chronological order, so one could choose to watch the star's movies in the order they are listed or in the order they were made; or one could read the IMDb synopsis of each film and watch the best-sounding ones first; or one could choose them as I did, strictly according to their availability.

Frugal Fannie that I am, I went to the local branch of my library with the IMDb list in hand. I then scoured the shelves for Bill Nighy titles. Upon finding one, I took it home with me—for free—for a week. I soon learned that other branches of the Hamilton County Public Library had different BN movie titles I could request. The library system would even transfer those DVDs to the branch I frequented! In this manner, I located and viewed four Bill Nighy movies last week. In the order in which I liked them, from least to most, they are: *The Constant Gardener*, *Enduring Love*, *Notes on a Scandal*, and *The Girl in the Café*.

The Constant Gardener is a political thriller from 2005. It is based on a novel of the same name by John le Carre and it was filmed in Kenya. The movie is about a man, Justin Quayle (Ralph Fiennes), who is looking into the murder of his wife, Tessa (Rachel Weisz). He is a British diplomat and she was a socially conscious lawyer. She was found dead in Kenya, where she had been compiling data against a multinational drug company. This company was using Africans as guinea pigs to test a drug that proved to have fatal side effects.

Bill Nighy plays the part of Sir Bernard Pellegrin, the head of the Africa Desk at the Foreign Office. He is the one who ordered Tessa's surveillance as he tried to block her reports. The movie ends with Pellegrin's part in the scandal being revealed and with journalists hot on his trail.

As to my thoughts on the movie, I will need to beg forgiveness on this one. This type of movie leaves me cold, since my brain does not think along political lines. In spite of that, I am reluctant to pan it for four reasons:

1. My beloved Bill Nighy is in it.
2. The cast and crew were so affected by the circumstances in the area of filming that they set up The Constant Gardener Trust in order to provide basic education for the villagers they got to know.
3. The plot was vaguely based on a real-life case.
4. Before falling in love with Bill Nighy, I happened upon the Johnny Worricker Trilogy. In the first episode of that series, *Page Eight*, beloved Bill stars with Ralph Fiennes and Rachel Weisz. Because of that, I feel an affinity for these two actors and I enjoyed seeing them again in this film.

Bottom Line on *The Constant Gardener*: As ever, Bill Nighy looked very handsome and did an admirable acting job, though he had far too few minutes on screen.

Enduring Love is a British film from 2004 starring Daniel Craig and Rhys Ifans. The movie starts with a beautiful day in an English meadow. Joe (Daniel Craig) has planned a romantic picnic with his lady love, Claire (Samantha Morton). As the couple open a bottle of champagne, a hot air balloon drifts into the field and it is in trouble. The pilot's leg is caught in the anchor rope. There is a passenger on board, a boy, who is too scared to help or to jump down. Joe and three other men witness this sight and run to the rescue. They secure the basket momentarily, but then the wind takes them all into the air. All of them ultimately drop safely to the ground except for one man who falls to his death. That evening, Joe and Claire dine with friends Robin (Bill Nighy) and Rachel (Susan Lynch). In retelling the story, we see how distraught Joe is from the experience. His emotions are not helped by the fact that he and fellow rescuer, Jed (Rhys Ifans), went to retrieve the body of the fallen man. It is at this point that the movie takes an odd twist as Jed feels an instant connection to Joe, a connection that becomes creepy—and then creepier still—as the weeks go by. Ultimately Joe realizes that Jed is romantically obsessed with him. Things get ugly from there.

Here are my thoughts on the movie:

1. I would have wanted to see this movie even if Bill Nighy did not have a part in it because it is based on a novel of the same name by Ian McEwan. Since I have read and loved another book by Ian McEwan—*The Children Act*—I was interested in knowing this story.

2. I love the title that McEwan chose for his book: *Enduring Love*. Does he mean everlasting, or does he mean something someone has to put up with? Joe is looking for enduring love with Claire, but he also has to endure the love Jed feels for him. But I wonder, even in a "normal" love relationship, are both aspects of "enduring" present? Such food for thought! I wonder if McEwan makes more of this topic in his novel.

3. But on to the movie, in it, Bill Nighy's character has a wife and a baby and they are friends with Daniel Craig's character and his fiancée. I enjoyed seeing Bill Nighy dressed cozily in a cardigan sweater and I much admired his handling of the baby,

but as ever, while Bill Nighy looked very handsome and did an admirable acting job, he had far too few minutes on screen for this obsessed fan.

4. And speaking of obsession, one comes out of this movie thinking about how awful it would be to be stalked by a crazy person. This served as a reminder to me—in the wooing of my Bill—to be sure I don't come off as a disturbed stalker.

5. Though the movie was very good, I can't rave about it because of its sinister nature—the Rhys Ifans/Jed Parry character was a deranged and scary fellow. While I know there are a lot of frightening people in the world, I try to keep my head in the sand in that regard. If I allowed myself to read about rapists, mass murderers, stalkers, and the like, I couldn't sleep at night. And I already have enough trouble in that regard.

Note to Bill Nighy: I am so sorry to be 0-for-2 in loving your films. Read on, though, better reviews to come...

Notes on a Scandal was released in 2006 and is based on a novel of the same name by Zoe Heller. It is about a young art teacher, Sheba Hart (Cate Blanchett), who is involved in many love relationships. There is her husband, an older man named Richard (Bill Nighy), and a fifteen-year-old student with whom she is having an affair. As if that isn't enough, a veteran teacher at the school, Barbara Covett (Judi Dench), has her romantic sights on Sheba. The plot is juicy, as is the fact that Bill Nighy has several major scenes in this film. Be forewarned, though, while his part is larger here—he's in about a dozen scenes—he simply is not the star of the show. Argh!! Just the same, here are the many things I liked about this movie:

1. I loved that Sheba was twenty or so years younger than her husband. Indeed they met when she was twenty and he was

her professor, so I liked the juxtaposition of the prior older man/younger woman relationship as compared to the current older woman/younger man relationship. Of course, they did make the younger man jailbait here, but even so, it is easy to see how Sheba might have missed that fine detail having lived the other side of the equation. What a lovely nuance!

2. Soon after Sheba and Barbara first meet, Sheba invites Barbara to her home for lunch. Barbara is a spinster and has designs on Sheba, so she is thrilled to learn more about the object of her affection. At the lunch, Barbara learns that beyond teaching, Sheba has many responsibilities. Yes, there is this older husband fellow, but there is also a teenage daughter and an adolescent son with Down syndrome.

3. After lunch, it is evidently the tradition of Sheba's family to turn on music and dance. The teenage daughter, of course, will have no part of such shenanigans. Meanwhile, Barbara is feeling much the same way. Richard pulls her by the hand and gets her to the dance floor, but the very, very foolish Barbara will only stand there and sway as opposed to throwing herself into it, throwing herself into his arms. Even so, the scene of Bill Nighy dancing is one that is so charming it needs to be rewound and watched repeatedly by his fans.

4. After lunch and dancing, Sheba takes Barbara out to her studio. Yes, Sheba is also an artist, but a stifled one. With all that she is currently doing, how could she manage to be creative? Regarding this loss, Sheba quotes her father as saying that one needs to "mind the gap" in life, "the distance between life as you dream it and life as it is."

5. Sheba is not the only isolated and deeply unhappy person in the movie. The same is true of Barbara, who at one point

beautifully reflects that no one understands her loneliness, "what it's like to construct an entire weekend around a visit to the launderette."

6. In the movie, I was mortified when Barbara came on to Sheba with "arm tickles," but I guess this proves how good the acting was to make me cringe. I loved the arm tickles, though. My cousin and I used to give them to each other when we had sleep-overs as kids. I didn't know it was erotic at the time; I just knew it felt good. I tried it with various men through the years and they just didn't get the charm of it. Men, it seems, want to get on to the main event.

7. While I will probably never find myself in the position of being involved with a teenage boy, nor in the position of having a spinster teacher proposition me, I still could highly identify with this movie—it is a tale of loss and loneliness.

8. But enough about Barbara and Sheba, Richard Hart has some great scenes. There is the not-quite-dancing with Barbara scene—and at the end of it, an adorable scene of him clowning with his son. Then there is a great scene of him as a frustrated family man trying to get his wife into the car when she is instead fussing with Barbara. And the best scene is Richard Hart's confrontation of Sheba as her romance with the teenager hits the news.

9. One of the perks of watching a DVD versus seeing a movie in a theater is that a DVD comes with bonus materials, not just the movie. For instance, there was a four-part section called "A Conversation with Cate Blanchett and Bill Nighy" in which they sat and chatted with each other. Though I have watched a variety of Bill Nighy interviews in my many Google searches and while he always exhibits an easy charm, he is somehow

stilted and uncomfortable in these brief takes. Cate Blanchett puts forth a lot of opinions while he says, "Yeh, yeh, yeh" and exhibits fidgety hands. Additionally, he's wearing a light gray suit, a classic Glen Plaid. It's rather shocking! Perhaps he just doesn't be-speak well when not in navy blue.

The Girl in the Café is the last of the four films. It is a British movie that was made for television, premiering in 2005. The movie was written by Richard Curtis, directed by David Yates, and produced by Hilary Bevan Jones. I read several reviews before watching this film. I learned that in this movie Bill Nighy plays the part of Lawrence, a civil servant working for the Chancellor of the Exchequer. He is a loner, perhaps because he is a workaholic or perhaps because he has few social skills. He meets Gina (Kelly Macdonald) by chance in a London café and invites her to travel with him to a G8 summit in Reykjavík, Iceland. Once there, they attend a dinner party where she confronts the prime minister of the United Kingdom over the politics of poverty relief in Africa. This angers the prime minister and embarrasses Lawrence, though he realizes she is right and tries to help persuade the Chancellor and others at the summit to do something about this issue.

Oh my God! That sounds so political! That's not my kind of movie at all! I actually thought that and would not have seen this movie except that my friend Kim — the one who is *not* into complaining on yachts — insisted that I must, sending me this library link so that like shopping on Amazon, I was one click from nirvana: https://catalog.cincin-natilibrary.org/iii/encore/record/C__Rb2770191__Sthe%20girl%20in%20the%20cafe__Orightresult__U__X7?lang=eng&suite=cobalt

I will confess that there are a lot of politics in this movie, and my mind simply does not do politics. So when Lawrence tells Gina that he is going to a G8 conference and she asks him what that means, I listened carefully for the answer because I did not know. The various elements being negotiated at the G8 conference made sense while I watched the movie, but not so much sense that I can parrot them back to you now. However, there was one part of the political debate that I understood well, the death of children due to starvation. Gina's character makes this issue crystal clear as she says a child dies every three seconds in Africa while snapping her fingers in three-second intervals to illustrate her point.

So the political stuff grabbed me and didn't grab me in equal measure, while the part that completely won me over—in a snap—was the character of Lawrence Montague. The movie starts out showing him in all his solitary pursuits: living alone, eating alone in restaurants, lost in his own thoughts at work so that even in a room full of people he was alone. And then out of pure chance, at a restaurant at which he stops for a cup of coffee, he finds nowhere to sit so he asks another solitary diner, this girl in the café, Gina, if he can sit with her. From there bloomed an amazing, wonderful, hysterical romantic comedy. The movie is often laugh-out-loud funny, and better than that, almost every scene in the movie has Bill Nighy in it. The movie is ninety-five minutes of bliss. I mean Bill-iss! I mean it is Bill-isimo! Stupendo and magnífico too!

Some specific things to love in this movie are:

1. I already knew that Bill Nighy is a terrific actor, but in this movie I learned that even the man's back is amazingly talented. As Lawrence starts to leave the café after meeting Gina, the viewer watches him walk to the door. But it's evident he's not just walking to the door; he's debating with himself if he should leave Gina behind or find out how to see her again. And all of this is conveyed through his back as he stops and

starts and stops again until he finally turns around to talk to her again. Without a doubt, he wins the Academy Award for the finest performance by the back of a body in a movie. I can't even imagine another contender for the award.

2. But beyond his back, there is also his chest starring in this movie. The viewer gets a glimpse of it as he buttons up his jammies in one scene and then — oh my God — there is a scene with him in the shower in which we see his naked chest as it peeks out behind a small towel. Chest hair! I'm swooning!

3. Though laughter comes abundantly in this film, the movie is also a very serious treatise on loneliness. Toward the end of the movie, Gina has said and done things to jeopardize Lawrence's career and his heretofore stellar reputation. Addressing this fact, Lawrence delivers these gorgeous lines: "We have a pair of unfortunate situations here: A man who has nothing in his life except his work. That is unfortunate. And then by a stroke of bizarre chance he finds someone who makes that not true for a day or two. But then suddenly it seems as though the price that has to be paid for that ray of light is some kind of disgrace. It doesn't seem quite fair." Of course, if Bill Nighy — in the role of Bill Nighy — likewise feels that he has nothing in his life except his work, he needs to look no further than the woman from Ohio who has tried wooing him with roses…

Here are a couple of things I am wondering about, and oddly, Google is no help in answering these questions. So enquiring minds want to know:

1. In this movie, beloved Bill actually sleeps with his love interest. Has that happened in other movies? In the Johnny Worricker trilogy there are women of interest, but I can't remember if he sleeps with any of them. (Note to self: Check it out!)

2. The cover of the DVD has a photo of Bill Nighy and Kelly Macdonald's characters holding each other as they gaze into each other's eyes. Bill Nighy's left hand is shown and there is no evidence of his Dupuytren's contracture. What's up with that? Why would they doctor the photo?

And as I review all four of these movies, I have still another question unanswerable by Google. Supposedly Bill Nighy's breakthrough role was in *Love Actually* in 2003, right? Supposedly movie roles now come to him without the need to audition, right? So with the exception of *The Girl in the Café*, why aren't his parts larger? Here are the movies in chronological order:

Love Actually, 2003
Enduring Love, 2004
The Constant Gardener, 2005
The Girl in the Café, 2005
Notes on a Scandal, 2006

Perhaps he had already signed on for *Enduring Love* and *The Constant Gardener* before he experienced the success of *Love Actually*. That could explain his small parts in those movies. But didn't his acting prowess deserve more scenes in *Notes on a Scandal* and the many, many other movies that followed in his career?

From what I've seen, beloved Bill has had starring roles in the Johnny Worricker trilogy and in *Skylight*, all written by David Hare. And he had a starring role in *The Girl in the Café* written by Richard Curtis. But other than those two writers—and me—no one seems to see him as the leading man he is. This saddens me, but also makes me like Bill Nighy more. It's impressive that his ego allows him to be part of a movie instead of its star.

As for my ego, it has allowed me to be prostrate on the sofa for many hours over many days as I have watched these stories. While many of my friends binge-watch TV, I never have, so this is totally bizarre-o behavior. Oh well, tomorrow's another day. Actually, it's Thursday, so it's movie day with Vera. Ha! Well at least that's a social activity as opposed to some form of addiction. Or is this hibernation? Or have I just stalled out in life?

Thursday, June 25, 2015

Dear Diary,

Today's movie schedule allowed Vera and me time to have a leisurely lunch at a nice restaurant, which was great because I had so much to tell her. Though the letter from Bill Nighy came a week ago, right as I got home from our last Thursday together, I refrained from emailing or calling her because I wanted to watch her open his letter in person. So after we sat down at Mitchell's Fish Market and ordered our meals, I slipped the letter out of my purse and passed it across the table to her. "Look at this," I said.

"What is it?" she asked. I just shrugged and made a very wide-eyed, innocent face. She looked down at it, the front addressed to me, the back announcing it was from BN in NYC. And then it hit her and she shrieked, "Oh my God, is it from him?!" At that point, I started shrieking too, bringing the entire restaurant into our conversation. Like that vintage TV commercial for E.F. Hutton, when Vera and Lorie talk, people listen!

With eyes closed, Vera joyously clutched the letter to her breast, as if it were a missive from the oncologist proclaiming her Bill cancer-free. After reading it, she asked, "Are you writing him back?"

"Wait, wait, wait," I said. "You're missing something major. What about those three X's on his letter?" She looked the letter over again and then looked up at me questioningly, not getting my point. "Do you think that means he loves me back? Is there a chance of that?"

"You mean on a scale of zero to none?"

Well okay, that answered my question. So I went on to tell her about my two botched attempts at writing fan letter number two. And I told her about my Google exhaustion and about being both done and finished. And I casually mentioned my four-film movie marathon. But then I made the mistake of telling her about Roberta's correspondence with Stephen Sondheim and she said, "Well, if Roberta got five letters from her guy, then you have to get five or more letters from yours. Where is your competitive spirit?"

"But what would I even be hoping for here? To be his pen pal?"

"Sure, that works. And to win the competition."

"I much prefer thinking he loves me. I prefer to visualize us together on the red carpet: he in his bespoke blue suit bespeaking his dressing style and willingness to spend cash and me in my TJ Maxx or Lands' End bespeaking mine."

"You sometimes buy off the sale rack at Macy's" she offered, and we laughed loudly, disturbing the lunch crowd at Mitchell's once again.

"Ya know, I can actually picture this, Vera. There I am getting dressed for the red-carpet event, trying on outfit after outfit and rejecting one after another. And then I see him, the king of self-deprecation, likewise trying on one navy suit after another trying to find something, anything that will work for the date."

"A match made in heaven," she said.

"From your lips to God's ears," I responded lightheartedly, but I meant it a little more seriously than she could know.

Vera and I finished our lunches and, to the delight of the other restaurant patrons, left for the movies. Today's film was *I'll See You in My Dreams* starring Blythe Danner and featuring Sam Elliott as her love interest. I often post a movie review on Facebook on Thursdays, and this is what I wrote today: "If you are up to watching a nice depiction of loneliness, this is a three-star movie. And I liked her wardrobe in it!" I didn't say more because I didn't want to give away the plot online, but I will tell all here. Blythe Danner's character is a widow. She is not looking to meet a man, but she does, and they hit it off! But then suddenly, he dies. The movie ends with her having a mundane day hanging out with her girlfriends. My original thought was a horrified, *What kind of ending is that?!* But then I reasoned with myself that although the bait and switch with romance and reality was jarring, she was continuing to live life one day at a time. What was her other choice? What is another choice for any of us?

It's interesting to me that this topic of loneliness keeps rearing its ugly head to me. I'm wondering, dear Diary, if that's why I am so over the top with this Bill Nighy guy, adorable though he may be. Am I looking for a relationship? I know Vera's suggestion that we be pen pals is abhorrent to me. I want so much more than that.

"But what exactly is it that you want?" a voice in my head shouted. Uh-oh, VOR is back.

"Oh, God. I don't know. Leave me alone!" PITS hollered back.

"Yes, you *do* know. You've told dozens of people what you want from a man at this point in your life, and it is…" VOR prompted.

"I want a man to call me on the phone every couple of days and leave a message that says something like, 'Hi, babe, how ya doin'?' I want said man to expect no response but just to take his joy from the fact that he spoke to my machine. Of course I want him to take me out to dinner every now and again. Maybe twice a month, maybe more. And let's not forget that he will buy me lovely gifts. Diamonds. Lots of diamonds. Yes, that's what I want, D&D, dinner and diamonds."

"So," VOR surmised, "this is what you want from Bill Nighy?"

"No! Not at all—I want more!"

"Hot sex all day every day, perhaps?"

"No," said a horrified PITS, or maybe it was her low-level libido speaking. "I can't even imagine that. Maybe because Hollywood and all those film makers in Great Britain have never pictured him that way either. I don't think the guy has ever been painted as a Lothario, at least in the movies I have found to date. Isn't that part of his charm?"

"So if you don't want the fuck, what the fuck do you want?" In response to my stony silence, VOR went on kindly, "What are you imagining, PITS?"

"I am imagining a cottage in the woods. It has a huge great room. One wall contains an enormous stone fireplace, and the weather in this pretend Brigadoon-ish locale always requires a fire. On the wall opposite the fireplace is a huge book case with all of his books and all of mine, happily co-mingling on the shelves. Among mine are several stories of great love that have withstood all obstacles, even those of time and death. We have the love of Robert Kincaid and Francesca Johnson in *The Bridges of Madison County* by Robert James Waller. We have the love of Julie Roseman and Romeo Cacciamani in *Julie and Romeo* by Jeanne Ray. And we have the love of Tin Win and Mi Mi, the young Burmese lovers, in *The Art of Hearing Heartbeats* by Jan-Philipp Sendker.

"Beloved Bill has a bedroom and bath off the great room, as do I. His is equipped with a state-of-the-art sound system so he can get his daily dose of Bob Dylan. Each of our rooms has a bed large enough to accommodate a guest when canoodling is called for, which is often, because it's a cold, hard world out there and everyone needs the shelter of warm arms. And then of course, someplace within the cottage there must be a kitchen from which delicious and low-carb food appears magically as beloved Bill and I live happily ever after."

VOR takes pity on the demented PITS and just says quietly, "You know that's all far-fetched fiction, right?"

And PITS is equally quiet and non-belligerent as she replies, "You know he included three X's in his letter, right?"

SATURDAY, JUNE 27, 2015

Dear Diary,

I spent all morning Googling my guy. In countless articles in the print media and in countless YouTube interviews featuring him, he is steadfastly charming. And in both still photos and film clips, he is almost always in his signature navy blue suit—his bespoke suit—and he graciously discusses that fact over and over and over and over again. I have been following him on Google for just a couple of months and I am sick of the topic, so I wonder how he must feel. Be that as it may, my beloved Bill will gladly discuss it again with any reporter should they ask.

While on this topic I should confess, dear Diary, that I have looked up the meaning of bespoke dozens of times. I just cannot get that word into my head. But today, on still another dictionary search, an interesting fact finally penetrated my brain—the word is an adjective! And here I keep trying to make it a verb. Come to think of it though, I like it better as a verb; it really be-speaks to me that way.

Back to the man, he is completely humble and modest. It is always in a self-deprecating manner that he speaks of himself while he has only the highest praise for every actor, actress, playwright, director, and producer with whom he has ever worked. It is not a far reach to guess that he probably feels the same way for every cameraman, makeup artist, costume designer, casting director, choreographer, etc., who has crossed his path. I would say he doles out kind words to a fault, but I find no fault with such magnanimity.

It is unbelievable to me, but beautiful Bill seems to have body image problems. I hope he knows he is just like the rest of mankind in this regard. But this fact helps explain why his signature light blue dress shirt will have only the top button undone. Should I ever be so fortunate to be in a relationship with this guy (Vera's opinion be damned!),

I will smuggle him into the dressing room in Macy's intimates department, where he can hear women cell-phoning their friends as they haplessly try on bras, the lady in one dressing room bemoaning the fact that all of them are too small while the lady in another dressing room is crying over the fact that they are all too large.

Beyond body image, Bill Nighy seems to have struggled with alcohol in the past. He is reluctant to call it an addiction; it was an unhealthy relationship instead, and he is unwilling to further delineate the situation. Likewise, details about his daughter and ex-"wife" and especially about the demise of their relationship are skimpy. He seems to want it that way, so I will dig no further, and I ask forgiveness for having earlier questioned his daughter's lengthy name.

On the professional side, this man has a huge résumé. Most of his work is British, which makes sense since he is too, duh! America found him thanks to *Love Actually*, but the rest of the English-speaking world has known his charm for loads of years. What a testimony to his un-inflated personality that he has worked multiple times with the same writers, directors, and actors. Apparently they love working with him as much as I love seeing him upon the screen.

Of most interest to me, his personal life seems quiet. He lives alone and likes it that way. He takes his walks and drinks his coffee. In one interview, he said he has been known to lie beneath trees as he takes pictures of light filtering through the branches. He is a solitary man.

While those seem to be the basic facts of his life, all my Googling and reading has also turned up these amplifications and additions:

- He does not like to dress more casually than his bespoke navy blue suit. He never wore T-shirts "even when he was supposed to wear them," as he never felt he had the right shape for them. He says he "couldn't do a T-shirt justice."
- Likewise, he "doesn't do unshaven well either." He feels it makes him look "like someone about to have a breakdown."

- He ended his unhealthy relationship with alcohol in 1992.
- He credits Diana Quick with helping him kick the habit.
- His substances of choice these days are coffee and Yorkshire tea.
- He also loves Marmite, which is a sticky food paste made from yeast sludge (a waste product from brewing beer), water, spice extracts, and lots of salt. Often used as a breakfast spread on toast, it is an acquired taste.
- His hand condition started in his twenties and does not hurt at all.
- There is an operation that can correct it, but he has chosen not to have it.
- Due to the condition, he calls his handshake "spooky."
- When he's working, he wakes up at 5, and when he is not working, he gets up at 10.
- He loves independent book shops.
- He loves dogs and stops people in the street to talk about their dogs.
- He loves football in general, and specifically he loves the Crystal Palace Football Club.
- He thinks about death twelve times a day and measures his life in Champions Leagues—how many annual football competitions does he have left?
- There isn't a day that goes by when he doesn't listen to Bob Dylan.
- He has two dogs, Smokey, a rescue dog, and Nelly, a posh terrier.
- He has a cat too, Ziggy, who has only one eye.
- He loves the poetry of Harold Pinter.
- And the writing of Ernest Hemingway, F. Scott Fitzgerald, and Ford Madox Ford.
- And speaking of writers, at one point in his life he wanted to be

a journalist and found a job as a runner on a hunting magazine called *The Field*. Going on to Paris to follow in Hemingway's footsteps was also a part of his plan.

- His song, "Christmas Is All Around," from the movie *Love Actually*, made it to number twenty-six on the U.K. charts.
- And here's an odd fact: He contributed a doodle to the National Doodle Campaign (2008), which auctions off celebrity doodles to benefit the Neurofibromatosis Association.
- And a final fun fact: He's been called "the thinking woman's crumpet."

In the same manner that I checked the meaning of the word "bespoke" dozens of times, should I need to convince myself that any of this is true, or at least reported as true, here are the sources I have been reading: an article called "Bill Nighy: I'm Greedy for Beauty" that appeared in *The Guardian* on February 8, 2015, and which was written by Nigel Farndale; an article called "I've Just Been Extremely Fortunate: Bill Nighy Is Having the Time of His Life," that appeared in *The Sydney Morning Herald* on October 12, 2013, and which was written by Stephanie Bunbury; and http://www.billnighy.info/about-bill-nighy/. (Of course the amalgam of information from this site might not be current.)

Well, dear Diary, I love the man, but enough is enough. I am off on a Saturday expedition. Hooray for me that I have found one. I am going to a quilt show in Miamisburg, Ohio. The round trip alone is ninety minutes and I delight in being away from Google for that long. I will be back with a report on the show soon…

…My how time flies when one gets away from electronic devices. Four hours have passed and I am back now from the quilt show. The quilts were lovely! I have never seen such superlative work! The designs were all original and the craftsmanship sublime! And kudos to those who installed the show itself; they made excellent use of the physical space, not to mention the ambient light!

So that's probably what Bill Nighy would have said about the show. Here is my actual report, though not so magnanimous. In all honesty, the quality of quilts was similar to what one would find at a state fair as opposed to a top-level quilt show, but I still enjoyed it. And to be honest, when the quilts at a show are too terrific and amazing, they thwart my creativity instead of feeding it. Simply put, I am a great quilt technician but not much of an artist. While I create all my own designs, they are based on traditional patterns, patterns I know how to execute well. For instance, my star points appear in toto and are never accidentally lopped off. If my fabric has trees printed on it, all my trees stand upright; none of them lies on its side. I am a good girl. I know how these things are supposed to be done, and I do them that way. But a great artist? No, I am not that. When I started to make quilts professionally, I created my own niche so I would not have to be compared to those fine fiber artists—I began to make quilts with words and symbols pieced into the design. To my knowledge, no one else does that. Whether you call my stuff art or craft—or crap—I stand alone in my field.

So the quilts at the show today did not rattle my nerves, though something else at the venue did. Beyond the quilt exhibit, there were six or seven vendors at the show selling all sorts of things, but mainly fabric as would be expected. After all, we quilters live by the motto "She who dies with the most fabric wins." But anyway, one of the vendors was a woman selling already made quilt blocks. She had a boatload of them. All very lovely, all in coordinating colors, all dirt cheap. For instance, she was selling star blocks that were six inches square. Each block was composed of two dozen littler squares and triangles sewn together to create the star, which is a time-consuming task. Her workmanship was outstanding—Bill Nighy and I would have no choice but to agree on that—and her price for each block was $1.50.

"Are you insane to be selling quilt blocks at that price?" I asked her. "The fabric alone is worth that much."

"My adult kids ask me the same thing," was her response, "and what I tell them is this: My stash of fabric is huge. The quilt blocks I make will indeed sell for that price. And if I weren't sewing quilt blocks and bringing them to quilt shows, my other choice in life is to be bored, depressed, and lonely."

Like the lyrics to the old Roberta Flack song, this woman was killing me softly with her words as she described my life. It was all I could do not to cry. I had no more questions for her but a bunch for myself. Could I give up making quilts for grandkids and get back to my signature stuff? Could I maybe sell my unique quilts on Etsy at whatever low price worked, just to stave off boredom and depression? I would need a following, but my stuff is so visual, couldn't I start putting my older work up on photo-sharing websites and places like that? Would my publisher allow me to use quilt images from my two quilt-related books to help get my name out there? Could I additionally sell my books on Etsy? Oh my gosh. So many questions. And I know exactly where to start my search for answers: Google. Good thing for me I am such an experienced Googler!

Unfortunately, once I got home and got my device back in hand, all these thoughts vanished as it occurred to me to Google this instead: "YouTube Charlie Rose and Bill Nighy." Some of these interviews are an hour long! An hour of watching and listening to my man! It's heaven! Oh my. Here I go again. The kerplop you just heard, dear Diary, is the sound of me going off the deep end.

SUNDAY, JUNE 28, 2015

Dear Diary,

It's Sunday, so I spoke to Roberta on the phone tonight, thank God! I could not wait to talk to her and to confess. "Bird! I have spent the entire past week Googling Bill Nighy. I am absolutely driving myself crazy with this, but I just cannot seem to stop. I Google until late at night and wake up early in the morning only to start again. Do you think this is some sort of adult-onset mental illness? I am exhausted, but I can't stop."

"This is so unlike you. You are usually so reasonable."

"I know! But in this case, I am pie in the sky and grandiose!"

"But why?"

"It's because of those three fricking X's, Bird. There is a part of me that is convinced that something in my letter resonated in him and that he loves me back, hence the X's. And when I say *resonated*, I mean it evoked something in him, rang a bell, touched a nerve, recovered some long-lost memory. I am thinking that beyond love at first sight, there is also love at first write."

"It's a given from your experience with the monthly column that people like your writing, so why shouldn't he?"

"I agree, but here's the crazy part: In spite of all this, I am hard-pressed to even imagine a relationship with him. He lives in London and I would never move there because I need to be here with the eight grandkids. Then I think, *Well, I could fix Thursday dinner for the kids and then fly off to be with my Bill on Friday and then return on Sunday night in time for Marmel School on Monday.*"

"But with flight times and time differences, what would that give you? Ten minutes together weekly?"

"No, actually, according to my research we would have almost twenty-three hours together. There are no nonstops, so I would leave

Cincinnati at 4 p.m. on Friday, stop in Boston, then continue to London arriving at Heathrow at 7:20 a.m. on Saturday. I would then leave Heathrow on Sunday at 6:40 a.m. flying through Charles de Gaulle airport in Paris and arriving Cincinnati at 2:16 p.m. I don't even know how to factor in the five-hour time difference except to say I am going to be very tired, not to mention broke. The round-trip fare is $1,424. Of course he might own his own plane, but I rather doubt it, as I don't even think he owns a car." Bird's silence on the other end of the line was worrisome. "So as you can see, I've been a little over the top."

"Yes," she hesitated. "A little…perhaps you have been. All because of those X's, huh?"

"Yes. The three X's." There was some silence before she rendered an opinion.

"Maybe that's just the way he signs his name."

So there I was, dear Diary, talking to her on my cell phone with one hand and with the other I grabbed my iPad and I Googled "Bill Nighy's signature — images," and two astounding things happened. First of all, Google actually pulled up a bunch of images showing his signature! (Isn't Google amazing?) And second, all those many images proved to me that the man often signs his name and then embellishes it with X's. I felt my adult-onset mental illness immediately dissipate. Hallelujah! Let my normal life resume!

MONDAY, JUNE 29, 2015

Dear Diary,

I had a dream last night. I was in the laundry room, up on a ladder, changing the fluorescent light bulb. Unfortunately, I lost my hold on the bulb and dropped it onto the ceramic tile floor. The bulb burst into thousands of pieces. I woke up breathless at the loss, thinking to myself, *That was a fragile ray of light.*

July

WEDNESDAY, JULY 1, 2015

Dear Diary,

I spoke to Anita today. Her mom is not doing well. After a week-long sojourn in the hospital, beloved Aunt Betty is debilitated and needs a lot of assistance. Hearing the exhaustion in Anita's voice, I volunteered to come help out in St. Louis. Yes, I love Aunt Betty so I am thrilled to be able to take a turn at care giving, but I am also thrilled to run away from home for a while, thrilled to have a new focus as I try to get past my own debilitation, my Bill Nighy addiction. I'm still a little shaken by my weeks of crazy behavior. As Big Irv would say, it doesn't add down and across. Nope. No way. It was totally out of character for me.

<u>THURSDAY, JULY 2, 2015</u>

Dear Diary,

Aunt Betty has been dependent on thrice-weekly dialysis for years now, and suddenly this treatment is not doing the trick, hence the recent hospitalization for this dear eighty-seven-year-old woman. I should Google how long one's life expectancy is on dialysis, but I am not really sure I want to know. I've been through Mom's death in 2002 and Dad's death in 2010 and Big Irv's death in 2014, and the situation here in St. Louis is not looking good to me. This sets a somber tone for my visit.

Though I grew up in St. Louis and have countless fond memories of my life here from birth through early adulthood, it's only sad stuff that is catching my attention so far on this visit.

1. As I traveled Highway 40 West en route to Garden Villas, the independent living facility where Aunt Betty lives, I passed Missouri Baptist Hospital, which towers over the highway. Those rooms on the top floors are medical offices, and it was in one of them that we got the news of Mom's lung cancer, the illness that would kill her within five weeks of diagnosis. I remember thinking at the time that our family's life had reached an end point while all those people I saw driving on the highway below still had places to go; hence, that patch of highway will always be the crossroads of life and death for me.

2. Reaching the retirement community was no less moving, as it is the same facility at which Dad lived when he gave up his condo in St. Louis. He lived at Garden Villas for a year but then needed more help, so we moved him to Cincinnati and within ten months, he too was dead. Garden Villas is a truly lovely place, but for Dad it was the beginning of the end. Wrenching is the best word to describe it now.

3. There are even Big Irv memories here in St. Louis, as he helped move Dad from the condo to Garden Villas. Then he helped move Dad from St. Louis to Cincinnati. Then in Cincinnati he helped with the moves from assisted living to a nursing home and then to hospice. As Big Irv poignantly noted, Dad went from a houseful of possessions to a boxful in four moves. Wrenching.

4. And speaking of Mom and Dad's old condo, I always drive by there when I am in town. It is in an area called Creve Coeur. Big Irv was the one who informed me that Creve Coeur means "broken heart" in French. Indeed, the city's logo contains two images, a fleur-de-lis and below it, a cleft heart.

How odd it is to come to this place of death and dying, this place of the broken heart, to figure out the next step of life and living for me…

Wednesday, July 8, 2015

Dear Diary,

Today is my last day in St. Louis. If nothing else, I am well-rested after this visit. On her dialysis days, Aunt Betty is gone for five hours, allowing me lots of quiet time. I packed two books for the trip but could get into neither of them, which is odd. One of the books is Paul Auster's *Sunset Park*. Auster is my all-time favorite author and I have read almost every word the man has written, but I just could not get into this one. Since his work can be taxing to the brain, I also brought along some fluff — Jennifer Weiner's *All Fall Down*. Usually her books grab me by the shirt collar, pull me in, and keep me turning pages, but not this time — I just don't have the patience to read. Looking for something to fill my time instead, I turned to old habits. I walked laps at the Frontenac mall like I used to with Dad; I ate lunch at the Pasta House like I used to with Dad; I browsed the aisles at Aldi's and Walgreens like I used to with Dad; and of course I visited Mom at the cemetery like I used to with Dad. Handily, he is buried beside her, so I got to visit him too.

Anyway, even when Aunt Betty was around, things were pretty calm. I got her up at 7 a.m. and tucked her in for the night by 10 p.m. In the intervening hours, she ate meals and watched TV. That was as animated as she got. And please note that at her current age, "watching TV" is a euphemism for having a snoozefest. Meanwhile, I enjoyed all the old movies she slept through. Indeed, this may explain my Bill Nighy movie marathon — watching stuff on TV is fun! I had forgotten that.

Beyond relaxation, I used some of my time here to get my July column in order. Woo hoo! How nice to have that done! Along creative lines, I have also thought — a smidge — about getting back to quilt making and/or about marketing my old quilt designs on Etsy.

A friend who tried selling her art via that venue says one needs to be online all the time to make it successful. Another woo hoo! Right up my alley.

Speaking of such, it is surprising, but I have not been tempted this week to Google my guy. I have an iPad and smartphone with me so I could have, but I have not. My only concession to that former way of life—I hope—is that I have a gnawing worry that he has indeed sent me roses, dozens of roses, during my time in St. Louis and that said roses are dying out on my front porch in the Cincinnati summer heat.

I also have a game plan in regard to HIM. I am going to think of him as a hobby. I do enjoy reading about him online, so I will… in moderation. I also enjoy his movies and I will continue to watch them…in moderation. Weekends are hard for us single folks. (Even Barbara Covett/Judi Dench knows this.) A Saturday night date with one of his films would be lovely. I just need to remember the story of the burning bush through all of this and allow Bill Nighy to light my fire without letting him consume me. As Dad always said, everything in moderation.

A Bit of Fantasy—The Mail

I see Bill Nighy between gigs. The U.S. *Skylight* engagement is over and work on *Their Finest* has yet to begin. He can linger in New York City or return home to London as his mood dictates. Sleeping in, visiting coffee shops, perusing book stores, and strolling the park can fill his days in either locale, and they do...for a few days and then the idyll becomes less idyllic. *Darn!* he thinks. *It's hard for me to be out of character! Indeed, who am I on my own without a character to play?* That disturbing thought is immediately ignored as he chooses to get back into his most recent character instead. Thus, he wonders what Tom Sergeant would do to pass the time. Oddly, the thought of sending roses pops to mind. And that nice lady from Ohio pops to mind. And then some voice in his head shouts, "Are you daft, man?"

So he nixes the flowers and instead he types her name into a search engine. After all, two can play that Google game. In this manner, a lot happens in rapid order:

1. He sees she has books in print!
2. He orders said books from Amazon.co.uk—one-click shopping and overnight delivery of course!
3. He reads her books!
4. And in the same manner that she fell for him after experiencing his work, he falls for her!
5. And so writing her a second letter becomes his obsession!

LORIE ECKERT
I LOVED YOUR THREE BOOKS.
I LOVED YOUR SLICE OF LIFE COLUMN THAT I FOUND ONLINE.
ONLINE PHOTOS OF YOU ARE LIKEWISE ENCHANTING.
TO BORROW FROM YOUR LETTER TO ME:
HOW ODD TO BE A "FAMOUS ACTOR" WITH A CRUSH ON
A SIXTY-THREE-YEAR-OLD WOMAN IN OHIO.
I HOPE YOU WILL WRITE ME AGAIN AT THE ADDRESS ON THE
ENVELOPE.

BILL NIGHY
X

Thursday, July 9, 2015

Dear Diary,

Oops. Having just pledged to do this Bill Nighy "hobby" in moderation, I failed miserably during my trip home today, spending most of those 360 miles spinning a fantasy about the man. Why did I do that? I could beat myself up over it, but instead I hear Big Irv in my head. He always explained away the unexplainable by saying, "It is as it is." Heeding this philosophy, I forgive myself and will try for moderation again tomorrow. Argh!

As I worry about moving on beyond my BN addiction, I just read over the column I will email to editors tomorrow. Its bottom line, comically, is forward march! I sure hope my psyche is listening. Seriously, though, here is an observation from today's travel that might help in that regard. As I drove across the Mississippi River heading to Ohio, I realized that leaving the past behind can be a very literal thing.

JULY 10, 2015

A Slice of Life: A Monthly Column

RUNNING OUT OF THINGS TO DO

I recently had a conversation with my son-in-law, Scotty B. He was telling me about his parents' new home and how they were working crazily to get it in shape. He didn't understand the reason they had sold the old house—which he felt was perfect in every way—and bought this new one, a fixer-upper. I suggested to him that perhaps they had run out of things to do in their retirement and that they were reverting to old interests as a hedge against boredom. They have rehabbed many a house. They are good at rehabbing houses. When in doubt on what to do next, why not rehab a house? He looked at me skeptically. Had I been his mother instead of his mother-in-law, he would have let loose with a long and protracted multi-syllabic rendition of the short word, *Mom.*

I went on to explain to this thirty-eight-year-old male that when I was his age and when my kids were young like his, I likewise could not fathom running out of things to do. Every time I transported the kids to whatever game, practice, class, or friend's house they needed transporting to, I always ached as I passed shop after shop I needed to go into but did not have the time for. *Look, there's the new bakery with the wonderful babkes—I'll hope to go there someday! Look, there's that gift shop I love—I wonder what darling things they've gotten in since my visit there a year ago. Look, there's the new and very posh salon— wouldn't a massage be wonderful?* I think he caught my drift. But then I confessed that as soon as my kids were grown and I had the time to stop, I somehow no longer had the desire to do so.

Trying to help me find ways to fill my time, he suggested that I take up volunteer work, but I have had quite my fill of that through the years. He suggested—perhaps hopefully—that I babysit grandchildren twenty-four/seven, but love those eight little kids as I do, I let that exhausting concept pass with a dubious shake of the head. He suggested I take up golf, but of course that is what he would do with his spare time if he had any, not what I would do with mine. (But I encouraged him to play golf because it is a time-consuming hobby and someday he will be in his sixties and need to pass some time.) Unfortunately, that was the end of his suggestions. He ran out of ideas before he solved my problem. Darn!

As I have established in previous columns, in the midst of plenty— meaning lots of kids and grandkids living nearby—I often feel lonely. And now I am recognizing this other truth about my life: I have run out of things to do, the translation of which means I am bored. And I'll fess up: I'm a little depressed too. Owning all three legs of the bored-lonely-depressed triumvirate, it occurs to me that perhaps I should look for something to do.

Well, if it works for Scotty B's parents to fall back on successful activities of their past, what about me doing the same?

- I have worked as a substitute teacher at the local school district, but I find I don't have the patience for little kids except my own.
- I have worked for a real estate investment trust as the administrative assistant to the president and vice president of the company, but I find it is not fulfilling to spend my life making sure there is enough coffee and soda pop on hand for the staff.
- I have worked as an assistant to visiting chefs at a nearby kitchen shop that offers cooking classes, but I find minimum wage hard to bear, especially with all the non-glamorous pot scrubbing and floor washing it entailed.

- I have worked as a personal assistant to a wealthy lady over there in Richville, but in spite of the fact that I loved the money she threw my way, I found it hard to handle all the crazy places she threw money. One week she would have me purge all Barbie dolls and Barbie doll paraphernalia from the ten-year-old daughter's bedroom, only to send me to the toy store the next week to buy lots of Barbies again because the daughter missed her toys. I hear that *every three seconds* a child starves in Africa, so without a doubt there is a better use for money than this.

- I have worked as a motivational speaker giving unique presentations that are illustrated by my artwork—quilts with words and symbols pieced into the design. I have spoken to more than 250 audiences in eleven states, but at sixty-three, I am too old to schlep from state to state with a carload of quilts. Plus, it is difficult to be a motivational speaker when often I am a depressed person.

But wait, wait, wait! Wait a minute here. I am not the sort of person to move backward in time. Forward march is more my motto. And so I have no choice but to look ahead to what comes next. Unfortunately, I just don't know what that is. Stay tuned…

SATURDAY, JULY 11, 2015

Dear Diary,

A new item on my weekly schedule: Saturday Night at the Movies starring the incomparable Bill Nighy. In choosing which film to watch tonight, there is good news and bad news. The good news: He has so many films from which to choose! The bad news: His part in many of them is minuscule! Supposedly the role of Billy Mack in *Love Actually* made him marketable in America, but evidently marketability and starring roles are not the same thing. Darn! Meatier parts would be wonderful for those of us wanting to devour the man. Regardless, in choosing a film to watch tonight, I enlisted Bill Nighy's aid. In an interview with *Buzz Feed News* entitled "Bill Nighy Examines 10 of His Film Roles" by Adam Vary, BN himself mentioned these films in this order.

1. *Underworld* (2003)
2. *Love Actually* (2003)
3. *Shaun of the Dead* (2004)
4. *Pirates of the Caribbean: Dead Man's Chest* (2006)
5. *Hot Fuzz* (2007)
6. *Valkyrie* (2008)
7. *Harry Potter and the Deathly Hallows Part 1* (2010)
8. *The Best Exotic Marigold Hotel* (2012)
9. *About Time* (2013)
10. *Pride* (2014)

My choice for tonight is *Valkyrie*…due to its availability on the library shelf today!

Saturday Night at the Movies

Valkyrie
DIRECTOR: Bryan Singer
WRITERS: Christopher McQuarrie and Nathan Alexander
RELEASE DATE: 2008
RUNNING TIME: 2 Hours, 4 Minutes
ALSO FEATURING: Tom Cruise, Kenneth Branagh, Tom Wilkinson, Terrence Stamp, Eddie Izzard, and Tom Hollander.

Wikipedia tells us *Valkyrie* is an historical thriller set in Nazi Germany during World War II. The film depicts an actual plot by German army officers to assassinate Adolf Hitler on July 20, 1944. Part of the strategy was to use Operation Valkyrie, which was a plan that involved the deployment of the Reserve Army to maintain order in the event of a national emergency, in this case, the death of Hitler. In the movie, Bill Nighy plays the part of General Friedrich Olbricht, a member of the German resistance. Olbricht is the one who recruits Claus von Stauffenberg, played by Tom Cruise, into the resistance movement. Stauffenberg becomes the leading member of this particular assassi-nation plan while Olbricht is just a participant. However, Olbricht's slight hesitation to carry out his part of the plan provides a major plot—and historical—element. Namely, Hitler was not assassinated.

Since anything of a political nature scrambles my brain, it is hard for me to report on exactly how the movie progressed from Point A to Point B and beyond. Additionally, since my father's entire family was lost in Warsaw thanks to Adolph Hitler and the Nazi regime, being "entertained" by a story of that time period is not quite possible for me. But it never occurred to me that there was a German resistance movement that was trying to oust/murder Hitler—I somehow missed that in high school history lessons—so I was very happy to learn about this part of history.

The Wikipedia article quotes Bill Nighy as saying, "One of the most disconcerting things imaginable is to put on a Nazi uniform. It's so associated with evil that it took me several days to get used to being in costume." I am comforted by his sensitivity on this topic. It also helps me to read these comments about the movie from Bill Nighy himself as mentioned in an interview that appeared in *The Oklahoman, NewsOK*, on January 2, 2009. These quotes further help me understand there were good people in the German army.

- "I never thought of him [Olbricht] as a Nazi. In spirit he wasn't. He had to pay lip service to the Nazi Party to stay alive...These men were in the midst of a country terrified into collective madness. They were honorable military men, ashamed that they had a commander-in-chief who was not only an incompetent corporal but also a lunatic. Olbricht was involved in the German resistance longer than almost anyone else. He risked his life every day for several years, plotting schemes against Hitler. And then, when the moment of real action arrived, he faltered."

- One of the eeriest and most moving experiences for Bill Nighy during the making of *Valkyrie* was filming on the exact spot in Berlin where Olbricht faced a firing squad. BN says Tom Cruise "made a little speech that night just to mark the occasion, out of respect and to recognize that we were being given this responsibility to show how these brave men lived and died."

In an interview with indielondon.co.uk, Bill Nighy continues in this vein as he talks about Tom Cruise's character: "Stauffenberg came from nine generations of military men—he was like the epitome of what was German then and what being a soldier meant." The implication being that Stauffenberg was not alone in his resistance.

While it is true that BN did not have a meatier role in this thriller, it is heartening that the story itself was of such significance.

Dear Diary,

I have been home from St. Louis for a week now and I am feeling a little bit down. Perhaps it's the sobering effects of Aunt Betty's condition that still linger? Or maybe I'm just a little tired? I am keeping busy with my normal schedule and with all the mail that accumulated in my absence. Yes, I am Googling my guy a bit, but it's all under control, more to pass time than as a crazy addiction. What I am feeling most is an odd disappointment every time I go to my mailbox and find no letter from Bill Nighy there. Likewise, it is sad to look out to the front porch and find no roses either. I realize I never sent a second letter, but there is that tiny hope he picked up on the hints I placed in my first letter and Googled his way to loving me just as I fantasized on my drive home from St. Louis. The only thing is, a second letter from him does not arrive in my mailbox. It occurs to me I should do something to increase that likelihood and to keep the thrill of the mailbox alive. It occurs to me I should send a second letter.

Notes to myself:

- Keep your expectations low.
- Pray for a response — not for a relationship.
- Remember that the real goal here is to go from flat to bubbly and that the mere possibility of a reply is the mood-altering drug to get you there.
- Sounds sensible, doesn't it? Keep it that way!

But wait a minute; it also occurs to me that if I am trying to increase the likelihood of the man contacting me, I should give him more than one way to do so. If I resurrect the idea of sending my business card, he would have four ways (4 ways!) to do so:

1. My home address
2. My email address
3. My home phone
4. My cell phone (That he can call me OR text me on my mobile phone is also rather wonderful!)

With these thoughts in mind, I will send a second letter and include my business card. His play closed in New York weeks ago, but the theater address is the only one I have, so I will send my missive there with a note on the front asking whomever to kindly forward it to Mr. Nighy. Of course I will add red rose stickers to my letter and my envelope. It was his trademark and now it is mine.

Wow! I'm feeling a little joy just thinking about sticking them on.

July 15, 2015

Hello again, Bill Nighy.

Thank you for your response to my letter. Receiving a note from you made my day. Well, actually, that's an understatement—I have gotten emotional mileage out of it for weeks!

Just so you know, I am a person who loves going to movie theaters but who rarely watches TV or DVDs at home. (I prefer to read.) In spite of that fact, I find myself watching whatever BN movies I find at my local library. Most recently I saw *Valkyrie*, and I will see *Pride* next. Of the various films I have seen over the last several weeks, I must comment on two. The lonely lives of Barbara, Sheba, and Richard in *Notes on a Scandal* haunt me weeks after seeing the film. And on a lighter note, I adored *The Girl in the Café*. I find that it, too, has a lingering effect—it causes me to frequent crowded coffee shops on rainy days hoping to share my table with you.

I close with the confession that it is a lot of fun to be a besotted fan. I haven't felt this way since the 1960s, when I was twelve years old and in love with Paul McCartney! Thanks, Bill Nighy!

Lorie Kleiner Eckert

Thursday, July 16, 2015

Dear Diary,

Just in case you're wondering, it was only yesterday that I mailed my letter to BN so no response yet, just renewed hope as I visited my mailbox today, which is good! Also good was my Google search of the day. I seem to have the notion that Bill Nighy is a little-known actor. Given his huge C.V., I know this is ridiculous, but the idea hangs around in my mind. I am sure it was this concept that allowed me to think I stood a chance to be in a relationship with him back in the day of my triple-X hysteria.

Trying to figure out how well-known the guy is, I have looked him up on Facebook to see how many followers he has as compared to other stars. While Facebook is the most popular social network world-wide (according to The Statistics Portal at http://www.statista.com), I wondered as I started this process if Facebook is as popular in England as it is in the U.S. Doing a Google search, I learned that there are 151.8 million Facebook users in the United States while only 30.3 million in the U.K. So a Facebook search is not 100 percent fair to a British actor, but it is the best I can do. Here, then, is the number of Facebook "Likes" for some famous folks I like, some famous folks Bill Nighy likes, and some famous folks with whom Bill Nighy has acted. I place them in numerical order as I try to gauge the level of fame for my guy.

- Charlie Rose   4,932
- Richard Curtis   6,126
- Tom Wilkinson   11,839
- Michael Gambon   12,188
- **Bill Nighy**   **45,253**
- Robert Redford   115,353
- Sam Elliott   123,559

- Paul Auster   132,411
- Ralph Fiennes   141,967
- Hugh Grant   160,084
- Richard Gere   374,411
- Michael Douglas   1,530,394
- Christopher Walken   1,619,620
- Matthew McConaughey 4,749,043
- Paul McCartney   6,464,899
- Bob Dylan   6,554,618
- Tom Cruise   9,942,265
- Johnny Depp   15,959,690
- Robert Downey Jr.   26,221,052
- Adam Sandler   52,504,670

Well, I love to be right, but I hate to be right at the expense of Bill Nighy. Huge C.V. and all, it appears he is not very well-known. As I explain this to myself, here are some reasons why…

1. The majority of Bill Nighy's career was spent working in England, and much of that work was on the British stage. Regarding stage versus screen stars, I know that here in the United States, Roberta is very familiar with American stage actors while I am very familiar with American film actors and that our rosters of "stars" don't often intersect. I assume the same would be true for British stage and screen stars. As an American movie buff, then, I may have a slight familiarity with British film actors, but I have no familiarity at all with British stars of the stage. So the guy's stardom is at its peak among English theater lovers.

2. Bill Nighy discussed his British film career in an interview he gave after the movie, *Pride*, was released in 2014. (The interview can be found on YouTube via DP/30 @ TIFF '14: Pride,

Bill Nighy.) In it he says that *Still Crazy* was a landmark film for him. It was the first time he played a "principal part" in a movie. Prior to that, he had "very small parts in movies." *Still Crazy* was a British film released in 1998, when he was closing in on the age of fifty, so even British movie audiences of the time might have thought him a "newcomer" even though he had a thirty-year career under his belt.

3. His landmark U.S. film was *Love Actually*, which premiered in 2003, when Bill Nighy was fifty-three. So though the man is now sixty-five years old and though he has been acting his entire adult life, we here in the U.S. really just met him a dozen years ago. In an interview on YouTube with Gordon Hayden (he is the film critic for Ireland AM and Spin 103.8) Bill Nighy said, "More people saw me in *Love Actually* than probably had up until that point seen me in everything else I'd done in the whole of my career."

4. Even with these landmark roles, very few of his post-2003 projects put him in starring roles. The Johnny Worricker trilogy, *Skylight*, and *The Girl in the Café* are the exceptions to the rule. But none of these is a big-screen movie role. Instead they are TV, stage, and a made-for-TV movie respectively. Additionally, the Johnny Worricker trilogy and *Skylight* were all written by Englishman David Hare. Likewise, *The Girl in the Café* was written by Englishman Richard Curtis. Therefore American writers, who turn out big American films, have no experience casting Bill Nighy in such roles. Voilà! An actor with a huge résumé who is still not widely known—at least in the U.S.

5. Looking again at the *Buzz Feed News* list of ten films enumerated by Bill Nighy, it is astounding to find no starring roles and even more astounding to realize how small some of the

parts are that he is touting, not to mention that in one of the films he is a vampire and in another he is a tentacle-faced squid. Indeed, he says in the interview that he thought he had reached a point in his career where he could only play men from "other dimensions," and that he was pleased when he again got parts as a "regular human being."

6. One final factor comes into play in all of this: the truth that he does not wish to be a leading man, or at least not a romantic lead. In *Bill Nighy: The Unauthorised Biography* by Sue Blackhall, he admits it is difficult for him to think of himself as an object of desire. It's even difficult for him to think of himself as an object of love! He credits his longtime agent, Pippa Markham, for understanding this fact and for steering him in the direction of character roles instead.

While it has taken me a long time to understand the size and nature of Bill Nighy's star, the same is not true for the man himself. In his typical and adorable style, he has this to say about his fame, "The good news—and the bad news—is my progress so far has seriously exceeded any expectations I might have had. My expectations were exceeded a decade ago. And it got better. And then it got even better. It's breathtaking. There was a moment where I thought, I have every-thing I could ever want...But I'm not a film star—I'm that guy. It's just as it should be and it's just as I like it. It's a nice level of notoriety. People think, *Oh, is that Bill Nigby?*" As much as I want him to have scads of starring roles—especially in romantic comedies—I admire him very much for this attitude about his celebrity. I was so taken with the *Bill Nigby* malapropism that I printed the whole quote out and read it to Vera today as we ate our ice cream after seeing the movie *Amy*, about British songstress Amy Winehouse. Of course, I packed the Facebook numbers in my purse to show her as well.

"It's interesting to juxtapose his level of stardom with what we just saw on the screen," she said. "How many people 'like' Amy Winehouse on Facebook?"

"I love you, Vera, for giving me the opportunity to pull out my iPhone and Google in public."

"Well, get to it…"

"Uh…Amy Winehouse…oh my…10,855,064 people 'like' her, even dead. Wow."

"Yes, but dead in part because of those ten million people loving her, which brings on the paparazzi and the so-called lifestyle of the rich and famous. It all goes hand in hand."

"I wonder at what point one crosses the line from famous to too famous," I said.

"And from human being to commercial entity," Vera added. "You should be happy for your Bill that his ego allows him to be a character actor, not a star."

"Actually, it works in my favor. Small roles allow him to be in more projects per year, giving me more projects to find and enjoy. The man is ubiquitous. Did you know he is the voice of various video game characters and the voice of various animated film characters?"

"I didn't know that. So you're going to play video games and watch cartoons now?"

I laughed. "No, but he has also recorded books *The Wonderful Wizard of Oz* by L. Frank Baum, *Moonraker* by Ian Fleming, and so forth. I might listen to those. Just think, I can turn him on at night and let him whisper sweet nothings in my ear as I fall asleep."

"And that's enough for you?" she asked. "Just his voice?"

"Yes," I said, but when she looked at me skeptically I tried to better sell my case. "I don't need the full Monty. A smidge of him will do." We both laughed at my remark, but then her look returned to skeptical, so I tried again. "True confession? I'm trying to use him as a mood-altering drug to keep me bubbly instead of flat. Low dosage is my goal."

That answer she liked.

SATURDAY, JULY 18, 2015

Dear Diary,

Today is Saturday and I have a goal…figuring out something to do. Argh! Why is this so hard? The kids are all busy today—doing what, I don't know. They are too busy to even tell me that. That's as it should be of course, but…just the same…argh!! What is there for me to do? Reading the newspaper over my morning coffee worked just fine, but as I tried to continue the reading streak with a book, I had no patience for it. Perhaps I should go to the launderette like Judi Dench's character. Or maybe…what? I surely do not know. Vera is so good at planning my Thursdays; perhaps I could hire her to oversee my weekends. As an added bonus, I always try to put my best self forward with her, which is so much better than this current self who is feeling rather bleak…and jittery! Have I had too much coffee or am I having a breakdown?

I never realized how much time Big Irv filled in my life. I miss talking to him. I miss worrying about him. I miss doing things for him. I even miss the drama he provided. My brain was often enflamed by his antics, and I miss feeling that alive. Speaking of explosive things, I remember the time I smelled gas in the house but he did not. General contractor that he was, he tended to manage that sort of issue for me. But since he didn't smell it, it was a non-issue—to him. After days of arguing, he finally called in his buddy, Jay, the plumber, who took one step in the house and smelled gas! The only problem was that Jay couldn't fix the leak because he had neglected to bring any tools with him that day. "What kind of plumber comes to do a job without tools?" I asked. The two men looked at each other—and at the floor—and tried not to look at me. Apparently, Jay's role was to come over and do nothing at all except pat me on the head and tell me not to worry. Such ridiculous antics with that man! But I miss the antics! And I miss the man! Go figure.

Enough with this scribbling! I need to get back on track and figure out something to do today! Thank God I have a game plan for tonight: Saturday Night at the Movies. But what is there for me to do today? Well, whatever it is, it starts with putting on makeup, doing my hair, getting dressed, and getting out of the house. This morning routine is as vital to my mental health as a mood-altering drug, and no one will ever accuse me of not taking my medicine. Once I am in the car, I will most certainly drive somewhere. Can't wait to see where it is.

Saturday Night at the Movies

Pride
DIRECTOR: Matthew Warchus
WRITER: Stephen Beresford
RELEASE DATE: 2014
RUNNING TIME: 2 hours
ALSO FEATURING: Imelda Staunton, Dominic West, Paddy Considine

Like last week's film, *Valkyrie*, tonight's movie is also based on a real-life story, another part of history about which I knew nothing. CBS Films describes *Pride* this way: "It's the summer of 1984, Margaret Thatcher is in power and the National Union of Mineworkers is on strike, prompting a London-based group of gay and lesbian activists to raise money to support the strikers' families. Initially rebuffed by the Union, the group identifies a tiny mining village in Wales and sets off to make their donation in person. As the strike drags on, the two groups discover that standing together makes for the strongest union of all."

Bill Nighy's character in the movie is Cliff Barry, who is the leader of the men's union in Onllwyn, which is the name of the above-mentioned mining community in South Wales. Though many of the union members and townspeople are initially antagonistic to the members of the Lesbians & Gays Support the Miners (LGSM) movement, Cliff and several of the women in the town warmly embrace the activists and help to bring the two groups together.

Eventually Bill Nighy's character comes out as gay. It is a very poignant scene. He and a woman friend (played by Imelda Staunton) are casually making sandwiches together when he reveals his secret. Her response is to tell him—equally casually—that she had known that fact about him for nearly two decades. And so they carry on as if nothing major had happened.

I liked many things about this movie. I liked that Bill Nighy had the courage to play a gay man. I liked that when his character came out of the closet, it was a ho-hum, no big deal, who cares type of experience. And I loved knowing that the Welsh miners ultimately came to London to march with Gay Pride a year later in 1985. That's my kind of politics—the Youngbloods play in my head once again, "Come on people now, smile on your brother. Everybody get together, try to love one another right now."

There are many *Pride* interviews with Bill Nighy online, so we get to learn some of the things he liked about the movie as well. He liked that it is about two things that are very close to his heart: the emancipation of gay men and women in his lifetime and the miner's strike. He calls the miner's strike a huge scandal—and a civil war—and says it was misrepresented and misreported when it occurred in 1984. It evidently was the longest strike in trade union history, and thus many miners were starving as it dragged on. Once the LGSM stepped in to help, though, they never missed a week to bring money and food to the miners. Bill Nighy likes how the stories of these two groups dovetail and he likes telling the story itself, as it is a little-known episode in history. (Whew! I'm not the only one who never heard of it.) He says he was so taken with the script that he didn't care what part he played in the film; he was just keen to be in the movie because it tells the incredible story with dignity and respect, and most of all, with humor.

One more thing to love about the DVD version of this movie is that many of the people depicted in the story are still alive, so there is extra material to view on the DVD, including interviews with these people. We not only get to hear their take on that period of history, but we get to know what they are up to now. I love it when a movie gives me that information! It saves me from having to come home and Google it myself!

Can't close without confessing to still another great thing about this evening, the treat I ate during the movie. It was a British candy called Maltesers that my Google gods tell me is a favorite of Bill Nighy. Short story long, I had a handful of items on my grocery list, so when I was hard-pressed for a destination today, I went shopping. Instead of going to the Kroger that is walking distance from home, though, I went to Jungle Jim's International Market. I chose it specifically because it's such a schlep to get there. It is fourteen miles—and twenty minutes—from home, making it a perfect place to shop for a gal who has loads of time on her hands.

Jungle Jim's is an enormous place. It boasts 200,000 square feet of shopping space and more than 150,000 products from around the world, and as soon as I got there, I realized I could hunt for British treats loved by my guy. I whipped out my iPhone and did a Google search for "Bill Nighy favorite foods," which pulled up Billnighyinfo. com and these specific items: "Yorkshire tea, Rowntree Fruit Gums, all kinds of English chocolate like Aero and Maltesers, and Marmite." Yes, all of those items were available at Jungle Jim's! Yes, I could have bought them all in one fell swoop! But I did not. Saturday will roll around again next week and I will need someplace to go. Therefore, I just bought the Maltesers, a candy similar to Whoppers malted milk balls.

I enjoyed my excursion. I enjoyed my candy. I enjoyed my Saturday Night at the Movies. After such a shaky start to the day, things turned out pretty fine. Whew!

Dear Diary,

I spoke to Bird tonight and told her how British candy saved the day yesterday. My emotional upset on Saturday morning concerned her, so I also told her about my visit with Dr. Popa on Friday. I think she loves the man as much as I do and often reminds me of the time he diagnosed me from the doorway of the examining room without even walking through the threshold.

"What's this about chest pain?" he barked back then as he opened the door to the exam room while reading my chart simultaneously. But when he looked up from the chart and took an actual look at me, all of the alarm dropped from his voice. "It's stress," he said. "I can tell from here that you are all knotted up."

"It's not stress," I argued. "I'm dying. I have this terrible pain behind my heart..."

"I'm sure you do," he interrupted me, "and I'll be glad to run every test in the book if you want me to, but the better plan is for you to go home and take it easy. You need to soak in a bathtub for twenty minutes today and then repeat daily as needed until the pain goes away." Because of our thirty-year doctor/patient relationship, I knew to trust his opinion. Of course it helped that he actually entered the room, listened to my heart, took my blood pressure, etc., but then I went home, followed his advice, and lo and behold, the man was right.

"Why did you go see Popa?" Bird asked.

"I am having sleep difficulties, both falling asleep and staying asleep. My appetite is off and nothing sounds good to me. And while I had his ear, I also complained about this sty that won't go away."

"And he said?"

"In order of importance, I am to keep my eye clean but otherwise allow my eye to resolve the issue at its own speed. Second, since he is on the same carb-aware diet he suggested to me five years ago, he thinks I am just bored with the food choices before me. He asked if any of the P's sounded good—pizza, pasta, or pastry—and encouraged me to indulge from time to time to feel more excited about what's on the plate."

"Is it any wonder we love this man?" Bird asked. "I am tempted to move to Ohio so I can become his patient too. But what about the sleeping? You've never had an issue with it before, have you?"

"Not at all. I always boast that genetically I come from a long line of good sleepers. So this is a first for me. I am losing confidence in my ability to sleep, and that really frightens me."

"So what did Popa say?"

"He thinks I am in mourning for Big Irv. He reminded me I needed an antidepressant to get through Dad's death but that I have had no drug intervention for Big Irv's."

"Do you agree?"

"Since I started to sob when he said that to me, I'm thinking he's right, but I sure don't want to go on an antidepressant. So Popa said to come back in a few months and we will make the drug decision then. He's hoping time will heal my wound, causing the sleep issue to subside."

"That sounds like a good plan. And during that time, you can pamper yourself. You can try some of those yummy P's and soak in a bathtub every day or two."

"If both of you are advocating this plan, I better try it."

"Ah, but I have another ingredient to add to the mix," Bird continued. "You love writing in diaries. How about buying a brand new journal, some sumptuous leather-bound affair, and then use it specifically to write about Irv. You've been so angry with him—and rightfully so—but I wonder, have you really grieved for him yet?"

"Oh, you're making me cry too."

"Good! I'm glad all this sounds right to you, because I have another idea too. You haven't sewn for a very long time. Oh sure, you make quilts for all those grandbabies of yours, but none of your signature quilts, the ones with words in the design. Those words and quilts came right from your heart. Surely there is a message or two inside of you waiting for creative expression."

"I might have to pass on that one, Bird. I have thought about quilting, but I just can't fathom it at the moment. When I am in a creative mode, ideas bounce around in the back of my brain like popcorn popping, but that isn't happening now. Hey! I'll tell you what, though, I could eat some popcorn! It's a 'P' word! But get creative and make quilts? Nah…"

Well, dear Diary, leave it to a lifelong friend to suggest great advice in life. If you split my head open with an ax right now, dozens of outrageous Big Irv stories would fall out. Writing them down is a more life-affirming way to exorcise those demons. I will go shopping for a new journal this week!

Tuesday, July 21, 2015

Dear Diary,

You know me, right? I am interested in reading my horoscope in *The Cincinnati Enquirer* daily and I have been known to cut one out when it says something perfectly perfect about me. But most of the time, I find they are not perfect and I ignore those little blurbs completely. For years I have been reading Big Irv's horoscope as well as mine. Sometimes his Cancer speaks a better truth to consider for the day than my Aquarius. Likewise, nowadays I am reading Bill Nighy's Sagittarian advice, allowing all three horoscopes to guide me in my crush on BN. Here are some interesting things I have cut from the paper recently:

- Aquarius—You are connected at a deep level, working through joint karma together.
- Aquarius—Someone is becoming more and more intrigued by the mystery of you.
- Aquarius—There's a time for playfulness and a time to let others know you have serious regard for them.
- Aquarius—It takes courage to lay your heart on the line.
- Aquarius—You'll gently nudge people into the right groove.
- Cancer—It's a good thing that your sense of what is possible is all out of whack.
- Cancer—There is no safer choice than to follow your heart.
- Cancer—Remember the many ways in which you are similar.
- Cancer—Relationships will thrive as you give enough to let others know you're interested.
- Sagittarius—Your Internet search engine will be your best friend.
- Sagittarius—You're earning someone's trust by doing what comes naturally.

- Sagittarius—If you work together, the results will be rather brilliant.

So again, dear Diary, you know me, right? Thus you will not be surprised to learn that I Googled the astrological probability of a successful relationship between a man born December 12, 1949, and a woman born February 12, 1952. What turned up was http:// www.compatible-astrology.com and from this site I learned a lot of great stuff!

- The Aquarius/Sagittarius mix is a great team, one of the best possible matches for a Sagittarius.
- We definitely have soulmate potential.
- We are both optimistic, upbeat, forward-thinking, and progressive.
- Other more clingy signs might see our relationship as detached or somehow lacking, but to both of us, it is fine the way it is.
- We both value our independence.
- We both fear making a commitment too soon, so there is the chance we could remain casual friends for a long time.
- Ours is one of those rare matches that can survive and thrive as a long-distance romance.
- We are both objective and rational and we like these traits in others.
- We also like intelligent and articulate partners.
- We both see sex as an intellectual exercise instead of seeing it as an emotional one.

Of course there was stuff that didn't sound as perfectly "us" on the website as well. It says that neither of us is practical or domestic, but that's not true. I am. It says we share many interests in politics, technology, and current affairs, but that's not true. I know nothing at all on these topics.

I am cheerfully ignoring those items as I turn to the next astrological source, a book I own called *The Secret Language of Relationships, Your Complete Personology Guide to Any Relationship with Anyone*. In this gem of a book, there is a big chart. On one axis of the chart, I located my birth date, and on the other axis, I found his. In this manner, I was instructed to turn to page 760 to learn about Bill Nighy's and my specific relationship. And so I learned that the week of December 11-18 is known as Sagittarius III. It is called the Week of the Titan. Likewise, the week of February 8-15 is known as Aquarius III. It is called The Week of Acceptance.

- The main issue between such partners is "calling the shots." It appears our relationship would be a power struggle. "Strong-minded, both partners know what they think and what they want, but too often the relationship demands the subservience of one to the other."
- The best-case scenario for us is friendship. The worst case is a love relationship, though love affairs can work when they "are more playful than serious in nature."
- But uh-oh, marriages between the two "may strike the world as master-slave" in nature with the Titan/Sagittarian dominating and the Aquarian accepting it. (Yuch, dear Diary, yuch!)
- Mary Todd Lincoln and Honest Abe's birth dates were similarly matched, as were those of Frank Sinatra and Mia Farrow.
- The most shocking thing I found on page 760, though, was a note to myself in the margin. It seems I have been in this exact matchup of birth dates before. That philandering college professor with whom my daughter set me up years ago was likewise born on December 12, though a few years before Bill Nighy.

It is my inclination to ignore this negative stuff, to hear only what I want to hear. And so I remind myself that one cannot generalize too far based on sun signs alone. There are other astrological elements to consider, and surely those other planets could line up to create a happily ever after.

With this thought in mind, I decided to turn to another astrological reference book so I took myself to Barnes & Noble to find one—hey, I needed to go there to buy a new journal anyway! In this manner, I found a book with an alluring title: *How to Seduce Any Man in the Zodiac*. It gives me the following information to consider about my Sagittarian:

- He is an adventurer going in several directions simultaneously.
- He is freedom-loving, fun-loving, and full of life.
- His childlike charm can steal your heart away.
- He gets bored easily, so he is on the move via airports and airplanes.
- In any given experience, he has one foot out the door.
- He needs to feel free to come and go.
- He fears stagnancy and confining situations that feel like they may last forever.
- His feelings toward love are cheerful but not committed.
- His enthusiasm is never-ending.
- He is both funny and a lot of fun.

Given these traits, this book advises me to "entice him with a startling wit and engaging sense of humor" and to "give him so much freedom that he feels like he's living in an airport." It also says that if I want a good time, he's my man, but if I want more, I should look elsewhere.

Oh gosh, dear Diary, as VOR and PITS will attest, I don't know exactly what I want. On the one hand, this is a great description of a man for me, and on the other hand, I want so much more. Argh! Perhaps I should channel my inner Scarlet O'Hara and "think about it tomorrow." Before putting away astrological thoughts, though, I must throw out a few intriguing tidbits:

- My ex-husband, to whom I was married for twenty-one years, is an Aquarian like me.
- Jimmy Jet, with whom I was in a relationship for ten years, is a Cancer.
- Big Irv, with whom I was in a relationship for nine years, was a Cancer too.
- Diana Quick, with whom Bill Nighy was in a relationship for twenty-seven years, is a Sagittarian just like he is.

It's all very interesting, isn't it?

SATURDAY, JULY 25, 2015

Dear Diary,

I am very grateful to Bird for suggesting I write about Big Irv. Spiffy new journal in hand, I will take myself to Saxby's for coffee and I will write there today. Beyond the fact that it is an adorable café, going there also gets me out of the house. And did I mention they have delicious ice cream? After indulging in that sweet treat, I will return home to another one: Saturday Night at the Movies starring beloved Bill Nighy!

It may be difficult to dredge up all the Big Irv stuff, maybe even depressing, but I have always said that each time I share what's troubling me with another person, I give away a little bit of my sorrow. The same holds true for writing it in a journal. So it's a double dip against depression today—I get out of the house and I get stuff off my chest. It's a great plan and I am grateful.

THE GOOD — THE BAD — THE UGLY — THE END
Part I — The Good Stuff

Mom, Dad, and Big Irv, these are the closest loved ones I have lost to death. These are the people for whom I have truly mourned. Or have I? Have I mourned for Big Irv?

When Mom died in 2002, I did all the appropriate things prescribed by the Jewish faith, but my main job was to get Dad through the nightmare. What struggling I did with death, I did through reading and re-reading novels and non-fiction that dealt with the topic. I read *Patrimony* by Philip Roth. I read *Talk Before Sleep* by Elizabeth Berg. I read *W;t* by Margaret Edson. I read *One True Thing* by Anna Quindlen. I read *Moon Palace* and *The Book of Illusions* by Paul Auster. These and other books focused my crying.

I had some guilt when Mom died because of course I was in on the decision-making for her care. Thus, I was there when we made the decision to call in hospice. I was there when she asked, "But what if I don't die?" And I was there when she actually, physically did. But, and this is a really big *but*, Dad was the one who called the shots. I just supported Dad's decisions.

When Dad died in 2010, my brother and I made all the horrible decisions. No, no, that's not exactly right. Dad gave us a couple of huge gifts in the year of his decline. He was the one who said he needed more care than he was getting in independent living at Garden Villas. And then after we moved him to Cincinnati into assisted living at The Lodge, he was the one who told us he needed more care than that. And then a bout of illness took him from Cedar Village Nursing Home to the hospital where my brother and I made the horrible decision to move him to hospice, where he expired before a week did. But it was not just that decision; it was all the little decisions I made in the ten months Dad lived in Cincinnati that troubled me, tortured me, after his death. I wondered if I had vetted all his new doctors properly. I had the same worry about the facilities into which I moved him. Would other choices have yielded other outcomes?

As with Mom's passing, I did all the appropriate things prescribed by the Jewish faith, but that didn't come close to helping me. And so I spent a period of time, two years actually, going back to the hospice center where he died. I made donations to the facility so I could sit guilt-free in their library, drink their coffee, eat their soup, and write in a journal. With each visit, of course, I honored the memory—or was I punishing myself?—as I walked past the room where I watched him take his last breath.

Again in this mourning process, books helped me. The journal I wrote in was actually a book that was written for Jewish mourners. It is called *Mourning & Mitzvah* by Anne Brener and it is "a guided journal." It talks about Jewish mourning customs and quotes Jewish texts. With this information in hand, it poses questions for the reader to contemplate and then it provides blank spaces for the answers.

Another book that helped was the National Book Award Winner *How We Die: Reflections on Life's Final Chapter*, by Sherwin B. Nuland. In this fascinating book, the author describes in detail how people die from the likes of cancer, AIDS, Alzheimer's, and in Dad's case, old age. It was comforting to learn that 85 percent of the aged will succumb to the complications of one of seven major conditions: atherosclerosis, hypertension, adult-onset diabetes, obesity, mental depressing states, cancer, and decreased resistance to infection. Indeed, many of the elderly who die will have several of these afflictions, if not all seven. Nuland concludes that the elderly "do not succumb to disease—they implode their way into eternity."

Translation: Dad's body was a house of cards. His death certificate proves this, listing many causes. It all helps me realize that the few decisions I made in Dad's care could not have impacted the impending implosion.

Though of course I will never suffer a loss that is comparable to that of losing my parents, Big Irv's death was very significant to me, yet I did almost nothing to actively mourn the man. Why was this the case? Oh my, the reasons abound, not the least of which is the fact that we were broken up when he actually died. Or maybe we weren't; maybe we were just in the middle of one of my hissy fits over THE MAN DOING EXACTLY WHAT HE WANTED TO DO EVEN THOUGH I THOUGHT HE NEEDED TO DO THINGS DIFFERENTLY! Sorry for shouting. I get that way in talking about and thinking about Big Irv.

What I liked about him so much at the start is exactly what was so exasperating about him in the end: He was a bad boy. Oh, how intriguing he was to this good girl, this girl who has always been neat, sweet, and in her seat, this girl who has lots of rules by which to live.

Big Irv was a general contractor who managed construction jobs. His biggest job ever was building some long stretch of interstate highway. I assume he was employing poetic license in telling his story, but he made his crew sound as unsavory as a prison chain gang. And so he assured me that he had to be ready to come out of his truck feet first when he dealt with these men. Speaking English with Big Irv was always a bit tricky. It sounded like we shared the same native tongue, but I often had no clue what he meant. So I asked him about coming out of his truck feet first. Isn't that the way everyone gets out of a vehicle? You open the door; you step down feet first, right? But that was not what he meant. He meant that from the high perch of his truck, he opened his door and while still sitting, swung his legs out the door, and then he kicked his legs forward, parallel to the seat—in attack mode—knocking away anyone who approached the truck. He did this to show his workers that he was the boss. This was one of the first stories of his life that Big Irv told me, and the image still floors me today. I spent many years teaching my children that it is not proper to fight; that instead they needed to use their words. Here was a man who lived by some other set of rules. Interesting…

Another trait about Big Irv that I was crazy about at the start but that made me crazy in the end was that he was not one to complain. Early on in our friendship, he helped me reupholster a desk chair. It was the kind that had a padded seat that unscrewed from the frame, allowing the fabric to be changed with relative ease. One just needed to remove the heavy-duty staples that held the current fabric in place and then wrap the naked cushion in the new fabric, add staples, and voilà, the deed was done. Removing the heavy-duty staples from the chair pad, however, can be tricky, and so it was that as Big Irv tried to get his screwdriver under one of the staples to pry it up, the screwdriver slipped and rammed into his other hand instead. Having once had a brief relationship with a hypochondriac, I was a little leery about how Big Irv would respond to this injury, but he didn't respond. When I asked if he was okay he said, "Yes I am, but even if I weren't, I wouldn't tell you." What I thought at the time was, *Be still my heart, a stoic man!* As we went through his lung cancer, kidney cancer, benign brain tumor, seizures, and abdominal aortic aneurysm together, though, his silence on his well-being was—on a couple of occasions—life-threatening. His bad-boy tendencies didn't help matters either.

There was that time, for instance, when he was horribly sick. He had a fever for days, he would not eat for days, and I could not get him out of bed for days. I was thrilled when the date arrived that he had an appointment with the radiologist because I needed someone to see him and figure out what was wrong! One of Big Irv's bad-boy tricks, though, was that he often chose not to go to scheduled appointments, and that was the game he played that day. We argued to no avail and then I went to the appointment by myself to seek guidance from the doctor, whose take on the situation was this: Patients who are too sick to come to doctor appointments need to be hospitalized. Dr. Huth backed up his opinion by showing me the newest scan of Big Irv's lung and the worsening condition there. A discussion of end-of-life care also entered the picture.

And so I went home to convince Big Irv that he needed to check himself into the hospital. We had already fought the Battle of Going to the Hospital once before when he was bleeding profusely from a hematoma that had formed behind his kidney surgery incision. Even copious amounts of blood—that we could not stanch—did not easily convince him to go to the hospital, so I had no idea how I would convince him now. In the end, it was my screaming and sobbing that did the trick. Seeing me collapsed in a puddle on the floor convinced him to allow me to drive him—no ambulance allowed!—to the hospital. Once he was admitted, he let us in on the secret that he had been passing blood clots in his urine for days. They kept him for over a week that time, thank God. Not only was he desperately ill, but I needed the respite care.

But I am getting way, way, way ahead of myself here. There was all the good stuff in our relationship before we moved on to the bad and then to the ugly. And I need to remember that too. After all, isn't it the loss of the good stuff I am mourning? The bad and the ugly? I don't miss those times at all.

Here are a bunch of good things about Big Irv:

- He liked to go places, which was something new for this homebody. And so we went to Toby Keith concerts, NASCAR races,

Cavalcades of Cars, monster truck exhibitions, boat shows, home shows, local festivals, state fairs, county fairs, movies, every Cirque du Soleil event that came to town, and the Ringling Brothers Circus too. We had season tickets to Bengals football and to the Broadway Series and we saw every performance of other local theater groups, as well, and if someone like Larry the Cable Guy came to town—Git-R-Done!—we were there. Additionally, I collect advertising tins and Big Irv felt compelled to take me to flea markets and antique shops and to buy me all that we saw, firmly believing that if you collect something, that's how you play the game. And let's not forget travel. From Indiana to Israel, we were there!

- He loved to spend money—obviously—but that was new for me, as I am a frugal Fannie. I told him I was accustomed to reading a menu from the right-hand side to the left. He thought that was terrific but instructed me to order the most expensive thing I saw on that right-hand side. His oft-stated belief was that you only need to have one more dollar than you are going to spend. Plainly, he did not remember things like needing to put children/grandchildren through college, but at our age—and since we were not mingling our finances—it was a fun way to live!

- He loved to dine out, with *dine* being the operative word. There was no fast food for this guy, no standing in a line. He liked to have a reservation and a special table. He liked to have a drink while we "picked at" an appetizer, and then he liked more drinks as we enjoyed our entrees. Dessert was always the happy conclusion to a meal. Invariably, he ran out of appetite when there were three more bites left in the dessert, which were then mine, all mine. We made a game of going to restaurants whose names represented every letter in the alphabet: Anthony's Fish Grotto, Bubba Gump's, Cracker Barrel, Don Pablo's, Ethel's Chocolate Lounge, Flat Top Grill, Golden Lamb, Hyde Park Steak House, etc. And though X, Y, and Z were particularly tough, we made it through the alphabet, and then we started all over again. I should also mention that he liked to dine "fashionably late," with 8 p.m. being his all-time favorite.

- He loved to drink. I often said of him that he only liked three food groups: steak, mayonnaise, and vodka. He drank his Absolut Vodka straight but called it a martini. The more he drank, the more he said "I love you." Additionally, he taught me to drink. It only takes one cocktail to get me buzzy, but for a wound-up-tight person, it is wonderful to know about such an easy way to relax. When we were both wound up tight, or when the world dealt one of us a blow, we would go to our favorite restaurant to dine, drink, and decompress. No psychiatrist's couch could be more effective than the banquette at deSha's.

- He was a party animal, so he made plans to dine with our friends regularly, plus he threw many a party at the house. He wanted our friends loose and happy as they enjoyed the foods he grilled or smoked, so our parties always had a bartender or two to keep things flowing.

- He had a pet name for me—Tootsie Wootsie—and I am one who loves nicknames. In my book, they are literally terms of endearment. While my kids might be Scott, Shana, and Lisa to the rest of the world, they are Popsy, Beanie, and Fred to me. And so I was delighted when Big Irv started to call me Tootsie Wootsie and its various derivatives, Toots, Tootser, Wootser, and T.W. Of course, I was also his "Little Lor." Whatever squabbles were to come our way, his use of one of those nicknames was easy shorthand for me. He was saying "I love you." There was also a ton of hand-holding to let me know he cared. We took lots of ribbing from our friends over it, but holding hands was literally part of our connection. Oh, and regarding our hands, they were well pampered. He liked for us to go to the "pretty parlor" together to get side-by-side manicures.

- And let's not forget he was a man with tools and the ability to use them.

- Beyond all the fun stuff and the practical stuff and the loving gestures, he helped me take care of my dad in a hundred different ways. When we moved Dad from his condo to Garden Villas independent living in St. Louis, we got Dad all settled in on day one only to hear him wonder aloud if instead of bringing this easy chair, maybe he should have brought that recliner instead. Big Irv got up from where he was sitting, opened the sliding door to Dad's ground-floor apartment, left through the slider, got his truck, backed it up to the living room, picked up the questionable easy chair, and took it back to Dad's condo to swap it for the recliner.

- After we moved Dad to Cincinnati and went through a rapid-fire period of six falls and seven emergency room visits, Big Irv went to the ER with Dad when I absolutely could not bear going again.

- And when Dad died, Big Irv was the one who went to pack up his stuff at the nursing home while I remained prostrate in grief at home. How could I not love him—eternally—for all of that?

- Oh my, it's so nice to remember this good stuff.

Postscript to today's tale: Pleased that I had reached a lovely stopping point with its fond memories and feelings of eternal love for Big Irv,

I capped my pen, ordered up my ice cream treat, and proceeded to read the newspaper I had brought along with me to the coffee shop. Before long, I found myself laughing out loud. It was today's horoscope for Aquarius—*not* the funny pages—that created my outburst: "Different things make you happy at different times of life. For some there will be enjoyment from good food, good drinks, and a bad girl or boy to share them with." I am forced to wonder if that blurb is merely comic or if it's a cosmic zinger? Either way, it feels great to laugh. I will hope to laugh some more during tonight's movie. It's a comedy called *Pirate Radio*. Can't wait!

Saturday Night at the Movies

The Boat That Rocked — aka *Pirate Radio*
Director: Richard Curtis
Writer: Richard Curtis
Release Date: 2009
Running Time: 1 Hour, 57 Minutes
Also Featuring: Philip Seymour Hoffman, Nick Frost, Chris O'Dowd, Kenneth Branagh, Rhys Ifans, and Emma Thompson.
Friendly Connections: There is an ensemble cast in the movie and it includes various actors with whom BN has worked before. He and Rhys Ifans were both in *Enduring Love* (2004). He and Kenneth Branagh were both in *Valkyrie* (2008). He and Emma Thompson were both in *Love Actually* (2003). Additionally, Bill Nighy has worked with (for?) this movie's writer and director, Richard Curtis, twice before. They did *Love Actually* (2003) together and *The Girl in the Café* (2005). Loving Bill Nighy as I do, I am glad he has the opportunity to play with his friends!

Special Note: This film had different names in different countries. It was released in the U.K. as *The Boat That Rocked* and re-titled *Pirate Radio* in North America, *Good Morning England* in France, *Radio Rock Revolution* in Germany, and *I Love Radio Rock* in Italy.

As for my review of the movie, I have to confess that I did not like *Pirate Radio* at all when I first started to watch it. (Sorry about that, beloved Bill.) Though I was committed to seeing the entire movie, after about thirty minutes I had to give myself some time off for good behavior. There were just too many weird characters, and the jocular tone of the movie was a bit jarring. Even laundry sounded more appealing than the movie, so I did a load, and then I went back to the film only to fall under its spell the second time around. Watching and reading lots of BN interviews after seeing the film helped me understand it better and like it even more.

So here we go again: Like *Valkyrie* and *Pride*, this movie is historically based, though it is another part of history about which I knew zilch. The movie is set in 1966. Apparently, the British government did not allow rock and pop music to be played on BBC radio stations at that time due to the so-called commercialism and low morals of such music. To get around this ban, radio stations broadcast to the U.K. from ships anchored in international waters. This movie tells the story of the fictitious pirate radio station Radio Rock and its crew of eclectic disc jockeys who broadcast from the North Sea while the British government endeavors to shut them down.

Bill Nighy's character in the movie is named Quentin and he is the owner and captain of Radio Rock. He is as flamboyant as the crazy mix of DJs he manages on board, and his costumes are adorable, taking him far from typical BN attire. In the opening scene, he is in a big plaid suit with a paisley scarf. Another scene finds him in a Chesterfield jacket made with a small plaid fabric and requisite velvet collar. When dressed formally as the captain, he's in a double-breasted suit with epaulets and a purple boutonniere. Yes, he has a navy blue suit on from time to time, but once it is embellished with a red scarf and red socks and another time with a purple tie and golden pocket hanky. Hats and sun glasses add to his rakish air, and his hair parted down the middle is likewise fun to see. Overall he is…sexy! Yes, that's it exactly. He fits well in the sex-, drug-, and alcohol-filled atmosphere of Radio Rock.

It appears the film was not highly rated by critics. It got a lot of flak over its, well, jocular nature. In one video interview with Movies Ireland, for instance, the interviewer said the movie was "a little too fairy tale-ish" and then called it a "light, fluffy" movie. While one is never going to see the real-life Bill Nighy go ballistic, it is interesting to watch him respond to this interviewer as he defends his friend, Richard Curtis', movie. And so he says, "These are the searingly honest, cheerful bits" of the pirate radio story, not the grim ones. The movie is "shamelessly designed to make you laugh and make you feel fabulous. It has no other intention. We set out entirely to amuse you. There is no other agenda." He goes on to say that the plan was to "thrill you," to "play you some of the greatest tunes that have ever been made and to make you laugh."

Bill Nighy also explains that pirate radio stations were an actual part of his growing up. He listened to Radio Luxembourg and then to Radio Caroline. They were the only chance for listeners to hear decent, non-stop pop music because the BBC played "records" for only two hours a week. These stations were a BIG DEAL to someone like Bill Nighy, a man who loves his music. In this same interview, to this interviewer who insisted on panning the movie to his face, Bill Nighy reveals a big chunk of himself when he says, "I left home on the strength of the first Bob Dylan album. I threw my suitcase out the window. There was a ludicrous faith in the music. There was a kind of a highway somewhere between the sound of his guitar and his harmonica. It drove me nuts and I had to hit the road. Literally, I hit the road. Looking for something. The music was inspirational."

To this man who loves his music, the making of this movie must have been a blast, and thinking about it with that concept in mind is wonderful for a BN lover. He said that throughout the filming one had to wonder if the camera was on, one had to wonder if they were actually filming or if they were having a coffee break. And then there was that "one great day when [they] had to dance all day long out at sea." The song that day was "Dancing in the Street" by Martha and the Vandellas.

What I liked most in the movie was Bill Nighy's wonderful wardrobe and his darling haircut. What I loved the most was his lewd and lascivious character. In a movie review that appeared in *The Guardian* on April 2, 2009, columnist Peter Bradshaw picks up on both of these elements when he calls Bill Nighy's Quentin "the elegantly louche proprietor of the good ship Radio Rock: a dandyish mantis of a man." I have to confess that I liked seeing beloved Bill in a role where he acted the part of a man who is irresistible to women, because that's the real Bill Nighy to me.

Continuing in confession, though, the above is what I liked/loved most about BN in the movie. The reality is that what I *really* liked most about the film was a scene with Rhys Ifans, a scene that was ultimately cut from the project, but which appears in the bonus materials on the DVD. In the clip, Rhys Ifans explains why he came back to Radio Rock as a DJ. He says he had "money, chicks, drugs, time on [his] hands and [he] still [hadn't] found what [he was] looking for." But then, in Guatemala, someone put some coins in a juke box and "Get Off of My Cloud" began to play. The dance scene that follows is priceless as we watch Rhys Ifans' character come joyfully ALIVE! He concludes his explanation by saying, "You see, the thing that makes sense in this crazy world is rock 'n' roll."

Director Richard Curtis tells us this scene, called "The Meaning of Life," was cut because the movie was massively longer than intended. But I loved the scene and its title. They help me understand the true takeaway from the film: For all of us who find ourselves complaining on our yachts, the key to happiness is finding whatever it is that floats our boat, and then pursuing it.

WEDNESDAY, JULY 29, 2015

Dear Diary,

After the high of seeing Bill Nighy in fabulous and funky fashions in *Pirate Radio*, I got my feet back on the ground today by watching an interview with my man in which he discussed his favorite look, the lounge suit. The video was dated November 1, 2013, and was in conjunction with the opening of *About Time*. In the interview, a woman named Grae Drake spoke with BN for Rotten Tomatoes. The interview is called "How *About Time*'s Bill Nighy Likes His Suits and Movies." At the very start of the interview, BN states that he is having his third cup of coffee and comments on what a bad idea that is, indeed saying there is no excuse for a third cup of coffee. Grae Drake asks if he will light up like a Christmas tree, but he quotes Woody Allen instead and says he will "just become slightly too wonderful." I love the line because that's exactly what he is to me, and then I loved the rest of the interview because he gets down to details about his "look."

Thus, Grae Drake asks Bill Nighy about his "history in suits" saying that she fully expected him to wear one for the interview and indeed she was not disappointed. His response was to say, "If you really want the best out of me, put me in a lounge suit." The American interviewer gets a little twinkle in her eye over this term, perhaps having visions of smoking jackets instead of understanding what it is he really means. And I will confess that the first few times I heard him use this term, I had visions of leisure suits in mind, though I can't imagine Bill Nighy in plaid polyester.

And so I turn to my Google search engine for a lesson in men's haberdashery. Here is Wikipedia's definition of a smoking jacket: "The classic smoking jacket is a mid-thigh-length jacket made from velvet, silk, or both. It has a shawl collar and turn-up cuffs and toggle or button fastenings, or may simply be closed with a tie belt." A website called DuchessClothiers.com states further that since *Playboy* publisher Hugh Heffner has been photographed in a smoking jacket—with a bunny-costumed lady on each arm—it has become a symbol of a debaucherous lifestyle. If this indeed was Grae Drake's mental image, I can see why she looked a bit buzzed.

As for my leisure suit mind-set, Wikipedia says, "A leisure suit is a casual suit consisting of a shirt-like jacket and matching trousers, often associated with American-influenced fashion and fads of the 1970s." The suit "only achieved widespread popularity in the United States when—with the creation and popularization of synthetic materials—unprecedented inexpensive prices met with a culture that had come to hate formality."

Of course, informality is not what Bill Nighy is going for in his dress. For a definition of his beloved lounge suit, I turned to an article on Debretts.com. Debrett's was established in 1769 and has been the arbiter of society etiquette ever since. At their website, I followed links from Etiquette to British Behavior to Dress Codes. There I found a variety of dress codes: Black Tie, White Tie, Morning Dress, Eveningwear, Smart Casual, and Lounge Suits. Who knew there were so many ways to dress? Certainly not I! Clicking the link to Lounge Suits, I got this definition: "Lounge suit is an expression only seen on invitations as a dress code. In conversation, the terms dark suit or business suit or possibly business dress or business attire are used. Lounge suits are worn for most business events, both daytime and evening and for many social events such as lunches, receptions, dinners, weddings, christenings, and funerals."

In describing a lounge suit to Grae Drake, Bill Nighy got very specific. Amazingly, all these elements rolled off his tongue as easily and blithely as a four-year-old reciting his ABCs:

- It is a two-piece suit,
- With a single vent in the jacket,
- And a single pleat on the trouser.
- It has a turn-up of standard depth on each trouser leg.
- It has two back pockets.
- It has adjusters on the waist but nothing vulgar as braces or anything of that kind. (Google tells me that braces and suspenders are the same thing.)
- And it has a medium-size, sober lapel.

And of course I know from other interviews that the suit will be custom made and navy blue. Gosh, if I just had his sleeve length, chest, waist, and inseam measurements, I'd be able to woo him with suits instead of roses. Beyond that, I love his attitude about dress. He always looks gorgeous, so why tweak the look? I also love his attitude for its broader implication to my life. As one who feels the need to apologize whenever I buy the same pair of shoes or jeans—or a sweater—in more than one color, I can have a new mind-set. When I find something that works for me, I too can repeat it, shouting gleefully, "Why mess with success?" So thank you, Bill Nighy. You're the best! No, no, I need to amend that. You are more than slightly too wonderful!

Thursday, July 30, 2015

Dear Diary,

Vera and I saw the movie *Mr. Holmes* today. It starred Ian McKellen as Sherlock Holmes. As the movie starts, he is long retired and trying to recall the details of the last case he investigated. At age ninety-three, however, memory fails him. I would like to say more about the movie, but at age sixty-three, memory fails me. It was one of those films that leaves my brain as soon as I leave the movie theater.

"I didn't care for that one," I said to Vera as we exited the Mariemont Theater and walked down the block to the ice cream parlor. "Among other things, those English accents still give me trouble."

"Even with your Bill?"

"Oh yes," I replied while chuckling to myself that WHEN he and I meet, speaking English with him will be as challenging as it was with Big Irv.

"I liked Laura Linney's role in the movie," she offered.

"I agree. She was good. But I'll tell you what, I will like her in anything she does because she's a Bill Nighy buddy. They were in *Love Actually* together so I have an affinity for her. Remember when we saw *Cinderella* and I found Helena Bonham Carter to be so gorgeous? Same principle at work. She was in one of the Johnny Worricker films with him."

"Do you think they should have cast your guy as Mr. Holmes?"

"Are you serious? No! My guy is young and sexy! I don't want to see him playing a man in his nineties!"

"Ian McKellen is probably the same age as your Bill."

"They are not even close in age! Why do you say that?" *Vera and age*, I thought. *Argh!*

"Just trying to get your goat and spur you on to do some research, so get to it. How old is Ian McKellen?"

Forgiving her, I Googled him. He was born in 1939, ten years before BN.

"Speaking of Bill Nighy in sexy roles," I said, "I watched *Pirate Radio* last weekend." After filling her in on that movie, I told her about the Martha and the Vandellas dance scene and how completely fabulous he was in it. "I read an online interview that he gave to a woman named Susan Daly at the independent.ie. In it, he says the dance scene was difficult for him. Evidently, he likes to dance but only in the privacy of his own home because he suffers from 'a mixture of reasonably profound self-disgust and intense vanity,'" I said, finger quotes and all.

"Really? Profound self-disgust?"

"Really. The man has lots of self-doubt. As recently as May of this year he gave an interview regarding his Tony nomination for best actor in *Skylight* in which he said he has 'average difficulty' thinking positively of himself. But I think he's above average in that regard."

"Definitely," she agreed.

"But you know what? If he liked himself even half as much as I like him, he'd be a different person and I happen to love him just the way he is."

After leaving Vera, coming home to make dinner for the kids, and cleaning up after them, I was pretty pooped, so laptop in hand, I got in bed and found myself Googling "Bill Nighy's perception of himself." The first thing that came up was an article from www.theguardian.com dated November 18, 2009. It was written by Patrick Barkham. The little blurb right there in the search results quotes BN as saying, "I have a perfectly average skewed perception of myself." Because of it, he says this about his films, "I try never to watch. It takes me so long to get over it and I'm always so downcast. I find it really distressing…You just see how far short it falls from where you might have imagined you were heading." He additionally says he does not read reviews or interviews either. And along similar lines, he does not bemoan times when he is misquoted. Instead, he blames himself for saying things he regrets.

Happily, this particular interview ends on a high note as Bill Nighy says, "In the theater, there are always a couple of shows where you just forget. Somehow you turn off that part of your mind which is out to get you, the bit that undermines you, the self-conscious bit, and everything happens by magic, everything flows, everything's good, every single action you perform, every word you speak, every time you react to something, it all seems to fly. That's the holy grail."

It is wonderful to hear this from beloved Bill. I hope he is often a frequent flyer in this regard.

After closing down my laptop, I continued to think about the interview and to identify with BN. It would be excruciating for me to read critiques of my work. Even if a review was 99 percent positive, my psyche would find the 1 percent implied—or explicit—condemnation and be sick over it for days. I am not one who believes in constructive criticism; it's all destructive to me, I guess because I want people to approve of everything I say and do. I wish I was more like Vera. She simply doesn't care what other people think about her opinions, decisions, or actions. As I wax poetic about Vera, though, I realize Big Irv was like her in this way and that the trait wasn't so charming in him. He was so sure of his opinion about the way things should be that he bulldozed me in a very big way. But that's another story for another day...

August

THE BOOK OF IRV

The Good—The Bad—The Ugly—The End
PART I—THE GOOD STUFF, CONTINUED

Big Irv and I met originally through Match.com. Our first date was aborted due to the fact that we did not speak English well together. Via the phone, he and I had agreed to have dinner together on Saturday, November 19, 2005. The exact time was left open, with him telling me he would call me during the afternoon of the nineteenth to firm things up. Since he had only my landline number at that time, I was tied to the phone all day—waiting—which is never a good position for a woman to be in. By my definition of the word "afternoon," he did not call. I waited around until five, and then in a huff, I left the house. My answering machine told me he called at 5:30. When he called again at nine, he was surprised to hear I was angry and he was even more surprised to hear my definition of afternoon. He thought any time before seven would qualify, as it would certainly give him enough time to "scoop me up" for an eight o'clock meal.

Lord knows why, but I agreed to go out with him the next night, though I didn't let him scoop me up. Dating safety mandated that we meet someplace instead, and so we did, at TGI Fridays. Since he did not have a photo of himself posted on Match.com, I feared what sort of man might actually appear at the restaurant, but as it turns out, he was easy enough on the eyes. He was about six feet tall, something under two hundred pounds, and built like a wren, meaning skinny legs and no hips with a big block of a body. He said his grandkids call him "Big Irv" due to his years at Gold's Gym, and I understood the name. He was balding but blond. He wore tight jeans with a gray crew-neck sweatshirt over a polo shirt. And he wore boots, a very odd accoutrement to me.

Our conversation came with ease. Whatever question I asked him about himself, he then asked me in return. Strangely, this is not a trait that many men possess; they seem to like being "interviewed" but never think to turn the table. In Big Irv's case, not only did he ask me about myself, but he listened to my answers and asked follow-up questions to learn more.

I learned an interesting mix of information that night:

- He has two younger sisters, one with whom he gets along and one with whom he does not. Indeed as kids, that sister tried to kill him with a butcher knife, though he could not quite recall why. As to the quality of their current relationship, he "didn't care one way or t'other" if he saw his sisters.

- He lost his dad to an abdominal aortic aneurysm when the dad was in his early fifties, and "lo these many years," his mother, who is in her nineties, still lives on.

- He had been married once and had one child from that union. Daughter Karen lives in Cincinnati with her three children. I wasn't sure if he was kidding or if he was reflecting on the nature of those three granddaughters when he stated his belief that women should be allowed to have only one child.

- In the years since his divorce, he had dated many women, most of whom were a lot younger than he. He was tired of that concept now and had made a conscious effort to "play with children his own age."

- Finally, in discussing his business, he confided that he had had financial difficulties in the recent past with his money going "hither, thither, and yon." However, the situation had improved and he had managed, finally, to get "his cockiness" back.

Bottom line, our first get-together easily passed the "time flies test" and was a harbinger for one of the truly good things about our relationship.

I liked a lot of things about Big Irv that first date and found lots of other things to be intriguing. The only real concern I had was in regard to his age. His Match.com profile said he was born in 1952, the same year as I, but somehow he didn't seem to be my age at all. The patterns of his speech made him sound older, if nothing else. There were many things in our conversation about which Big Irv said, "I shan't worry about that," but I was thinking maybe I did need to be concerned about this topic.

We proceeded to go out a couple of times a week after that, and in those dates I casually asked questions as I tried to figure out his age. In what year was his daughter, Karen, born? What year did he graduate from boarding school? Where was he when JFK was assassinated? The man had no answers to these questions. Ultimately, we laughed over the following two truths:

1. As an engineer, he could look at a building and figure out—in his head—what it would cost to tear it down and then rebuild it on the spot.
2. But there were absolutely no numbers he could add or subtract that would allow him to figure out the answers to my personal questions.

Finally I asked to see his driver's license and learned he was ten years my senior. It is not my nature to directly confront people, but with me being a decade younger, was he really playing with children his own age when he played with me? Oh, and if you're wondering how he managed to botch up his age on his Match.com profile, he said a website called RealAge.com assessed his age as being ten years younger because he was so fit.

As much as Big Irv would have liked it, we did not have a date on New Year's Eve that first year because I attended my nephew's wedding out of town instead. I spoke to Big Irv by phone that evening and he told me this would be the last New Year's Eve he planned to spend alone. I thought that was his cryptic way of saying we were an item. By the time the next new year rolled around, Big Irv told me he thought we should do something official about our status. I thought this was his cryptic way of proposing, but in case it was an instance of him not actually speaking English to me—though it sounded so much like English—I did not respond. Perhaps if a proposal was what he'd intended, he'd pull out a ring someday so I would know. However, neither of us brought up the topic—if indeed it was a topic—ever again.

It seems in retrospect that direct communication was not our strong point. Here are a couple of examples.

- I told Big Irv that my ex-husband likes to send me email notes that say "L.D.," which is his shorthand for "let's discuss." Big Irv's response was that his notes would say "N.F.D." for no further discussion, or as he actually said it, "no futhuh discussion."
- After we had been together for a while, I said to him on a few occasions, "Other than that roll of hundred-dollar bills in your pocket, do you have any money?" His response was always to give me the Cheshire Cat's grin, straight out of *Alice's Adventures in Wonderland.* That grin was often the response to a probing question.

So back to his maybe proposal, with all of this non-communication going on between us, perhaps he thought I agreed with him that we needed to do something official about our status and so without futhuh ado and without futhuh conversation, he moved himself into my house. Huh?

"I have some good news for you," he announced on Sunday morning, July 8, 2007. "In honor of my sixty-fifth birthday today, I've decided to move into your house."

Well gosh, it's hard to go ballistic on the birthday boy on his really big day, so I remained calm. "What does that mean, exactly?" I asked.

"Things have been slow at the office so Krista had no work to do. I sent her over to my apartment to pack everything up. She put it all in storage for me."

Oh, it was Krista's doing, was it? Big Irv had nothing to do with it, right? Certainly I didn't! I was baffled and confused, but probably not exactly angry. And indeed my original thought was that we would discuss it the next day when his big birthday had blown by. But in waiting for the next day, it occurred to me that perhaps this was God's way of making me put both feet down into this relationship. I tend to be leery of romantic relationships, so I try to compartmentalize them. For a good time, call Big Irv. But maybe I needed to let him in more than that. So in the end, I said nothing.

Before the big surprise move-in at the twenty-month mark of our relationship, Big Irv and I had been spending loads of time together, including weekends back and forth at his place or at mine, more frequently at mine. Thus, Big Irv had a ton of stuff at my house already: clothes, toiletries, electronics, you name it. To his credit, I will say that when the man moved in, he brought nothing extra into the house, not an extra shirt or framed photograph, not a wall-hanging, pot, or screwdriver. He knew me well indeed. A two-hundred-pound man was all he could force on me at once. And just for the record, it was years before we located the Krista-packed box that contained my possessions from his place.

This living together, though, turned out to be the beginning of the end. I am not proud to say it, but by July 2012, I surprised him and moved him right back out again. Turnabout is fair play?

It's funny to read this over and to realize that some of the stories I have written today, under the heading of "The Good Stuff," are actually not so good. Knowing the pain Big Irv and I caused each other by the end, I wonder if I would do things differently if given the chance to live this over again. Like, you know, not go out with him in the first place after he stood me up on day one?

This tantalizing question comes to me because of my film choice for Saturday Night at the Movies, *About Time*, which deals with time travel. Yes, I already saw this movie when it came out in 2013, but it's a wonderful film, and the prospect of writing in The Book of Irv again was so daunting, I needed to be assured of liking my reward.

Saturday Night at the Movies

About Time

DIRECTOR: Richard Curtis

WRITER: Richard Curtis

RELEASE DATE: 2013

RUNNING TIME: 2 Hours, 3 Minutes

ALSO FEATURING: Domhnall Gleeson, Rachel McAdams, Lindsay Duncan, and Tom Hollander

FRIENDLY CONNECTIONS: As of 2015, Bill Nighy and Tom Hollander have worked together in six movies: *True Blue* (1996), *Lawless Heart* (2001), *Pirates of the Caribbean: Dead Man's Chest* (2006), *Pirates of the Caribbean: At World's End* (2007), *Valkyrie* (2008), and *About Time* (2014). Additionally, this movie represents the fourth time Bill Nighy and Richard Curtis have teamed up. Their previous collaborations are: *Love Actually,* 2003; *The Girl in the Café,* 2005; and *The Boat That Rocked,* 2009. It is reported that *About Time* will be the last film Richard Curtis directs, which is truly a shame since a Richard Curtis/Bill Nighy movie is—borrowing from John Keats—a thing of beauty [and] a joy forever.

According to Wikipedia, this is the plot of *About Time*: "At the age of twenty-one, Tim Lake (Domhnall Gleeson) is told by his father (Bill Nighy) that the men of his family have a special gift: the ability to travel in time. This supernatural ability is subject to one constraint—they can only travel to places and times they have been before. After his father discourages Tim from using his gift to acquire money or fame, he decides that he will use it to improve his love life."

Time travel, of course, can be tricky due to the so-called "butterfly effect," meaning one small change in the past can accidently affect other bits of history without intending to. So it is that Tim meets the girl of his dreams and manages to get her phone number. But then he turns back the hands of time to help solve a friend's problem (of course this problem happened on the same night he met the girl) only to realize that in doing so, his own life did not play out in the original manner and so he did not meet the girl, nor did he have her phone number. Using other information he knew about the girl, though, he is able to re-meet her and make a relationship work. Thus, he marries and has children with Mary (Rachel McAdams).

In another example of time travel gone astray, Tim tries to help his sister, Kit, who is in an unhealthy and unhappy relationship and who has an alcohol problem. When Tim turns the clock back to the time before Kit entered the bad relationship, it also turns time back to the period before the birth of Tim's first child, a daughter named Posey. When he comes back to the point in the future where Kit is doing well, never having been in the bad relationship, he also comes back to a future where Posey does not exist and his first child is a son instead. At this point, his father explains that travelling back to change things before his children were born would mean those children would not be born.

Ultimately it happens that Tim learns his father has terminal cancer and that time travel cannot change it. His father has known for quite some time but kept travelling back in time to effectively extend his life and spend more time with his family. Wanting to impart a big life lesson before dying, the dad suggests to Tim that he live each day twice in order to be truly happy. He elaborates, saying that the first time around Tim should live the day in a normal fashion with all the tensions and worries that stop us from noticing how sweet the world can be; on the second go 'round, though, he should be sure to notice. Tim follows this advice and also travels back into the past to visit his father whenever he misses him.

But then it happens that Mary wants to have another child, whose birth will end Tim's ability to travel back in time to visit his father, and so Tim and his dad have a last—and tearful—goodbye. It is a beautiful scene that does not translate well on paper. So I guess that is a tribute to wonderful acting. It contains all of four words.

Dad to Tim: "My son."

Tim to Dad: "My dad."

For someone like me, who has lost a dad and misses that dad daily, those words are not only wrenching, they make every minute of watching the movie worthwhile, even for the second time around.

One could easily write off this movie as being complete fluff; after all, time travel is not a reality. But the purpose of time travel in this movie is to allow Tim to live each day to its fullest and happiest, albeit when he lives it for the second time. In a *New York Times* interview by Jesse McKinley dated October 25, 2013, this aspect of the movie is discussed. Richard Curtis tells of a conversation he had with a friend in which the friend asked him if he was happy. Curtis was surprised to find that his answer was, "Not particularly." While "what was wrong" was not immediately apparent, it got Richard Curtis thinking about what a perfect day would be. Thus, he began to write the script for *About Time*, allowing his characters the ability to revisit—and repair—all the days of their lives.

Bill Nighy is also a part of that *New York Times* interview. He has this to say on the topic: "It's the thing that everyone struggles with all of the time, that idea of not having the day stolen from you by the static in your head, either regret for yesterday or fear for tomorrow. And while I've struggled with that like everybody else, I have been for the last few years actively trying to resist it…When you get to my age, you look at the clock, and you think: I better pay attention. And why not try and have an active search for beauty wherever you might be? That is the quest." The article goes on to say that he "has gone so far as to stand still in the middle of busy streets or lie under trees in

London squares, simply trying to relish the moment [he's] in."

As an aside, this interview manages to discuss all four films Bill Nighy and Richard Curtis worked on together. In the process, it tells this lovely tale of their first joint venture, *Love Actually*. Richard Curtis said he had no intention of casting Bill Nighy in the role of Billy Mack, but that changed after Bill Nighy did a read-through of the script—as a favor from Richard Curtis to the casting director. Richard Curtis said, "At that read-through, the only laughs were every line that Bill said." What a lucky break for all Bill Nighy lovers that the casting director got that favor!

Back to the *About Time* interview, it ends with a Bill Nighy quote. He said that *About Time* made him think about life and what it all means. His conclusion from such thoughts: "Be here now. Which is so much easier to say than to do."

WEDNESDAY, AUGUST 5, 2015

Dear Diary,

My mailbox has not been kind. I sent letter number two to beloved Bill three weeks ago and there has been no response. Darn! I know I expected and prepared myself for this exact outcome, but just the same, darn! Peeks out to the front porch likewise yield no missives in floral form. Fortunately, the Internet is full of the man, so I content myself with finding him there. Last week's movie — in which his character was simply known as "Dad" — has caused me to search for information about his relationship with his father. Indeed, the movie has caused me to think about dads altogether, mine included.

I was down in Tennessee recently and listened to a friend there speak Southern style as she referred to her "mother and daddy." I had to wonder, why such a stiffness for the female parent and such warmth for the male? In my own childhood, this was likewise the case, not in what I called them — it was Mom and Dad — but in how I perceived them emotionally. Both of my parents were terrific people. My mom was the stay-at-home version of the mother role, and as such, she was there to make life run smoothly. She put complete meals on the table daily. She cleaned the house — even washed dishes in the bath tub once when the kitchen pipes froze up in the winter. She laundered our clothes. Back in the days before permanent press, she even ironed everything. She paid the bills, always on time. Nary an experience with disconnection of power due to a late payment of the bill. She was truly Wonder Woman. But I only know this in hindsight. While living my childhood, she was wallpaper — always there, but only peripherally noticed. Dad, on the other hand, was the star of the family! Oh, how we loved him on those rare occasions that he was home from his work in retail at a time when my brother and I were still awake. Perhaps it is in the immediate family that absence makes the heart grow fonder while familiarity breeds contempt?

As a stay-at-home mom myself, I noticed the same phenomenon. This one vignette says it all: I put love notes in my kids' lunchboxes daily; their dad put one in a couple times a school year. Should you check the little box of childhood keepsakes that each of my children has, I am certain you will find many of Daddy's love notes while none of Mother's. Hmmm…I may choose to come back as a dad in my next lifetime.

In reading about Bill Nighy, I am thinking the same mother/father dynamic holds true. I find various things about his dad, Alfred Nighy, and little about his mother, Catherine Josephine Whittaker Nighy. Here is what I have found:

In an article that appeared in *The Telegraph* on September 4, 2013, written by Gaby Wood, Bill Nighy mentions both parents. Gaby Wood's narrative tells us that BN's father ran a garage in Surrey, that he based his style on Bing Crosby, that he died of a heart attack when beloved Bill was twenty-six, and that BN regrets enormously the fact that his dad was not around to witness his success. No similar summary of his mother's life is given. These quotes about his parents also appear in the article:

- "My dad was a lovely man…He was very gracious, and principled, and reserved."
- "If I ever played a part where I had short hair, after my father died, my mother would go very quiet, and it was because she was moved by the resemblance."

Could there have been a tinier mention of his mom? And while I know the Internet is immense, and many comments about her must exist, thus far I have found only one other interview in which he speaks of her. It is in an article written by Ariel Leve in 2007. The topic of discussion is Bill Nighy's love of Bob Dylan and of the fact that he listens to Bob Dylan *every single day*. Ariel Leve asks if it would be a deal-breaker if BN's significant other didn't like Bob Dylan and tells us his reply is very serious when he says, "No, no…I understand that the world is divided. It started with my mother—'He's a very good songwriter, but he should leave others to sing.' I have to live in the world with these people. So I have to let it go." Oh my. It's tough to be a mom when any of the million off-the-cuff comments we make can be used against us for all eternity.

But back to the love of his dad, in an interview with Charlie Rose in May 2012, after *The Best Exotic Marigold Hotel* premiered, Bill Nighy says his character in the movie, Douglas Ainslie, was a tribute to his dad. He elaborates by saying, "Doug Ainslie is a man who was a civil servant. He did a job he hated for about thirty-five years and he was married the same amount of time to a woman he continuously and deeply disappoints. She only has to look at him to be depressed. He's a decent man. He always seeks the decency option. Instinctively! He is drawn to what he thinks is right. It's heroic, and interesting! It also exhausts him to disappoint someone so much for so long. It's grueling."

Charlie Rose asks Bill Nighy at that point whether these character traits were spelled out in the script or if all of this was Bill Nighy's vision of Douglas Ainslie's character. BN replies, "This is how I see the man, but it chimes with the writer's intentions of a decent, honorable, long-suffering man." Bill Nighy goes on to say that both the Douglas Ainslie character and the Lawrence Montague character in the movie *The Girl in the Café* are a tribute to his dad. He says it is an understatement to say Lawrence Montague was a reserved man, that in fact he was disabled by self-consciousness, and though Bill Nighy's father wasn't like that exactly, his father was a very decent man, a shy man, a man "not in as much trouble as" Lawrence or Douglas, but a "very particular kind of Englishman."

So there it is, Bill Nighy's version of worshipping at the shrine of "Dad" just like I do, just like my children do. Is it any wonder I was torn up by those two lines/four words in *About Time*:

Dad to Tim: "My son."

Tim to Dad: "My dad."

My dad, indeed. Bring out the hankies. I think I'm going to cry.

Oops! Evidently, I wasn't quite done with this entry, dear Diary. I have one final thought to add to this topic of dads: Big Irv did not wax poetic about his father, and in fact I heard very little about the man beyond the medical history that he died young of an abdominal aortic aneurysm. The only other story I recall is that a teenage Irv once arrived home after curfew—and escorted by a policeman—and that his father's response was to "thump" him. I never asked him exactly what that meant in his version of the English language, but it's not good according to Merriam-Webster.

THE BOOK OF IRV
_____

The Good—The Bad—The Ugly—The End
PART II—THE BAD STUFF

Here is something that is abundantly clear: I tend to get myself into trouble in relationships because I neglect to stand up for myself. For instance, in 2002 when I was still in a relationship with Jimmy Jet, I should have been assertive and told him: "The only way I will be in a relationship with you is if you take your drugs to avoid severe mood swings." But I never said that to him. Thus, one day after he went on a sunny spending spree, I found myself looking at a large canoe docked in the middle of my family room. Instead of learning to be more assertive, I have learned not to get too deep into a relationship in the first place; hence, I never would have gotten around to suggesting cohabitation with Big Irv. That was just too scary. Dinners out and weekends together were quite enough for me.

But he did move in, so I figured God wanted me to learn to stand up for myself, and I tried. It was my routine to wake up at 6 a.m., do a quick, twenty-minute exercise routine with weights, and then go out for an hourlong walk at seven. It was Big Irv's routine to sleep in whenever possible. For my exercise, he had set me up with weights from his vast collection. Instead of the lady-like dumbbells that were one-piece pink or purple products, the ones I use have a metal bar, with small metal weights added on and held in place with special nuts and bolts. Due to this construction, they jingle and jangle ever so slightly when moved, especially when doing hammer curls, a bell ringer-like maneuver. And so it was over dinner one night that Big Irv mentioned he heard me working out that morning. In my heart of hearts, I would like to believe that it was an observation and not a complaint, but my psyche would never agree. And so we had a conversation about surveillance. Huh? I explained to him I am very sensitive to criticism. I told him that in my couple of experiences with cohabitation, I have had one man tell me that I put forks in the dishwasher incorrectly—they should be tines down, not up. I have had another guy tell me I use my garbage disposal incorrectly—one should continuously pulse it on and off instead of just turning it on and letting it run. I have even heard that I put mail in my house's mailbox incorrectly—I am told that since it is a roadside mailbox, letters should be propped up for easy handling by the mailman, not put down flat. I get hurt by these things instead of angry. So I instructed Big Irv to keep his mouth shut about what he observed or heard me doing, like weightlifting. I had no need to be under surveillance! Astoundingly, speaking up worked, and so our next go 'round with the issue went something like this:

Me: "This is the craziest thing!"

Him: "What is?"

Me: "A couple of days ago when I took Lila to the baby class at the library, one of the other little kids hit me in the head with a maraca. I thought it was no big deal at the time, but then today, I noticed I have a goose egg on my forehead! Is that unbelievable?"

Him: "Oh. I've been looking at that bump for all this time wondering how it got there. But I have been chastised on the topic so I knew better than to ask. I figured if something had happened, you would have told me, but since you did not, I assumed it has been there all along and that I have never noticed it until now."

What can I say? He's an educable man. Wow! Perhaps this living together would be okay after all. I was pretty proud of myself for teaching the old dog a new trick. Confidently, we moved on to the next old adage, the one about letting sleeping dogs lie.

Having spent weekends with the man before cohabitation, I knew our sleep patterns were vastly different. As I have just mentioned, I am a person who is up early and on the go. Back then—when I used to sleep well—my eyes were at half-mast by 11 or 11:15 p.m. and I was ready for bed. I was usually asleep before my head hit the pillow. Indeed, my sleeping skills were envied by many. Big Irv, on the other hand, loved to stay up late, needed a sleeping pill to knock himself out, and then arose from his slumber with difficulty. If left to his own devices, he would stay in the den watching TV until 2 or 3 a.m., he would sleep in until noon or 1, then putter around the house before finally hitting the shower between 4 and 5 p.m. I guess he was having this sort of ideal day when he had difficulty calling me in the "afternoon" for our first date.

Though this was Big Irv's dream day, he allowed it only on an occasional Saturday or Sunday in the early months of our relationship. As a person who likes a lot of quiet time, I just used those hours to read when I was at his place or to get things done around the house when we were at mine. So, yes, on weekends he stayed up late a lot, and slept late a lot, but he still managed to get himself up with enough time to go out for brunch. He groused that all those half-day café-type places closed by 2:30, but he loved to go out to brunch on weekends, so he managed to get us there in time to do our midday dining.

As for weekdays, I might be a wishy-washy person disinclined to confrontation, but there was no way he was sleeping in daily at my house, so we made a pact that he would be off to work by 9:30. We fought about it a lot, but in the end, I simply would not let that sleeping dog lie.

Somewhere along the line, things started to change in the character of our fun times due to his desire to sleep. If you are not starting your day until 2:30 p.m., there is not a whole lot of day to be had and a lot of activities need to be scratched from the agenda. And then at some point, sleep took over the majority of our dance card. I never knew whether to blame his natural inclination to sleep or to blame all the circumstances of the time. The chronology of our life gives ample reason for exhaustion. He moved into my home in July 2007. It was in December 2009 that Dad's health declined to the point that we moved him from St. Louis to Cincinnati. In a grueling ten months in Ohio, we moved him from independent living to assisted living to skilled nursing care to hospice and then back to St. Louis for burial. As draining as all that was, two more things gave Big Irv the desire to hide his head under the covers. The first was that he did not like the concept of hospice and was completely unhappy with—and unsupportive of—that decision. And then in a terrible twist of fate, on the same day my brother and I chose hospice for Dad, Big Irv had the test that led to his cancer diagnosis.

It is an understatement to say Big Irv liked to sleep. This fact was probably the largest stumbling block of our living together, and then of course it only got worse when chemo brain and the effects of radiation got added to the mix. Many of his doctors thought his sleeping would cause pneumonia and kill him, but in the end, it killed our relationship instead.

But I am jumping ahead again. I need to mention another factor that tore us apart. When he and I met, he had one child and three grandchildren living in Cincinnati while all of my kids lived out of town and I had no grandkids yet, though the first one was on the way. As an aside, I should say he didn't get along with his daughter that well, so we did not socialize very much with Karen and the girls. That was his model for dealing with adult children and grandchildren. But back to my kids, in the years Big Irv and I lived together, my three kids were prolifically procreative, and with burgeoning families in tow, all of them decided to move back to Cincinnati. Shana moved back in 2008 when she and her husband were expecting their second child. Scotty moved back in 2010 just weeks after he and his wife had their second child. And Lisa and her husband moved back in 2012 as they started to think about a second child. Shana ultimately had a third child, and Scotty's wife did too. By the time of the ugly blow-up in our relationship, five of my eight grandchildren were born and they were coming to Marmel School on Mondays, plus they and their parents—eleven people—were coming to family dinners on Thursdays. To add insult to injury, those dinners were at 5 p.m. to accommodate the schedules of the little kids and not 8 p.m. to accommodate Big Irv.

To his defense, that was a lot more kids and grandkids than he bargained for when he started going out with me. And let's not forget that in his perfect world, I would have had a more manageable head count of one child, one child-in-law, and one grandchild. But that was not our reality. But then I must also defend myself. I never hid the fact from him that my kids and grandkids meant the world to me. Indeed, early on when I told him of my previous relationship with Jimmy Jet, I told him of our frequent argument:

Said Jimmy Jet in anger and dismay: "Your children will always come first!"

Said I with equal venom: "Yes, that's right! They will always come first! What don't you understand? They leapt from my womb. You did not!"

Just in case Big Irv and I did not have enough stressors already, one bad diagnosis after another was about to come his way. He had two independent cancers (not metastatic), one in the kidney and one in the lung. He also had a benign brain tumor (complete with seizures) and an abdominal aortic aneurysm in need of repair. It would have been nice for us to pull together through the whole nightmare, but his bad-boy tendencies severely interfered with my need to be neat, sweet, and in my seat. And as he "came out of his truck feet first" at all of those doctors, nurses, and hospital administrators, it felt like I was constantly in between them, taking the brunt of the blows.

- Even before his first surgery, he read all the consent forms and argued with hospital administrators, insisting they strike clauses from the standard forms, especially those granting permission to insert an IV.
- One surgery even had to be postponed due to his refusal to sign the standard forms.
- Likewise, a procedure was postponed—at the last minute—because he chose not to have it done that day in spite of the fact that the hospital had brought in some special piece of equipment for that purpose alone.
- He fought with the kidney surgeon over picc lines versus IV for that surgery.
- After kidney surgery, he fought with the hospital pharmacist—a woman I know socially—over drug doses and intervals for said doses.
- He was enraged with the kidney surgeon for NOT making house calls during the profuse bleeding experience and let the man know it.
- During the hospitalization that followed my screaming and crying fit, the hospital staff threatened to restrain Big Irv as he fought with them about putting in an IV line.
- He fought with the lung surgeon over how much tissue she would remove and allowed her to take only the smallest sliver, though she promised him it would shorten his life.
- He fought with the radiologist about the amount of radiation he should have.

- He similarly fought with the oncologist about chemo treatments and agreed to have chemo only sporadically, the normal protocol be damned.
- He called the oncologist a motherfucker on a couple occasions—to the man's face.
- He was likewise verbally abusive to the ambulance technicians who picked him up off the floor at the local Olive Garden and transported him to the hospital after he had a seizure.
- As for me? I was embarrassed and then mortified by his behavior. I was angry and then enraged.
- Of course, I Googled every diagnosis. I also Googled every procedure. I kept a huge notebook of all CT scan reports, MRI reports, and the like. I Googled every word in every test result that I did not know. I asked questions at all doctor appointments and took notes on the answers. I Googled some more when I got home. All of this gave me a thimbleful of knowledge. Big Irv Googled nothing. He read nothing. And he knew it all.

Beyond bearing witness to all of these medical interactions, I also found myself in the role of translator as I turned Big Irv's brand of English into a form that was useful to his doctors. For example, he actually liked the vascular surgeon who was going to repair his abdominal aortic aneurysm. This man had followed Big Irv's condition for years. It was awful timing that in the midst of all of his other medical issues, this doc felt it was urgent to do the aneurysm repair. Big Irv had prepared himself mentally for such surgery for years, so he was actually on board for it, but in his pre-op visit, with me sitting in the exam room, Big Irv failed to tell the vascular surgeon about all his other medical issues. I was dumbfounded as the two men merrily chatted about what date would be good for surgery. From my corner of the exam room, I proceeded to give those guys the timeout signal.

When they finally noticed me madly tapping the palm of my right hand against the fingers of my left hand in "T" formation, I gave the doctor the lowdown on the long list of issues with which Big Irv was already dealing. Being in a different medical network from the other doctors, he had no clue. After conversing with those other doctors in the other medical network, though, it was deemed that the aneurysm surgery was not a possibility at that time. Big Irv's lungs were not strong enough for surgery.

Similarly, I was the interpreter between him and his neurologist. Brain surgery for his meningioma was not a possibility even though the tumor was pressing on his right frontal lobe. In this manner, it caused problems with rational thought and with get-up-and-go. It also caused the seizure. The neurologist had no choice but to manage the tumor and seizure through medication. Thanks to the seizure, Big Irv was unable to drive for a period of time. Thanks to the drug to prevent further seizures, he was unable to drink. Big Irv liked the neurologist, so it was friendly banter as he argued with the man about drinking and driving. The no-driving dictate post-seizure was non-negotiable. It was mandated by state law. But there was some room for discussion on the drinking issue, so he got the doctor to state that on occasion he could have a drink—one martini would be okay. There I was again, madly giving the timeout signal to the two men from my little corner of the room. "Let's speak English together here," I said. "What is your definition of 'a drink'?" I aimed my question at the neurologist.

He looked at me like I was crazy but then defined terms: "A drink is a couple or a few ounces of liquor."

"And what is your definition of 'a drink'?" I said, this time aiming the question at Big Irv, who did not reply, so I did it for him. "I think you take a ten-ounce glass, fill it with ice cubes and then pour on straight vodka. Is that correct?" He silently nodded his agreement.

"And when you are drinking, you usually drink a couple of those across the evening. Is that correct?" And again we got a nod. And in that manner, his drinking days came to an end.

It was exhausting speaking English with Big Irv, and all of his medical issues were daunting in any language. Even if he were a model patient, that would have been the case, but instead he was the polar opposite. I coaxed and cajoled him, I threatened him, I even tried to scare him into doing what the doctors thought was necessary. But he would have no part of it. He made his own decisions, most of them contrary to expert advice. Through it all, I clapped him on the back and mockingly congratulated him for his steadfast belief in himself, all the while telling him I would be sure to play Frank Sinatra's "My Way" at his funeral.

SATURDAY, AUGUST 8, 2015

Dear Diary,

I was at Saxby's today writing in The Book of Irv. I came away two ways angry.

- I am angry with myself for being such a bitch to him. Did I really rub his nose in Sinatra? And I recall telling him with great regularity that he was "an ass and a half," which is hardly a term of endearment.

- I am also angry with him because he really was an ass and a half. Enumerating his antics is rage-provoking. There were a couple of points at which I wanted to hurl the journal across the coffee shop. Instead I made a different kind of scene, as I sat there and sobbed.

I am looking for some comic relief to my day. Bill Nighy to the rescue. Tonight's film is *Hot Fuzz*. I hope I love it.

Saturday Night at the Movies

Hot Fuzz
DIRECTOR: Edgar Wright
WRITERS: Edgar Wright and Simon Pegg
RELEASE DATE: 2007
RUNNING TIME: 2 Hours, 1 Minute
ALSO FEATURING: Simon Pegg, Martin Freeman, Nick Frost, Jim Broadbent, and Cate Blanchett (sort of)
FRIENDLY CONNECTIONS: Cate Blanchett and Bill Nighy worked together on *Notes on a Scandal* in 2006. Jim Broadbent and BN both lent their voices to the animated film *The Magic Roundabout* in 2005. After *Hot Fuzz*, they will go on to another animated film, *Arthur Christmas*, in 2012 and they will both appear in *Harry Potter and the Deathly Hallows: Part II* in 2011. In 2009, Bill Nighy and Nick Frost will go on to work together in *The Boat That Rocked*. But there is a larger connection for the actors than this. The connection includes Edgar Wright and Simon Pegg as well. Specifically, Frost, Wright, and Pegg have created three films that are called the "Three Flavours Cornetto Trilogy." *Hot Fuzz* is one of the films in the trilogy. The other two are *Shaun of the Dead* from 2004 and *The World's End* from 2013. Each of the movies features a different flavor of Cornetto ice cream. (The Cornetto is an ice cream confection made by Unilever and sold in the U.K. Competitors in the U.S. are Nestle, which calls its product a Drumstick, and Sweetheart Foods, which calls its product a Nutty Buddy.) Beyond the fact that the three films feature this ice cream treat, they have little in common. *Shaun of the Dead* deals with an apocalyptic zombie uprising and *The World's End* deals with an alien invasion that takes place during an epic pub crawl. All, however, are crazy comedies and all feature Bill Nighy in some small role.

Hot Fuzz is the movie of the day. It is labeled a satirical action comedy film. It is one of the movies Bill Nighy listed in that already mentioned article in the *Buzz Feed News* in which he discusses ten of his films. *Hot Fuzz* is fifth on the list. My usual complaint about his movies is that he does not have a large enough part in most of them, and quite frankly, it is nearly impossible for him to have a smaller role than he does in this one. He appears for approximately one minute in an opening scene, then for less time (!!) toward the end of the movie. The only good thing I can say is that his first scene is within the opening five minutes of the film so it is easy to find, watch, rewind, and then find, watch, rewind, etc. I guess things could be worse. Cate Blanchett is also in the movie, but as Bill Nighy explains it, "They put [her] in one of those protection suits with a huge helmet on so you couldn't see who she was, and then they had a competition for you to guess where Cate Blanchett was in the movie. If you guessed where she was, you got two tickets for the premiere." On behalf of Cate Blanchett fans worldwide I say, "Argh!!"

Describing the plot, *Hot Fuzz* is about Police Constable Nicholas Angel (Simon Pegg), who is a high-achieving member of the Metropolitan Police Service. He is promoted to Sergeant, but it comes with a transfer to the small village of Sandford, Gloucestershire. He is transferred because he is too good at his job, which makes his colleagues look bad by comparison. At first glance, Angel finds the new town to be devoid of any crime. There is a local Neighborhood Watch Alliance (NWA) helping to keep the peace as everyone prepares for the "Village of the Year" award contest. In the new position, Nicholas Angel is paired with a witless new partner named Danny Butterman (Nick Frost). While on the beat, Angel suspects and proves that a sinister conspiracy is afoot with the residents and with the NWA. Where is Bill Nighy in all this? His character is the top cop, the one who sends Police Constable Nicholas Angel off to the hinterlands for being too good a cop.

In the unauthorized biography, Bill Nighy says he took the part in *Hot Fuzz* because he loves Simon Pegg and Edgar Wright and because they write "really funny jokes." From all I read about my man, I think this is an important topic to consider—jokes. He has said repeatedly of his stage experiences that he thinks it is really "bad manners" to make an audience sit in a dark theater for two hours without giving them some good jokes to laugh over. Additionally, in a *Playbill* interview dated March 31, 2015 (written by Robert Simonson), he says a "world-class joke" is built like a clock. "If you deliver them with all the 'ums' and 'ahs' and 'dot-dot-dots,' they go off like bombs." This is important to Bill Nighy. He is a man who will not watch his own work on the big screen for fear of all the ways he has fallen short in the performance he tried to give. But getting a good laugh from an audience is one of the few ways he has of knowing he has done a good job. A laugh from an audience is a pat on the back to this man, so of course he loves a comedy.

Back to *Hot Fuzz*, Bill Nighy describes it this way: "It's a big, daft, stupid cop movie." He says this with love and admiration. Though I would use the same words to describe the movie and mean them seriously and literally, given my love of Bill Nighy—and my understanding of the significance of humor to him—I will cut him, Edgar Wright, Simon Pegg, and Nick Frost some slack here and say, if you're into comedy, you might want to give this one a try. And if you don't like it, perhaps indulging in a Cornetto, Drumstick, or Nutty Buddy after the show would make you feel better. I'm off to get mine now.

Sunday, August 9, 2015

Dear Diary,

I spoke to Roberta tonight; I mean Dr. Roberta. She asked lots of questions as she took my emotional temperature.

Q: How's the sleeping going?

A: No change.

Q: How's the eating going?

A: Pizza is my new best friend. Two slices a day keep the food doldrums away.

Q: What about the Irv journal?

A: Writing in it and weeping.

Q: Sketching any new quilts yet?

A: Not even a doodle of a design.

Q: And the next visit with Popa is…?

A: Not until October.

On the topic of quilting, Roberta was pleased to hear that I have a quilt retreat coming up next Friday through Sunday at that great B&B in Indiana. We both agree that three days away with like-minded lady friends will help with the bored-lonely-depressed triumvirate. As much as she hopes the getaway will spark some creative part of my brain, I'm not counting on it. My plan is to sew a "Kids' Comfort," which is a very basic, lap-sized quilt that the Ohio Valley Quilters Guild distributes to charitable organizations. Making such a project is very easy in that the guild creates kits for them that include a pattern and coordinated yard goods. Indeed, the fabrics are already cut to size. All I have to do is sew the pieces for the top together, layer it with a batting and a backing material, quilt the three layers together, and then put a binding on. All are quilting tasks I can do in my sleep. This mindless work buys me a weekend with great women. What a deal!

And speaking of being with others, I told Roberta about my latest plan to have a family reunion in St. Louis over Labor Day weekend. Aunt Betty's health continues to decline and I want my kids and grandkids to see her, so I will take them to St. Louis for that purpose. By some stroke of luck, all of them are free that weekend, so off we will go. Our favorite restaurant there, The Pasta House, has a private room that holds eighty. I plan to fill it with both sides of the family, the whole mishpocha.

"You're welcome to come to St. Louis for the party, Roberta," I said. After all, it's her hometown too and she's known my extended family since we met at age five. "Shall I try to tempt you with all my relatives—who you know and haven't seen in forever—or with the Pasta Con Broccoli, Toasted Ravioli, and Pasta House Salad that I plan to serve?"

"If I come, it would just be to support you. Do you need me now that the journal I suggested has caused you to weep over Irv again?"

"Oh gosh, I thought I slid that by you."

"You know me better than that."

"Actually, knowing you are a speech therapist makes you a good person to talk to about one aspect of my agony. I have been listening to old voice mail messages from him and they tear me up."

"You have old voice mail messages from Irv?"

"Yes, on my cell phone. There are eight of them. I am clueless as to how I managed to save them."

"So they tear you up. Does this mean they make you angry or they make you sad?"

"Both, actually. Half of them are his standard message. He used to say, 'Hey when you get this, give me a call.' That used to really annoy me. Why couldn't he save time and just tell me what the heck he wanted?"

"And the other half?" she said, laughing at me.

"It's not so much the content as it is his voice alone…in all eight messages. It was such a deep, rumble-y kind of voice. I found it soothing. Did you know he intentionally spoke quietly so people would have to pipe down and listen to him? He actually cultivated that habit. And by the way, that annoyed me too! The combination of his soft voice plus my old ears added up to communication difficulties for us. Like we needed more problems."

"I just read an article in the *Huffington Post*," Roberta said, "about 'the strange science of sexual attraction,' and voice is evidently important in selecting a mate."

"The sound of a man's voice has always been important to you, but I just assumed it was because you're a speech pathologist," I replied.

"This article suggests it's way more important than that. It said, for instance, that a woman's voice is most seductive when she is at the most fertile point in her menstrual cycle. In fact, a woman's voice at peak fertility can literally make a man's skin tingle. So Irv's voice could have been that kind of a turn-on for you. How do you feel about Bill Nighy's voice?"

"Oh gosh," I laughed, "the British accent alone is very charming. So charming in fact that this week I changed the settings on my iPhone and now the voice of Siri is a British male. But darn, he doesn't sound anything like beloved Bill. Seriously, though, Bill Nighy's voice has been very important to his success. In his early days as an actor, radio parts were easier to get than stage roles, which was great because radio work allowed him to play parts he wouldn't have had elsewhere. It also allowed him to work with great older actors whom he got to observe—and learn from—at close range. And if all of that isn't enough, the hundred or more radio plays he did taught him how to convey a lot through his voice alone. So yes, Bill Nighy has a great voice, a very evocative voice."

"I guess that makes sense. Facial expressions and body language can't help at all when you do radio. The voice is all there is," Roberta said. "How nice for him to start his career that way."

"Actually, he continues in radio work today. In the last decade, for instance, he's done at least one show a year in a series called the *Charles Paris Mysteries* on BBC. And I guess his parts in animated kids' movies work on the same principle." When I told Roberta that BN's radio work is relatively easy to find and listen to on the Internet, we got off the phone in order to go search for him there.

Hey, here's a thought! That both Roberta and BN have careers built around voice will give them a lot to talk about when I am dating him and they meet. Ha!

TUESDAY, AUGUST 11, 2015

Dear Diary,

Uh-oh, something sad was in the mail today. The second letter to my guy came back to me. Evidently Bill Nighy is no longer in New York and the theater is unable to forward the letter to him in London, or wherever in the world he may be—literally. Honestly, though, I got a bit of a jolt finding the returned letter among the rest of my boring mail, so writing to the guy is fulfilling its purpose.

The returned letter prompted me to Google "fan mail to celebrities." In this manner, I came up with a couple of interesting interviews with a woman named Shelley De Angelus. One was on NPR with host Neal Conan and the other was in the *Wall Street Journal*. The one in print was written by Joanne Kaufman. Both interviews are from April 2009. Shelley De Angelus is the office manager at Mail Mann Inc., in Los Angeles. This company offers fan-mail and fan-club services to film stars, TV stars, musicians, and singers. The company boasts clients such as Richard Gere, Samuel L. Jackson, Anna Paquin, Joe Cocker, and Elijah Wood. De Angelus states that her firm gets "thousands and thousands" of letters or emails every week, saying the volume of snail mail has decreased considerably since the advent of the Internet. (Chalk one up for me; perhaps a real letter has a better chance of reaching a star—and the star's heart.)

Speaking of the letters, she says some of the fans are very devoted. They write two or three times a week, telling their favorite star about their daily activities. In such a manner, "they become like family" to the employees of Mail Mann Inc., the only ones who actually read the letters. Unless a letter is particularly touching, none is sent on to the star. On the positive side, De Angelus says 99.99 percent of the mail she reads is very respectful, very supportive, and very appreciative of the celebrity's work. On the negative side, she says she is surprised by the intensity of the expectations expressed in the letters and urges letter writers to be realistic. She mentions the fourteen-year-old who wanted the star to take her to the prom as an example. Perhaps this is cute from a fourteen-year-old, but not so cute when the teen's mother writes with the same request.

Just in case you are wondering what such a service costs, there is a setup charge of $250 and a minimum monthly charge of $125. For this money, Mail Mann picks up letters from the post office or from the celebrity's home and they retrieve emails and deal with correspondence per their clients' wishes. Mail Mann believes "people who want their mail done understand that the fans make their careers."

An article in *BBC News Magazine* tells of another company in the fan-mail business. The article is written by Jon Kelly and it appeared March 20, 2013. Sylvia "Spanky" Taylor's business is in Burbank, California. (People write to her clients c/o Spanky Taylor with no other company name given.) She and six employees process up to 20,000 items of mail each month. Her clients have included Johnny Depp, Rob Lowe, and Michael J. Fox. Taylor says television stars generate more mail than film stars because "if they're in your home every Sunday evening, you feel much more familiar with them." (So, again, in the game of trying to get a fan letter to a celebrity, score one for me. My guy is not a TV star, so he gets less mail; thus, perhaps mine will get through to him or, more to the point, catch his attention.)

A problem Taylor faces is how to dispose of the mail once she has processed it. Any food gifts are thrown away. Like Halloween candy, it is hard to know if someone has stuck a needle in it. Other gifts, such as plush toys, get distributed to local hospitals. And the letters themselves are shredded and recycled.

Lynn Zubernis is an expert in the psychology of fandom. (Oh lord, who would have thought such a specialty existed? I shall have to

Google it someday.) She says such disposal of fan letters is unsurprising to "most disinterested observers" but not to "committed fans." These fans hope their letter will stand out. It is maybe not an expectation, but it is certainly a hope. Zubernis says, "While the relationship between the fan and the celebrity may exist only in the mind of the former, it stems from a deeply rooted human need for community and belonging."

As for this "committed fan," I want to know how to send a letter to my man. Does he use such a fan-mail service or is there a different plan to consider? Getting specific in my next Google search, I typed this in to my device's search engine: "Fan mail to Bill Nighy." Immediately there was a link to something called fanmail.biz, which told me the talent agency that represents him is Markham, Froggatt & Irwin in London. Since I had already read about his agent, Pippa Markham, I figured this link was correct and visited their website. Once there, I found an alphabetical listing of all the celebrities they represent and right there in the N's was Bill Nighy. (By the way, daughter Mary Nighy is pictured beside him, as she is a client too. I was a bit surprised to see that Bill Nighy's former "wife," Diana Quick, was not a client as well.) Going to Markham, Froggatt & Irwin's FAQ section, I found this information:

> Question: How do I send fan mail, charity requests, or autograph requests through to your clients?
> Answer: Please send any fan mail, autograph, or charity requests via post. Please send to the below address, marked for the attention of the actor you wish to approach with a SAE so that a response can be sent back to you. We send mail on to each actor weekly. Due to the volume, we cannot track each request and we are therefore unable to provide an update on any requests sent. Please do not include money for postage.

Please note that some of our clients are overseas and we are therefore unable to pass on any fan mail to them. This will be noted on their individual page, so please check before sending.

Again, we cannot accept responsibility for any fan mail sent to these clients.

With all these caveats in place, here is the address to use:

Name of Actor/Actress

c/o Markham, Froggatt & Irwin

4 Windmill Street

London W1T 2HZ

With a solid address in hand, I was eager to get my missive back in the mail to Bill Nighy. I jammed my letter into a slightly larger envelope—thus, he could see my earlier attempt to reach him— added more of "our" trademark rose stickers to the new envelope and drove myself to the post office. I was advised by the postal clerk that I needed to add "Great Britain" to the address so it would not accidentally go to London, Ohio. Following those instructions, I bought my stamp and mailed my letter.

When I returned home, I researched the fan-mail topic a bit more and was chagrinned to find a YouTube video made by Ringo Starr in October 2008. In it he repeatedly sends his fans peace and love—and thanks—as he tells them, "I'm warning you with peace and love, I have too much to do, so no more fan mail." This plants the idea in my head that as I sit here hoping for another response from Bill Nighy, he could possibly send me a negative response asking me to please get lost. Even if he sent his rebuff with peace and love and many thanks included, it would be an embarrassing letter to receive. Oh gosh, being a big fan is not for the faint of heart.

<u>THURSDAY, AUGUST 13, 2015</u>

Dear Diary,
I saw *Ricki and the Flash* with Vera today. We had bagels at Bruegger's before and ice cream at Graeter's after. Yum! Though the movie only got a 64 percent approval rating on Rotten Tomatoes, we liked it a lot!

"I can't imagine not liking a movie with Meryl Streep in it," Vera said.

"Agreed! Definitely! But thank goodness I feel that way. Had I not loved her work, I might not have seen this particular film and thus I would have missed Rick Springfield. Is he gorgeous or what?"

"Rick Springfield? We're on to Rick Springfield now? What happened to Bill Nighy?"

"No, no, never fear. I was only browsing, not buying. Bill Nighy is still my main man. In fact, I never told you I ended up writing him a second letter—but before you get too excited about it, you need to know the letter bounced back to me on Tuesday. He had the nerve to leave the only address I had for him in New York."

"Do I detect some Google sleuthing in your future?"

"Nope! It's in my past. Been there, done that. I found his agent in London and mailed my letter to her!"

"Very efficient," Vera said. "Perhaps you stand a chance. Of getting your letter to him."

"I agree. I definitely stand a chance of getting to him. I read online that at the height of his career, Johnny Depp got 10,000 letters a week, but he's a STAR! As much as I want beloved Bill to be a star, he is not. He's a character actor. As such, he has said in a variety of interviews that he does not get much fan mail, and I am inclined to believe him. Additionally, most fan mail these days comes in the form of email, while I am sending a real, live letter for the man to have and to hold. Therefore, when his agent delivers his fan mail to him, it's my letter she will be delivering." There was silence on Vera's end, though she was looking at me strangely, so I forged ahead. "It appears you are dumbstruck with my logic, so I will continue by saying the only glitch in this plan is that the agent forwards letters to her clients' homes, but my guy is never home; he's always off on location."

"Well, I guess he'll have to return home sometime," she offered, trying to be positive for my sake.

"Let us pray," I laughed. "Seriously, though, in all my research about fan mail, I read an article about a woman whose profession is to answer letters for celebrities. Prior to this career, she was a psycho-therapist counseling schizophrenics, patients with multiple personality disorder, and other neurotics. The article said her exposure to people with inflated expectations and economy-sized fantasies serves her well in her current career. She talkin' about me?"

"Oh, thank God!" Vera shrieked, "I wasn't sure how serious you were about all this."

I laughed along with her on the outside while worrying about that very thing within.

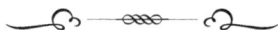

Text Messages:

Lorie to Vera—Beyond being faithful to beloved Bill, I see that Rick Springfield has been married for thirty-one years.

Vera to Lorie—Good Googling, girl! And you're a good girl, Googler. But why are you Googling? Aren't you supposed to be packing for your quilt retreat?

Lorie to Vera—I am a master procrastinator. I hate packing for trips! And beyond packing, I need to send my column to editors in the morning and it's not quite ready to go yet either!

Vera to Lorie—What's the topic of the month?

Lorie to Vera—After seeing BN's movie *About Time* a couple weeks ago, I am stuck in thoughts of dads so I am writing about mine.

Vera to Lorie—I'd ask you to send me a copy, but your to-do list seems long enough already!

Lorie to Vera— :)

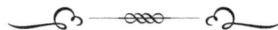

AUGUST 14, 2015

A Slice of Life: A Monthly Column

CAN'T HELP LOVING THAT FAMILY OF MINE

I am genetically predisposed to loving my family. I got this condition from my beloved father, the late Morrie Kleiner. You will understand this illness of mine better when I describe the eightieth birthday party we threw Dad in 1999.

Worrying there wouldn't be enough to do at the party, we planned a program. We would ask the assembled guests to share Morrie Stories—or a Moishe Moment for those who preferred his Yiddish name. My daughters created a large poster wishing their grandpa a happy birthday and decorated it lavishly. We then cut it into ten jigsaw puzzle pieces. Each storyteller would be given a puzzle piece after telling his or her tale. One by one, the puzzle pieces would be fit back together and taped onto the wall until the birthday message was revealed. Dad really liked the idea of the Morrie Stories and decided to tell one himself. And though all the stories told about Dad that night were lovely, they paled by comparison to his tale.

My father was not of a generation or upbringing that was comfortable with the words "I love you." With the advent of grandchildren, however, he became able to hear those words uttered in his direction, but he still couldn't say them back. The closest he came was to utter a quiet "me too" in response. But in the course of telling his Morrie Story, Dad used his own inimitable style to let us all know exactly how much he loved us without ever saying those words. He started by telling us about a walk he had taken with his dear friend, Harry. After hearing all that was going on in Dad's life, Harry commented, "Do you realize how lucky you are, Moishe?" Dad's voice cracked a bit as he agreed with Harry's commentary on his modern-day life. But then Dad mustered the strength to tell us the three components of his good luck that went much further back in time.

Dad was the youngest of four children. His siblings were eight, ten, and twelve years older than he. The big gap between the first three children and Dad was caused by his family's move from Poland to England and then on to the United States, and the first major piece of luck in Dad's life occurred before he was born. His family was scheduled to come to the United States on the Titanic, but they were denied passage because Dad's brother—an infant at the time—had contracted chicken pox.

Moving from his earliest good luck to his most recent, Dad spoke of his battle with meningitis the summer before. He told about months of daily drug infusions and weeks of such weakness that he could not stand up to shower, shave, or brush his teeth. Through it all, Mom was there to help. She learned to administer those chemotherapy-like drug treatments and she creatively made their bathroom handicap-accessible. Because of Mom, he was able to convalesce at home instead of a nursing home and he knew what a blessing that was. Mom not only faced and mastered each obstacle, but when Dad began to recover his strength, she even let him go along with her to the grocery store to practice walking while holding onto the cart! It was with her loving support that Dad was lucky enough to walk his way back to health.

While both of these stories amply illustrated his good luck, Dad had one more to tell. As a little boy and even a young man, Dad had always envied friends with large families, for he was not so lucky. The only relatives he had were his parents, siblings, and one cousin with a wife and three children. Later, Dad's family would help bring another cousin and her husband and child to this country, but that was a bittersweet addition to the family as the rest of the European relatives were lost in the Holocaust at that same time. Dad spoke of an early memory on this topic. He remembered how elated he was as a ten-year-old child when his eldest sibling, his sister Fannie, planned to marry. He assumed all of her new in-laws would be his relatives too. The reality of her marriage was not what he expected. He had gained only a brother-in-law and in the process had lost his beloved sister, as she moved away from home to live with her new husband. The pain of that loss was assuaged as the years rolled by and Fannie added three children to the family.

Dad was the next to marry, and as the expression goes, he "married well," for he married a woman rich in family. Mom's mother was one of six and her father was one of nine. There were aunts, uncles, and cousins galore. And then Dad's other sister married and added a spouse to the family. And then Dad's brother married and added a spouse to the family. And then the years rolled by and each of those marriages produced children...and then grandchildren...and in Fannie's case, there were even great grandchildren.

Thus, Dad found himself at the age of eighty standing before a large audience composed of all those people who one by one had become part of his now-large family, and he ended his remarks exactly as he had started them. He told of his friend Harry who recently asked him, "Do you realize how lucky you are, Moishe?" Dad's gaze encompassed the room as he said, "Yes, Harry, I know," and then he put his head down on the podium and cried.

Like Dad, I am lucky too—in three ways! I am lucky to have acquired the love of family from this marshmallow-soft man. I am lucky to have been part of the group he so cherished. But most of all, I am lucky to have called him...my dad.

A Bit of Fantasy—The Male

I'm thrilled—but it doesn't surprise me at all, really—that Bill Nighy is making a movie in Cincinnati! It was just a matter of time, because the Greater Cincinnati area is a Mecca for movie makers.

- In 1988, Dustin Hoffman and Tom Cruise filmed *Rain Man* here.
- In 1994, it was Melanie Griffith and Ed Harris working on *Milk Money*.
- In 2011, George Clooney came home to shoot *Ides of March*.
- Bill Nighy's buddy Cate Blanchett was here in 2014 to film *Carol*.
- In that same year, Don Cheadle came to Cincinnati to create the Miles Davis biopic, *Miles to Go*.
- Recent newspaper articles have boasted about an upcoming movie, *Melody and Mistletoe*, with Mariah Carey.
- Such articles also mention a future movie called *Marauders* with Bruce Willis.

So of course the great Bill Nighy was bound to come here to add to his oeuvre of hits. Yippee yahoo! The man is *here*!

I read in the paper that he is filming in Over-the-Rhine, an area of Cincinnati that I know well, an area full of funky and fabulous dining. I did not think he would go to Pontiac's for barbecue or to Senate for audacious hotdogs—he'd probably want a quieter atmosphere. I was certain he wouldn't go to Bakersfield for the world's best margarita—he doesn't drink. I figured instead that he would go to a Cincinnati institution, to the Graeter's ice cream parlor. I had been frequenting the Graeter's in OTR for days assuming someone would tell him he needed to give our city's signature ice cream a try. I assumed it was only a matter of time until he showed up, and good lord, it appears today was the day! In walked Bill Nighy in his navy blue suit and light blue dress shirt. I read recently that he does not button the cuffs of his shirts, and sure enough, unbuttoned sleeves peaked out at me. Wow! His clothes were impeccable. His coiffure was coiffed to perfection. His gorgeous skin called out to be touched and left me breathless.

Thank goodness I had been rehearsing my lines for days, or else some combination of fear and awe would have left me mute. Instead, as he walked past me on his way to the counter, I said, "Certainly you recall *The Girl in the Café* (my all-time favorite of his movies); well, I am the girl in the ice cream parlor."

A quizzical look covered his face, but then he caught my meaning and a bemused expression replaced it. "I'm not exactly sure what that means," he said.

"It means you are welcome to join me at my table. If you look around, you will see that all the other tables are full, but there is an empty seat here and you are welcome to take it."

He looked around at the empty ice cream parlor but likewise "saw" the crowded café in the movie scene I was trying to re-create. "Well, thank you. I shall join you. But first let me get something to eat. What do you recommend?"

"For an ice cream lover, this place is a ***dream*** come true. It has the best ***cold licks*** in town. And their chocolate chips? They are ***stone*** sized." He actually laughed out loud at my reference to the dream sequence in the movie in which he got to play guitar—hot licks—with the Rolling Stones.

So he got his ice cream—one scoop of chocolate chip and one scoop of black raspberry chocolate chip, the two best flavors in the shop—and then he came to sit with me. And because I did not want to interrogate him—he gets quizzed by reporters all the time—I said instead, "I know you suffer from terminal shyness, Lawrence Montague, but certainly there is something you'd like to ask me. Something you'd like to know about me?"

And so with a slightly befuddled look on his face, he scratched his head and then came up with a question. In keeping with the characters of the movie we were rehashing, he said, "Have you been to any G8 Summits lately?"

Laughing, I held out my hand to shake his and to introduce myself. "I'm not really Gina Taunton; I'm Lorie Kleiner Eckert, and I am very happy to meet you."

"Oh my!" he replied. "You're the woman who wrote me, the woman who came from Cincinnati to New York City to see me in *Skylight*! Yes, that's it! You schlepped all the way to New York City."

With an expression that was part grin and part grimace, I nodded my head yes as I agreed with him. "Do you mind?" I asked, looking him directly in his beautiful eyes.

"That you saw me perform in New York?"

"No. That I finagled a way to find you in Cincinnati? Were I a crazy person like Rhys Ifans' character in *Enduring Love*, you could think me a stalker."

"I think you're lovely. As for me, I am as terminally shy as poor Lawrence Montague in that movie. So if we were to meet, it was up to you to make it happen."

"Poor Lawrence did manage to ask Gina for her phone number," I reminded him.

"Ah," he said, but before he could say anything else, I handed him my business card that lists four ways (4 ways!) to contact me. As I handed it to him, I wore the same part grin/part grimace expression

I had worn before, while his expression was one of pure delight. He threw back his head and laughed.

Time flew by as in a dream, and before long he finished his ice cream. He stood up from the table with my card in hand and smiled at me before he headed for the door. But then he stalled before actually leaving. He turned around and came back toward our table. He leaned down and kissed me on the cheek. And then, like the *real* Lawrence Montague, he did a little jump for joy. He pocketed my card and walked out the door.

I have to confess that Lawrence did not kiss Gina—or jump for joy—that early in the movie. Such actions were improvisation on Bill Nighy's part...and they were thrilling. What can I say? I liked the man's moves! Better still, I liked our version of an afternoon delight.

TUESDAY, AUGUST 18, 2015

Dear Diary,

I am still aglow from the quilt retreat weekend. It was lovely and I am grateful for many things:

- I am grateful for a whole weekend of something to do.
- I am grateful for the camaraderie of quilt ladies. Unlike most of my other friends, they do not care about my hair or makeup or clothes. In this circle, a desire to sew is all that matters.
- I am grateful for my thirty-plus years of quilting experience, which allow me to go on autopilot at times like this when creative juices are not flowing.
- I am grateful for those same years of experience, which allow me to know that creative quilting juices will flow again…someday.
- I am grateful for the pats on the back I got for my very mundane Kids' Comfort project. Quilt ladies are a nurturing and supportive group.
- I am grateful for the life stories shared during the time we spent together. It is interesting to note that there is a distinctive inhalation of breath heard when a woman starts to tell a tale of woe to her friends.
- I am grateful for the supportive pats on the back I got when I was one of the women producing that distinctive sound.
- I am grateful to learn that as woes go, mine could be worse.
- I am grateful for the lovely B&B. I am as comfortable there as I am at home. And the breakfasts they serve? Outstanding!
- I am grateful for the B&B's remote location, which disables cell phones and gives a true break to this Google addict.
- I am grateful—and delighted—that on withdrawal from reading Bill Nighy stories online, my mind took it upon itself to create a Bill Nighy fantasy instead. My whole drive home—ninety

minutes—zipped by as scenes and dialog came to me, and even a kiss.

- When even the drive home from vacation is outstanding, you know you've had a good time, and for this I am very grateful.

SATURDAY, AUGUST 22, 2015

Dear Diary,

Last week at this time, I was at the Hickory Road Inn having a sumptuous breakfast with lovely lady friends. Today I am at the Starbucks café in my local Barnes & Noble. Coffee in hand, I try to gather the strength to write about the ugly stuff that happened with Big Irv. When I confessed it all to the ladies, the bare bones were all they needed to be on my side. They kept bringing me back to the continuous loop I told them about, these words that run in my head:

1. I feel guilty because I broke up with a man who was in the process of dying of lung cancer.
2. But he put me in the position where I had to choose him or choose my children and grandchildren.
3. I promised him—repeatedly—that if he ever put me in that position, I would choose my children, but that is exactly what he did, and exactly what I did.
4. But I feel guilty because I broke up with a man who was in the process of dying of lung cancer.
5. And on and on I go.

The other divorced woman understood it at a visceral level, knowing how hard it is to be a girlfriend and mother at the same time, knowing how awful it is to have to virtually apologize to some man for loving her children. But the other ladies got it too. Even the woman who did not have children took it personally; in a similar situation, she would want her mom to choose her! So no matter how much information I piled on about how sick Big Irv was, they kept bringing me back to these bare-bones facts. I am not convinced it will be so cut and dried when I actually write it all down, but that is the task of the day.

While on the topic of loving those kids of mine, I have always tried to read books that they read in order to bond with them. In this manner, I have read all sorts of things through the years, such as:

- *Interstellar Pig*
- *Where the Red Fern Grows*
- Pick-a-path Books
- *Staying Fat for Sarah Byrnes*
- *Maus*
- Lots of Paul Auster's stuff
- *The Beach*
- I'm even reading Junie B. Jones books these days to bond with the older grandgirls.

With this concept in mind, I plan to bond with beloved Bill tonight by watching a movie he loves as opposed to watching a movie in which he appears. Thus, tonight I will see Adam Sandler's movie *Punch-Drunk Love*. Certainly it will be better than *Interstellar Pig*, right?

OK. Enough stalling. Time to write in The Book of Irv. Argh!

The Book of Irv

The Good—The Bad—The Ugly—The End
Part III—The Ugly Stuff

- Had Big Irv only been disrespectful to everyone in the medical profession, that would have been enough to upset me.
- Had he only pretended to know more than trained physicians, that would have been enough to upset me.
- Had he only chosen to go against standard medical treatment repeatedly, that would have been enough to upset me.
- Had he only withheld critical information from doctors and from me, that would have been enough to upset me.
- Had he only risked his life for fear of going to the hospital, that would have been enough to upset me.
- But instead, he did all of these things, and then for good measure, he added a new bit of insanity to the mix: more sleep.

Big Irv had this long-held belief that if you are not feeling well, you should sleep until you feel better. In the aftermath of chemo, radiation, multiple surgeries, and hospitalizations, he further stated the belief that it is not unreasonable to sleep sixteen to twenty hours a day. His doctors were horrified at the concept. They felt he had to be up and moving to prevent pneumonia. As for me, I might have fallen for his sleeping sixteen hours a day had the other eight hours been consecutive hours, but instead, he was awake in bits and snatches across the day and night. Whether those bits and snatches added up to eight hours—or even four hours—were difficult to gauge and completely irrelevant. Such a sleep schedule wasn't a workable system for my life. In the same way that he had heard the jingle-jangle of my dumbbells, so did he hear (and get disturbed by) every sound produced by my children and grandchildren on Mondays and Thursdays and whatever other days they dropped by the house.

I was greatly conflicted over his enormous need to sleep. The poor man had been through a lot medically, so of course he was tired. And then there was the fact of his brain tumor. Was it possibly affecting his get-up-and-go and his rational thought? Was it giving him another good reason to be in bed? And then there was the fact that he was so stoic and wouldn't tell me if there was something new that was wrong, which could be the case as well. But given his history of loving to sleep, was it possible he was just indulging that desire? My brain hurt from trying to tease it all apart.

In his few waking hours, we fought constantly over his need for sleep. He didn't want my kids coming around to disturb him, but that was not negotiable. I tried to convince him to move to The Lodge, an independent living facility within walking distance of the house, the same place my dad had once lived. We all liked it there, plus it was close enough to home that I could be there daily to help him. I could still monitor his well-being. I could still cook his favorite dishes. I could still pick up his meds and put them in his daily reminder boxes. I could still take him to his doctor appointments. Meanwhile, he could sleep to his heart's content without hearing the pitter-patter of little feet. He refused.

I went in search of extended stay hotels. There were a couple in the vicinity, though not as close as The Lodge. I offered to take him there and show him all the amenities. He likewise refused.

I tried likening our situation to the case of an Alzheimer's patient. There comes a time when it just does not work for the loved one to live at home anymore. Such a time had arrived for us. He argued that was not the case. That everything could be perfect as it once had been were I only to ban the kids from my house. He reminded me that he would readily eject his daughter and grandkids from his life should I ask him to, and he thought it only fair that I return the favor. Of course I would never ask such a thing from him, nor could I allow him to ask it of me. In fact, I warned him, if he ever forced me into a position in which I had to choose between him and my kids, he would definitely lose.

Finally Big Irv and I hit on a mutually agreeable solution: On those days when the kids were scheduled to be at my house, he would move himself to a hotel for the night. This would mean he had to move to a hotel on Sunday night to be sure he was out of the house at 9:30 on Monday morning when Marmel School started, and that he would need to move to a hotel on Wednesday night (!) to be sure he was out of the house at 5 p.m. for Thursday dinners. He actually managed to do this one Sunday night. But then the scheme fell apart spectacularly.

It was on the afternoon of Wednesday, July 17, 2012, that I encouraged him and encouraged him to get out of bed and shower so he could move to the hotel. He kept telling me he'd get up in a few minutes, but he never did. The evening passed with the same scene being played out between us, as did the next morning and afternoon. A new element entered the negotiation on Thursday morning as he encouraged me and encouraged me to cancel the dinner, which I refused to do.

Ultimately the kids arrived for dinner while he lay in bed with one wall separating him from all the commotion. Evidently he felt it futile to negotiate further with me, and so he decided to send a text message to my daughter instead. In keeping with his one child/one grandchild thought process, he had zeroed in on my daughter Shana and her daughter Lila as the only ones in my clan that he liked, so he wrote to Shana: "Death for the noise makers. If it is Lila, she may scream." An hour later, he wrote her again, "I do love you, but you are stretching the boundaries of my love and tolerance. Thank you for your help. Next week I will take you out to lunch and shopping."

Since Shana's phone was in her purse, she did not see these messages until later that evening. When she found them and shared them, I seemed to be the only one to pick up on the fact that he was coming on to my daughter. The others only noticed the death threat—or what they perceived as a death threat—for all the children other than Lila. The reaction was swift. Within a couple of days, the adult children and their spouses decided it was unsafe for their children to come to my house if Big Irv was there. They said I could use any of their houses to run Marmel School and to hold Thursday night dinners, but none of that was going to take place at my house any longer, period.

I consulted with my attorney. I told her that if he and I were living in his house instead of mine, I would have moved out long ago. I told her that if he was not dying of cancer, I would have broken up with him long ago. And I told her that I doubted the man would harm the little children, but my opinion did not count in this case. I had the mandate of my adult children to deal with. Thus, I asked what I could do legally to get him out. Was there any legal recourse here at all?

It appeared that ours was a unique situation. Real estate law might not apply, since he was not exactly a tenant. Neither would family law apply because we did not have children together. I asked about domestic relations court only to learn that since we never married and since Ohio is not a common-law state, we could not use that court, as it is for married people only. But, the attorney informed me, no matter where we tried to place the case, any change would take at least sixty days to effect.

In the end, I got Big Irv out by tricking him. I did not tell him that my kids refused to bring the grandchildren over. I just acted like the next Marmel School was coming up, and thus I got him to get out of bed on that Sunday and move to a hotel so the house would be ready for kids on Monday morning. By some stroke of luck, he managed to be well enough/rested enough to actually get up and go. I was beyond relieved. It would have been quite embarrassing to have to hold Marmel School elsewhere. It would have been humiliating to admit I did not have control over my own home, my own life.

Big Irv and I then had some difficulty speaking English to each other regarding the second night he spent in the hotel. He called me on Monday afternoon to say he decided to stay for another night. He said the hotel was closer to his office. That made no sense, as he had not been going to the office. I was thinking perhaps he slept through checkout, and since they were charging him for a second night he might as well use it. I was thinking Mr. Stoic was not feeling well and was too sick to get out of bed though unwilling to admit it. I was thinking perhaps he had enjoyed the silence, no kids, no grandkids, not even the jingle-jangle of dumbbells. But I said none of that, and instead of playing twenty questions with him to ascertain why close proximity to the office was so appealing, I just let it go, because I was thrilled for a second night of nirvana without him.

The next morning, he called. "I guess I'll be home about 3 today," he said.

"Oh gosh," I replied, "I thought when you stayed away the extra night it was because you enjoyed the silence there as much as I enjoyed the opportunity to make noise here without disturbing you."

"No. I stayed because the hotel is closer to the office," he replied.

"You actually went to the office?"

He hesitated before replying, "No. But it is closer."

"Oh…yeah…sure…closer, you're right," I agreed, dumbfounded by his cockamamie reply. "But…um…why don't you stay in the hotel a couple more nights? This is Tuesday and you'll just have to move there again on Wednesday in honor of Thursday night's family dinner. Why move back and forth so much?"

And so he agreed to that plan—probably because it meant he would not have to get out of bed and shower anytime soon—and by the time Thursday night rolled around, I was so pleased with the new arrangement that I made it impossible for him to come home. The fact of the matter is that Donna, the woman who helps me keep the house clean, is the only person who owns a key to my home. The rest of us just come and go through the garage door's keyless-entry system. Though I am not very handy mechanically, I do know how to program a new code into the outside key pad. I also know how to climb up on a ladder and change the code that allowed Big Irv's remote-control device to work. Two small actions on my part, and lickety-split, I managed to lock him out of the house.

He was as stoic in handling this news as he was in handling illness. Eventually he came over to pick up some of his clothes. I had packed them for him and handed them off at the door, not daring to let him in. And across that threshold we chatted a bit. No, we agreed, we were not breaking up; we were just no longer cohabiting. Of course I would still help him with all of his medical stuff. He'd call me soon and we'd get together. That word "soon" was so Big Irv-like and vague that I almost laughed, but I managed not to. Nor did I laugh when he said, "I am so nice and easy to get along with, I don't know why you are treating me like this." With those words still hanging in the air, he trotted off. The date was August 1, 2012, which was more than eighteen months after his cancer diagnosis and almost two full years before his death.

Saturday Night at the Movies

Punch-Drunk Love
DIRECTOR: Paul Thomas Anderson
WRITER: Paul Thomas Anderson
RELEASE DATE: 2002
RUNNING TIME: 1 Hour, 35 Minutes
Featuring: Adam Sandler, Emily Watson, and Philip Seymour Hoffman
FRIENDLY CONNECTIONS: Though Bill Nighy is not in this movie, Philip Seymour Hoffman is. He and Bill Nighy worked together in *The Boat That Rocked* in 2009.

In that my main complaint about last week's movie, *Hot Fuzz*, was that Bill Nighy had such a small part in it, it is odd tonight to watch a film that does not feature him at all. The idea to see this movie had its genesis when I Googled "Bill Nighy's favorite movies" and found a blog written in 2012 by Video City, which is evidently "an actual shop" in London. They reported that Bill Nighy stopped by the shop and volunteered to help out with their blog by writing a list of his favorite movies for them. He then left the shop, went out to dinner, and returned with a list. It was two movies long:

1. *Punch-Drunk Love*
2. *Lost in Translation*

I chose to see *Punch-Drunk Love* because I have heard Bill Nighy speak of it in various interviews. The man is nuts about this movie! As much as I would love to love it too—in his honor—I must confess I did not like it at all.

Punch-Drunk Love's Tomatometer rating on Rotten Tomatoes is 79 percent, so there are a lot of people in BN's camp when it comes to liking this film. The movie is about an unmarried man named Barry

Egan (played by Adam Sandler), who owns a company that markets novelty items such as themed toilet plungers. He is also a man with seven sisters who ridicule him constantly. Between his loneliness, his meaningless work, and the emotional abuse of his sisters, he exhibits fits of rage. Trying to assuage his loneliness, he calls a phone-sex company, but unfortunately the company's real business is to extort money from men who contact them. Thus, Barry has to deal with four henchmen who come to collect money from him.

Beyond all of these issues, Barry makes a startling discovery he hopes will change his life. There is a promotion by the makers of Healthy Choice products that pairs product purchase with the earning of frequent-flyer miles. Barry discovers a loophole in the promotion by which he hopes to amass millions of frequent-flyer miles via the purchase of large amounts of Healthy Choice pudding.

Into this crazy mix comes a woman named Lena Leonard (played by Emily Watson). Lena is a friend and co-worker of one of Barry's sisters, and she has taken a liking to Barry after seeing his image in a family photograph. In fact, she is so taken with him that she orchestrates their meeting via a "chance encounter." As it turns out, Lena travels extensively on business, so Barry follows her to Hawaii where a romance develops.

Ultimately the four phone-sex henchmen, Barry, and Lena violently collide and this experience threatens the budding love affair. Fear of losing the relationship sends Barry into a fit of rage and he fights off all four of the henchmen using a tire iron. In the end, Barry explains the phone-sex episode to Lena and begs her forgiveness. He promises to use his frequent-flyer miles to accompany her on all future business trips. She forgives him and takes him up on his offer, and the movie ends with the assumption of happily ever after.

Here is Bill Nighy's take on all of this as stated in the biography.

The author says the original source is from the Rotten Tomatoes website:

1. "It is one of the wittiest and cleverest expressions of love [he] has ever seen."
2. "[He] loves the fact that it's this fucked-up love story."
3. "[He] loves it stylistically, the jokes, the visual attitude of it."
4. "[He] loves the apparent arbitrariness of the plot, which hinges on the fact that you get free air miles with a particular brand of chocolate pudding."
5. "Everyone in it is magnificent."
6. "Adam Sandler gives one of the greatest light entertainment performances [he's] ever seen."

In his comments, Bill Nighy goes on to say, "What most of my favorite films have in common is that they all make me laugh. And they all give me hope. You feel considerably better when you come out of the cinema than when you go in. You have insight, you are thrilled, you think everything might just be worth it."

I will agree with Bill Nighy 100 percent about loving movies that thrill me with their insight, as I am a person who is looking for the answers in life in every movie, play, or TV show I see, in every book I read, and in every set of lyrics or conversation I hear. However, I found no such insight in this particular movie. Sorry, Bill Nighy, I tried. But I am happy for you that you like this one, and thrilled that it gives you laughter and hope.

SUNDAY, AUGUST 23, 2015

Dear Diary,

I had a very interesting conversation with Bird tonight. I told her about the movie Vera and I saw last Thursday, *The End of the Tour*. It is the true story of a journalist from *Rolling Stone*, David Lipsky, who spent several days interviewing author David Foster Wallace. Part of the interview takes place as the men travel together to Minneapolis for the end of David Foster Wallace's book tour for *Infinite Jest*, a work that has been called an "encyclopedic novel" due to the fact that it is almost a thousand pages long and that it includes 388 "endnotes."

"Did you ever read *Infinite Jest*, Bird?" I asked her.

"No. I haven't read any of David Foster Wallace's work. How about you?"

"Me neither. It was the fact of his ultimate suicide that caused me to want to see the film. Obviously he had great success as a writer, so one would think he had *everything* in life. And you know me, I am always intrigued by the sad equation that having everything doesn't equal happiness. When I saw the movie about Amy Winehouse recently, I was watching the same story unfold."

"So if great success is not the key to happiness, I guess we're supposed to look to the small stuff," she replied, "as mundane and boring as that sounds. Though I must confess, some of the small stuff of life gave me great joy on Wednesday night."

"Good news. Tell all," I said.

"Audra McDonald was appearing in Philly at the Merriam Theatre and I was there to see her!"

"Good for you! I know you love her work. How phenomenal was she?"

"She was truly great. She appeared with Seth Rudetsky, who accompanied her on the piano. She brought down the house a couple of times, especially when she sang 'Summertime' from *Porgy and Bess* and when she sang 'Somewhere Over the Rainbow' from *The Wizard of Oz.*"

"Did I remember to tell you she was in *Ricki and the Flash?* I only know her work through you, so I was surprised to see her act instead of sing."

"I wonder if that's still playing. I should go see it," Roberta replied. "But back to the small things in life. What was your pleasure this past week?" she asked.

"Well, there was something in *The End of the Tour* that got me all bubbly and excited. Quite frankly, the feeling still lingers all these days later. You'll be surprised to hear it's something that made me think about Bill Nighy."

"What was it?"

"When the two Davids go to Minneapolis, they meet up with a couple of women who are friends of David Foster Wallace. One of the ladies went to college with him. But guess how the other one met him?"

"I'm thinking she must have written him a fan letter."

"Bingo! How on earth did you guess that?"

"I don't know what possessed me this week, but following in your footsteps, I did a quirky Internet search. I was going to mention it to you next."

"Quirky? What does that mean, Bird?"

"I Googled 'celebrities who marry their fans,'" said my good friend, who supports me in all my craziness.

"Were there links to follow from there?" I asked, incredulous.

"Yes, indeed. I'll send you the best one when we hang up."

—————◦◦◦◦—————

And so it is that I have found a bustle.com article dated December 11, 2014. It is written by Kaitlin Reilly and titled "17 Celebrities

Who Married Their Fans, Because Life Really Can Be That Good." I would love it if all these matches were made via fan mail, but in reality the big fan met the big star in some other way. For example, we have:

1. John Travolta and Kelly Preston—She evidently fell in love with him when she was a teenager and he was the star of *Grease*. They have been married since 1991.
2. Kelsey Grammer and Kayte Walsh—She was a huge fan of his and they met due to her work; she was a flight attendant. They met in 2010 when he was a married man. He got a divorce and married her in 2011.
3. Nicolas Cage and Alice Kim—She was a waitress at a restaurant and he was her customer. She asked for his autograph and got his phone number as well. They married in 2004.
4. Matt Damon and Luciana Bozan—She was a bartender at an establishment into which he ducked to escape a mob of fans. They met in 2003 and married in 2005.
5. Patrick Dempsey and Jillian Fink—She was his hairstylist. They met in 1999 and have been married ever since.
6. Conan O'Brien and Liza Powel—She was in his audience when he was taping his talk show. He saw her and the rest is history. They wed in 2002.

As for this big fan, I'm thinking I will keep up the letter-writing campaign. I know it's just two weeks since I resent the second letter, but in a couple of weeks, I think I'll write him again. Evidently there are lots of ways for big fans and big stars to meet. This plan worked for David Foster Wallace's fan; why can't it work for me? Maybe life really can be that good.

And speaking of such, I can't close without mentioning another bit of joy from Roberta tonight. Beside the "17 Celebrities Who Married Their Fans" link, she also sent a link to a YouTube video of Bill Nighy singing "Make Someone Happy." It's from a movie called *Arthur Christmas*, an animated film in which BN is the voice of GrandSanta. His performance of the song is charming. When it ended, a second video began to play immediately. It was called, "Arthur Christmas – Bill Nighy Voicing GrandSanta," and in a split screen format it showed Bill Nighy speaking his lines into a microphone at the same time as it showed GrandSanta spouting those words. The rendering of his lines was fascinating to see. Oh, how I love the Internet...and Bill Nighy.

THURSDAY, AUGUST 27, 2015

Dear Diary,

There aren't a lot of great movies to see at the moment. I would have just gone to lunch today and skipped the movie, but Vera wanted to see *Learning to Drive* because it stars Patricia Clarkson, an actress she likes from the TV series *Parks and Recreation*, a show I have never seen. The movie also stars Ben Kingsley. It is about a female writer living in Manhattan who decides to take driving lessons after her marriage crumbles. The Sikh instructor she hires has marriage problems too. Their ensuing friendship helps each of them find the strength they need to keep traveling the road of life.

"Did you like the movie?" Vera asked when it was over.

"Sure. It was a nice enough film. I actually identified with the main lady."

"You did? How so?"

"In getting dumped by her husband, she had her independence thrust upon her. One could say that in our relationship I dumped Big Irv, but that was not really the case since the relationship carried on until he died, at which time..."

"You had your independence thrust upon you," she said, finishing my thought. "It's interesting to think of your situation that way. Patricia Clarkson had to learn new things after her husband left her, like how to drive. Have you been learning new things too?"

"Oh gosh, a couple of minor things pop to mind like how to sleep through the night and how to fill my weekends with activity. It's tough." We looked at each other solemnly. I knew she understood, but what exactly could she tell me? So, I forged ahead with movie chatter. "My favorite thing about the movie was the actress who played Patricia Clarkson's daughter. Her name in real life is Grace Gummer."

"She's Meryl Streep's daughter," Vera informed me.

"I know that! But she is also Mamie Gummer's sister! And Mamie Gummer is the one who appeared in *The End of the Tour* as the big fan who met David Foster Wallace through writing him a letter. Is there some cosmic connection in this double dose of Gummer sisters? Is the universe bringing me one Gummer girl to remind me of the other? Is it telling me it's time to write my man again?"

Vera laughed. "It's said that all roads lead to Rome. But with you, all thoughts and conversations lead to Bill Nighy."

"Well thank you! That reminds me, I want to tell you that I watched *Punch-Drunk Love* the other night because it is one of his favorite movies. And I must say it was awful! So never fear, good buddy, Vera, when beloved Bill and I are together—even after we're married—you will still be my movie partner!"

When she stopped laughing, she said, "How do you know about his favorite movies?"

"You'll be surprised to hear that I Googled it. By the way, I also know his favorite books. They were listed in the unauthorized biography. The only thing I have read on his list—or even heard of—is *Skylight*, by David Hare. You read more than I do, though, Vera. Maybe you will have read some of them. I'll text you the list when I get home."

And on that promise, we parted ways.

Text Messages:

Lorie to Vera — Have you heard of any of these books? *Parade's End* by Ford Madox Ford, *The First Forty-Nine Stories* by Ernest Hemingway, *A Dance to the Music of Time* by Anthony Powell, *Amongst Women* by John McGahern, *Collected Poems & Prose* by Harold Pinter, and as I already mentioned, *Skylight* by Sir David Hare.

Vera to Lorie — I know most of the authors but none of the titles. Are you going to read any of them?

Lorie to Vera — Hemingway and I don't get along and I am allergic to short stories. By the time I figure out what is going on, the story ends. Very frustrating! I am likewise non-thrilled with poetry.

Vera to Lorie — What about the others?

Lorie to Vera — I just Googled the list. *Parade's End* is made up of four novels all dealing with the First World War. *A Dance to the Music of Time* is told in twelve volumes! It deals with English political, cultural, and military life in the mid-twentieth century. *Amongst Women* is about a man who was a guerrilla leader in the Irish War of Independence. He has three daughters and a wife upon whom he heaps his fury after the war. I'm thinking I will pass on all these reading opportunities.

Vera to Lorie — Even though your Bill loves them?

Lorie to Vera — Should he and I ever meet, I will beg his forgiveness. But perhaps he'll give me a gold star or two for not only seeing but reading *Skylight*.

Vera to Lorie — :)

Lorie to Vera — OMG! I was just Googling *Skylight* and found this interview with BN around the time of the Tony awards last May. OMG! http://www.broadway.com/videos/156126/skylight-tony-nom-inee-bill-nighy-offers-options-for-mispronouncing-his-name/#play

Vera to Lorie — Just watched it, OMG!

Lorie to Vera — From my mouth to Bill Nighy's ears?! More cosmic connections?

Vera to Lorie — Ha!

Friday, August 28, 2015

Dear Diary,

I have watched the link I sent to Vera at least a dozen times. I found it on Broadway.com. It is called "*Skylight* Tony Nominee Bill Nighy Offers Options for Mispronouncing His Name." It is part of a series called "2015 Tony Nominee Secrets" and it is dated May 13, 2015. The OMG moment happened when they asked him about the most shocking thing a fan had ever said to him at the stage door. His response was that a woman once preceded her comments to him by saying, "After we're married." This so rattled him that the words reverberated in his head, "After we're married?!" Recovering from this remembered shock, he goes on to acknowledge that she gave him an ashtray from Spain, which he thought was very nice!

———— ⋘ ————

Back in high school when we dissected frogs, we first stuck a metal probe into the frog's head to scramble its brains. His answer to this question is having the same effect on me. OMG!

FRIDAY, AUGUST 28, 2015 – CONTINUED

Dear Diary,

I'm still thinking about that interview. Another of the questions reverberates in my head. They asked him what makes him cry. Here is his answer: "I could tell you, but then I would be involving you in something close to gossip, and I know you'd never forgive me for that."

This answer is interesting because it is very similar to an answer he gave in an interview that appeared in *The Guardian* on February 8, 2015. Interviewer Nigel Farndale asked him to confirm his status as a single male. He replied, "I don't come home to anyone. I live alone, and if I was in a relationship and I were to tell you about it, I would involve your readers in something approaching gossip, and I know they would never forgive me for that."

I wonder if this is a stock answer ready to be pulled out for questions that are far too personal to answer? Interesting…

I'm off to bed now, dear Diary, as tomorrow is a big day. I plan to finish writing in The Book of Irv. Unlike beloved Bill, I plan to tell all about my relationship and about my tears. Whom do I go to for forgiveness?

THE BOOK OF IRV

The Good—The Bad—The Ugly—The End
PART IV—THE END

The next year passed without seeing much of Big Irv. We would talk
or text from time to time, but we did not manage to get together with
any frequency. For example, on March 10, 2013, we texted as follows:

9:51 a.m.—Big Irv: Want to find a burger together tonight?

10:01 a.m. —Big Irv: Hello?

10:05 a.m.—Big Irv: Hello?

10:10 a.m.—Me: Sorry, didn't hear the bing-bong indicating a new
text. Sure. Where do you want to meet?

10:20 a.m.—Big Irv: Flipdaddy's?

10:26 a.m.—Me: Sure. What time?

11:41 a.m.—Me: How about 7:30?

3:13 p.m.—Me: Does 7:30 work?

Then 7:30 came and went without hearing from him. I assumed
he fell ill—or fell asleep—between 10:20 a.m. and 10:26 a.m., but
I did not know for sure. It was easy to imagine that he was playing
with me and trying to hurt me. When he finally called at 9 p.m., I
did not choose to pick up the phone. He left a voice mail message
that said he would phone the next day, but he did not. It took six
days for him to text again, this time to ask me if I was free for lunch.
Speaking English with him was so dicey, I wondered if this meant he
was asking me out to lunch or if he was just chatting me up about my
life. Whichever the case, I did not respond. I was hurt and angry but
not so angry that I did not worry about him. Who knew? Maybe he
was really sick during those times of silence.

A whole year passed like that until he became so ill that he needed me. He called me, hallucinating, not knowing exactly where he was. When we finally figured that out and I went to see him, he was in a rat trap of a hotel. No, I shouldn't exaggerate; let me be more specific here. He was at a hotel in a seedy part of town that was closed down a short time later because it was a den of drugs and prostitution. He had instructed the front desk not to disturb him, so his room had not been cleaned for some length of time. Somehow he had procured food, so Styrofoam boxes of past meals littered the room. When I opened the boxes, I saw the food was covered in mold. The employee at the front desk was kind enough to give me several large garbage bags and I filled them all while Big Irv watched from the bed. I also went to the desk to replenish the room's stock of toilet paper and Kleenex. How long had he been without those commodities? I got fresh towels, too, to replace the ones all over the bathroom floor.

I tried to convince Big Irv that he needed to go to the hospital, but of course he would not go. However, a few days later he was forced to call an ambulance for himself because he could not breathe. The hospital ultimately admitted him and placed him in the ICU. His doctors said later that they did not expect him to live so they were surprised when he rallied. It turns out he had a growth in his lung called a broncholith. That was the bad news, but then there was good news too: A new medicine existed that could help with this malady. Also adding to his recovery was the fact that he had been too sick and confused to take any medication pre-hospitalization. Feeding and hydrating his body had also been neglected, so a week in the hospital helped a lot with his condition in general.

When eventually he was released, he was sent to a nursing home for rehabilitation. In the six weeks he spent in rehab, he continued his stunning recovery—it's amazing what a little food, water, and prescription drugs can do.

When it was time for him to leave rehab, I suggested he move to an independent living or assisted living facility where his meals would be provided, where cleaning service and laundry service would happen magically, where we could pay to make sure someone handed him his prescription drugs on time, where if he fell ill, someone would be right there to notice it immediately. He scoffed at all that. He hadn't felt this well in a long time! He was sure all of his illnesses were in remission! And so he chose his own brand of independent living: He bought a house.

During Big Irv's time in the hospital and rehab, he made me his power of attorney so I could take care of his finances. And so I learned that he had racked up some bills in the year we were apart. Instead of being the guy with a roll of hundred-dollar bills in his pocket, he went the plastic route and there were now several credit card companies clamoring for payment. I requested copies of all of the statements over the past year and in this way learned he had been dating someone during that time. Even reading the menu from right to left and ordering the most expensive thing on it, he could not have spent as much as he did at all those restaurants were he alone. And again, there seemed to be the alphabet game of gastronomy in play:

- Annabel's
- Buckhead
- Cock & Bull
- Don Pablo's
- El Toro
- Flipdaddy's
- Great Scott
- IHOP
- Joe's Crab Shack
- Longhorn

- Max & Erma's
- Outback
- Pompilio's
- Red Lobster
- Taqueria Mercado
- York Street Café

Yes, I see that he—and she—missed some letters of the alphabet. But to compensate, they visited various letters more than once (not to mention they visited various restaurants multiple times), and so add to the list:

- Betta's Italian Oven
- Bombay Brazier
- Buca Di Beppo
- Buffalo Wild Wings
- Cancun Mexican Bar
- Chez Nora
- City BBQ
- Gordo's Pub
- J Alexander's
- Lone Star

Yes, I was hurt. Yes, I was pissed off! But more than anything, I was baffled. How did he have the energy to get up out of bed and dine in fifty-seven restaurants in a year's time? Other credit card charges equally gave me pause, especially the ladies' second-hand clothing store he frequented and the couple hundred bucks he dropped at the Hustler store, which is owned by Larry Flynt. (Google says he is "one of the fifty most powerful people in porn.") Well, whoop dee doo, Big Irv, don't you know all the classy places to shop?

I wrote down all the offending expenditures on what turned out to be a three-page consolidation sheet. With this list of charges, this rap sheet in hand, I confronted the man. "So, I'm thinking you were dating someone in the time between moving out of my house and now."

"No," he said, all doe-eyed and innocent, completely nonplussed.

"Uh…want to take a look at this list of purchases you made over the last year?" I handed it to him and he leafed through the pages but was seemingly baffled by it all. "You've been to dozens of restaurants and spent far more than you could spend on just one person. Who were you dating?"

"I wasn't dating anyone!" he protested.

"You sound like that cartoon we laughed over in whatever men's magazine. Remember it? A woman opens the door to her bedroom and finds her husband in bed with someone else. When she asks who the woman is, her husband replies, 'What woman?'"

His response was to give me his Cheshire Cat smile. I guess he was fondly remembering the cartoon. Pissed-off purple, I rose to my feet, clapping. "Standing Irvation!" I shouted. "Great performance! But I repeat the question: Who were you dating?" I was thinking to myself that he could easily claim to be seeing his daughter or granddaughters or sisters or mom, but he gave off no acceptable lie. So then I thought, *If he isn't dating anyone, what is he doing that is so awful that he cannot admit it to me? If he were doing drug deals, for instance, would he be paying for meals during the exchange?*

"Why don't you leave those papers here and let me look them over and see what I can remember."

"Sure, Big Irv. Here you go, buddy," I said, knowing I would never see that list again. As an aside, I was wrong about that. I did find the list again as I cleaned out his house after he died.

As another aside, in the weeks between his leaving the rehab facility and this conversation/confrontation, he had pretty much given up driving. He never said he'd had a couple of accidents, but neither could he explain the scratches all over the side of his truck or the reason why the hood of the truck would not stay down without a bungee cord to hold it. Therefore, he needed me to go to his post office box for him weekly. So, with other women and drug deals running through my head, I asked him, "Now that I am picking up your mail, is there anything shocking I'm going to find? Love letters from whomever, for instance?"

He laughed at that. "No, not a thing," he assured me without giving the question a second thought.

And so I was rattled a couple of weeks later to find a bill from Big Irv's dentist in the P.O. Box. The patient listed was a woman whose name I did not know. To protect the not-so-innocent, I will call her Suzie Q. The bill was for $1,624.76 to be exact. I called the dentist to ask why Suzie Q's bill was Big Irv's concern. Forgetting about HIPAA privacy rules, the receptionist blithely reported that he had brought her in for dental work and said to charge his account for services rendered. Was it with glee that she added the information that they seemed quite the happy couple as they played around together in the waiting room?

OH GOD! I can't write any more of this! I am out of here!!

Saturday Night at the Movies

Glorious 39
DIRECTOR: Stephen Poliakoff
WRITER: Stephen Poliakoff
RELEASE DATE: 2009
RUNNING TIME: 2 Hours, 9 Minutes
ALSO FEATURING: Romola Garai, Eddie Redmayne, and Juno Temple
FRIENDLY CONNECTIONS: In this movie Bill Nighy has two daughters, one played by Juno Temple and the other by Romola Garai. He has been cast as the father of these women in the past, working with Juno Temple in *Notes on a Scandal* in 2006 and with Romola Garai in *I Capture the Castle* in 2003. Additionally, writer/director Stephen Poliakoff and Bill Nighy have worked together on two different TV movies. In 2003, *The Lost Prince* was released, and in 2005, *Gideon's Daughter* was released. The Poliakoff/Nighy team is so strong that Bill Nighy won a Golden Globe Award for Best Performance by an Actor in a Mini-Series or a Motion Picture Made for Television for *Gideon's Daughter*. I like that Bill Nighy works with the same directors, writers, etc. repeatedly. The fact that he gets "invited back" tells me he is easy to get along with.

Glorious 39 is tonight's movie, and it is a psychological thriller. In the same manner that *Valkyrie*, *Pride*, and *The Boat That Rocked* taught me about parts of history I was unaware of, so did *Glorious 39*. Specifically, the movie is about appeasement, in this case, British Prime Minister Neville Chamberlain's policy of trying to placate Hitler's aggressive foreign policy with diplomacy instead of going to war. Evidently England was still reeling from World War I, so Chamberlain's policy of "peace in our time" was lauded by many. Today, however, this approach is viewed as a cowardly and mistaken policy that encouraged Hitler's aggression. Even so, the movie covers that period of time when the appeasement policy was in effect, the time before World War II, the glorious summer of 1939.

In this film, Bill Nighy plays the part of Sir Alexander Keyes, a Member of Parliament and a World War I veteran. He is the father of three adult children, the eldest of whom was adopted before Alexander's wife gave birth to the other two children. The Keyes family lives an exalted lifestyle, thus we see them in two different residences, one an enormous estate in Norfolk and the other a home in London where they go when Parliament is in session.

At the start of the movie, there is a birthday party for Alexander Keyes that is organized by the eldest child, Anne. Two of Anne's friends are at the party. Over dinner, one voices a criticism of the Prime Minister and his lack of action against Nazi Germany. The next day, Anne finds some gramophone records in an area of the Norfolk estate that she is not supposed to enter because it houses her father's "manuscript papers." The records look harmless enough since they are labeled "foxtrot." Thinking she will soon be dancing, she listens to the records and finds that they contain recorded meetings and telephone conversations instead of music. Trying to figure out what she has stumbled onto, she turns one of these records over to still another friend. When both the friend who was outspoken at dinner and the friend who listened to the foxtrot record turn up dead—both "apparent suicides"—she turns to the second dinner party friend for help, and the next thing we know, he too is dead.

It turns out that Anne's father, Alexander, believes Britain will be completely destroyed unless it secures a peace treaty with Germany. Indeed, their London house is the location at which pro-appeasement meetings are taking place, with Alexander as the chair of those meetings. Furthermore, it turns out that Anne is the only member of the family who does not share his beliefs. To his credit, he does not likewise murder her, but he does lock her up and keep her sedated, "to keep her safe." While all of this is in the name of Chamberlain's appeasement policy, and its grand-sounding purpose of "peace in our time," the movie makes it look like the real purpose of the appeasement policy is far less grand. It looks like the upper crust of Great Britain will do anything to preserve their privilege.

I liked this movie for many reasons:

1. It was a very palatable history lesson.
2. It provided many opportunities to see Bill Nighy's handsome face, by which I mean he turned up in a great many scenes, quite an improvement over *Pride* and *Hot Fuzz* and, of course, *Punch-Drunk Love.*
3. It was fun to see Eddie Redmayne in his small role at Alexander Keyes' son, knowing he will soon go on to star in *The Theory of Everything.*
4. Finally, I loved the way Alexander Keyes spoke to his older daughter in this movie. He often called her "darling" or "my dear." Though these are generic terms of endearment, I would gladly answer to them should my beloved Bill ever manage to meet me, love me, and call me by such names.

There is one thing I did not like about this movie. Given that I adore Bill Nighy, it is difficult for me to watch him exhibit acts of cowardice even though I know he's just playacting. I felt that way about him in *Valkyrie* when his hesitation at a crucial moment helped spoil the plot to kill Hitler, and I felt the same way in this movie. Though he would have had a much smaller part in *Glorious 39*—and indeed would have been killed off in the role—I would have preferred him to be the friend who voiced criticism of Prime Minister Neville Chamberlain and his lack of action against the Nazis.

<u>SUNDAY, AUGUST 30, 2015</u>

Dear Diary,

It has been a weekend of thirty-nines. Last night there was Bill Nighy's movie, *Glorious 39*, and today there was Scotty's birthday party. How do I have a thirty-nine-year-old son? But, lucky me, I got to hang out with all the kids and grandkids as we celebrated him today. I am very grateful for our togetherness and for the good time we had, especially since the weekend has had a pall over it due to my writing in The Book of Irv.

I am not sure what to do about that project. On the one hand, I am thrilled that next weekend I will be in St. Louis for the family reunion and therefore I will not be able to write the final pages in that miserable journal. On the other hand, I am not sure how I can leave town without getting closure on the story. Perhaps I should schedule some time to finish writing it before I leave next Friday. But that's like volunteering for a root canal, isn't it?

And speaking of pain, whenever Big Irv reminisced and looked back on the way I moved him out of my house, he said he had felt brittle about being kicked to the curb. That has been a disturbing image to live with. I wonder how he would characterize what happened next, at the end. Would he see the part he played in the drama, or would he see only what I did in response? And does that matter? After all, I was raised on the bromide that two wrongs don't make a right. All of his wrongs and all of mine don't either.

September

THE BOOK OF IRV

The Good—The Bad—The Ugly—The End
PART IV—THE END, CONTINUED

All right, deep breath taken, I continue my tale…

After speaking to the dental receptionist, I Googled this Suzie Q person. I expected to find her on Facebook or LinkedIn. Instead, I found a police report that contained her name. She had been arrested for "forgery, criminal tools." I have no clue what that means. The police report also gave her address and her age. She lives somewhere close to Big Irv's office and is thirty-seven years old. I have a pretty good idea what that means.

I should mention that when I asked Big Irv about this, we talked without the aid of an interpreter and so I am not really sure what all these words mean, though they sound so much like English. Thus, he told me he had been hanging out with some old friends, the "children" he used to see before he met me. In fact, he volunteered, the stuff he bought at the Hustler store, he bought for these children. As far as this particular child, this Suzie Q, he was feeling guilty because he turned her in to the police over a drug issue, and so when she got out of prison, he helped to fix her teeth. He was pretty proud of himself for giving her money in that manner instead of giving her cash, which she would have used for drugs. Kudos from me was not forthcoming. But actually, I was proud of myself. I finally figured it out—Big Irv really had mastered the English language except for when he was avoiding the truth or outright lying. I am sure he could have told me all of this in a way that made sense; he just did not choose to do so.

As for my choices, I was not really sure what to do. Here was a man whom I had loved and lived with. Here was a man who was dying from cancer. I already felt great amounts of guilt over kicking him out of my home given that specific circumstance. I mean, really, what kind of ogre does such a thing? Now, I had every reason to walk away from the man and leave him to his own devices. Except, who would come to his aid? His daughter helped him as infrequently as was humanly possible. His sisters helped him not at all (at least from what I could see and what he reported, if indeed he was telling the truth). There was a nephew, Patrick, who came around from time to time, but that was it. I chuckle to remember the niece who set up a CaringBridge page for him when he was in the rehab center, but interestingly, no one ever signed up to come care for him.

Legally, I was Big Irv's everything: his power of attorney, his health-care power of attorney, his executrix, his heir. I asked him if he wanted to change any of that. He did not; all he wanted was to go back to the way things had been before my kids moved back to town, la la la. Of course, that was not an option. What I offered instead was to become his employee, to help him whenever he needed help, but to pay myself—from his funds—for my time and for my expenses. With no other offers on the table, he agreed to that. And so we limped on together. He had chosen his house for its proximity to his office instead of its proximity to my home, so I was not close enough to come by on a whim. I was Johnny on the spot for his bills. That was easy. I had his mail forwarded to my home so I could take care of issues as they arose. I also spoke to him on the phone daily. But other than that, I followed his daughter's lead and saw him as infrequently as was possible, which in my case turned out to be once every couple of weeks.

When I went to see him, I picked up groceries, prescription drugs, and lunch along the way. I would bring these into his house along with his clean laundry. I would sit with him and chat as he ate, and then when he got tired and went back to bed, I would clean out his refrigerator, put away his groceries, empty the dishwasher, reload it with all the dishes in the sink, put away his clean laundry, and gather up his dirty laundry. I also gathered up his trash and hauled it away to my house, as I had learned the hard way that trash put out at the curb on the wrong day got a police citation and fine and he could not be counted on to know which day was which. While at his house, I also portioned out his pills into a seven-day pill reminder box and called in refills for any meds that ran out. On weeks that I did not see him, I did not know if he managed to take pills. I didn't ask. I didn't need to feel any further guilt in his regard.

But speaking of guilt, I did feel it over a new issue. As I sat and chatted with him during his lunch, it often occurred to me that I should take him to bed and hold him. Like the old song, I wanted to give him the shelter of my arms, but I never allowed myself to do that. I could blame it on my kids, on a vague fear that they would find out and be angry with me for fraternizing with the enemy. But we adults need to take responsibility for our choices, and so I was the one who chose to turn that particular cold shoulder on Big Irv. I regret it. What a wonderful and simple gift it would have been: warm arms to hold him.

Back to my plan on how I could help him as his paid employee, it worked for a while until his health started to decline. Overnight he lost fifty pounds—a quarter of his body weight. I looked into many age-in-place options for him, such as Meals on Wheels, but as expected, he could not be counted on to be awake for deliveries or even to hear a knock or a pounding at the door. Likewise, he could not be counted on to let a cleaning crew in. Likewise, a couple of friends stopped by to see him, but he did not respond to their knock. His daughter, his nephew, and I all had keys to the house, but we could not be counted on to come by to let others in.

I reminded Big Irv how healthy he had been when he left the rehab facility. I reminded him how important it was to take medicine regularly and how vital it was to eat and hydrate his body. I suggested—countless times—that he move back to the rehab place or to a similar facility to have all those systems in place. I waxed poetic about him having easy access to a clean apartment and clean clothes. And amazingly, after talking about it every night for weeks, he finally consented to have me look at facilities.

I spent a lot of time in that endeavor, responding to all his stated needs. For instance, he needed a place that offered covered parking for the truck he no longer drove. He needed a place that would allow him to have the dog he planned to buy. He needed a place that allowed him to bring his barbeque grill and his smoker. On and on it went until, by golly, I found the place that could accommodate it all, The Seasons. Additionally, said facility would meet the needs of the bon vivant in him—the dining room at The Seasons had an acclaimed chef. He could dine there three times a day.

We spent almost an hour every night on the phone hashing and rehashing the decision. Beyond my hourly wage, he "paid" me by calling me Tootser, and quite frankly that meant a lot. It kept me in his corner. Eventually, he allowed me to put down a deposit on the place. Eventually, he allowed me to hire a service that would take care of the move. They would visit the current house and the new apartment. They would confer with him about what he wanted to move. They would pack up his house, move it all to the new place, or to storage, or to Goodwill. And before moving day was done, they would hang every wall hanging and put away every dish, article of clothing, and toiletry item before leaving him comfortably settled in the new place. We set the moving date for the July Fourth weekend. On June 25, he backed out of the deal on the grounds that he needed a first-floor apartment as opposed to the one we had rented on the second floor.

"With a first-floor apartment," he said, "I can exit The Seasons easily to get in my truck and go where I need to go."

"Where do you plan to go? You haven't left your house in ages! You haven't driven your truck in ages! Where do you plan to go now?"

"Tootser, I'll need to take the dog for a run."

"Give me a fucking break here, Big Irv."

"You can't keep a pup cooped up in a one-bedroom apartment," was his calm reply.

"If you back out of this deal," I told him, "do not count on me to negotiate another deal. I have spent countless hours on this, and I simply cannot spend another moment of my life on your insanity! The building has an elevator! Your second-floor apartment has easy access to the elevator! You can take the elevator to the fucking first floor!"

"No. I'm going to wait for a first-floor apartment to become available. And don't worry your pretty little head over it; I will handle the negotiations with The Seasons and the mover."

I am ashamed to say that my pretty, irate little head and I stopped speaking to him soon after that. I did not even call him for his birthday on July 8, 2014, which was also the seventh anniversary of the day he surprised me and moved into my home. Had some time passed and let me calm down, would I have gotten back on board as his friend, as his Tootser? I don't know. What happened instead is that he died.

I got a call from his daughter on July 16 asking me if I had spoken to him recently. Of course I had not. Neither had she. Evidently she had been phoning him, but he had not returned her calls. Upon hearing that the last time he had phoned me was July 5, she enlisted Big Irv's nephew, Patrick, to go over to the house. Patrick had a key but was afraid to use it, afraid of what he would find inside. Instead he knocked on the door and then pounded on the door. A big swarm of flies inside the house responded. Seeing that, Patrick called the police, who entered the house and found Big Irv dead on the bathroom floor.

It was comforting to hear the police describe the scene inside the house. There was a bowl of cereal sitting on the kitchen counter with a carton of milk open beside it, waiting to be poured on. The TV in his bedroom was tuned to one of the "Speed" stations he loved. Evidently he had been in his beloved bed watching some car race before he got out of bed to get some food, before he went to the bathroom and died. The police ruled it a natural death and so no autopsy was performed, but we assume his abdominal aortic aneurysm burst and he died quickly. From the condition of the body, the police reported, he had been dead a day or two. It is very fitting to me that we don't know exactly when he died, since in the beginning of our relationship it was so hard to ascertain exactly when he was born. Life is funny like that sometimes. Even Big Irv would have chuckled over the symmetry.

—∞—

Back in our heyday when Big Irv and I did so many things together, we went to Temple weekly in spite of the fact that he was Catholic. He seemed to have an affinity for Judaism and for my rabbi. In fact, our trip to Israel was a congregational trip. During those good old days, Big Irv met with the rabbi to discuss conversion. Since Big Irv came to services regularly, and since he had been to Israel with the congregation, and since he was dying of cancer, the rabbi proposed a conversion plan that was beyond simple:

- He needed to have a conversion ceremony that could be as large as he wanted it to be or as small as just the rabbi and me.
- He had to write a statement as to why he wanted to convert. Such a statement could be one sentence long or it could be book length.
- The only caveat was he could not say, "I want to convert because Lorie is Jewish."

Had he asked me for help in writing his statement, he probably would have confessed that his only reason for converting was me. So I would have suggested the following rationale, which is a bad boy's dream come true, allowing him to do exactly what he was told NOT to do in such a creative way that it would be acceptable. *My reason for wanting to convert is that I have always enjoyed the teachings of the Old Testament and I am particularly taken with a quote from the Book of Ruth, where Ruth tells Naomi, her Israelite mother-in-law, "Where you go, I will go, and where you stay, I will stay. Your people will be my people and your God my God. Where you die, I will die, and there I will be buried."*

But Big Irv did not ask for my help and so I did not offer any. I did not put any words into his mouth. There could have been a hundred reasons for not getting around to converting, the least of which was the issue of writing a speech. Therefore, he lived and died a Catholic and was buried a Catholic as well.

I mention the burial because I feel guilty about that too. I could have made arrangements to bury him in a Jewish cemetery in a joint plot that I would someday inhabit, but I did not. I did not want to go through eternity with him and I did not want to make it difficult for my children to visit my future grave because it would mean visiting his as well. I am painfully aware that once again I chose my children over him. As it turns out, though, I think opting for a Catholic cemetery was a good choice. He is buried at Gate of Heaven, in his family's plot, near people he had known and loved in his lifetime. It's right out of the Book of Ruth, just like I hoped it would be for him.

Thursday, September 3, 2015

Dear Diary,

Last night after finishing The Book of Irv, I soaked in a tub, ate a tub of ice cream, and gave myself over to other more pleasant things. Thus, I Googled "Bill Nighy in the news" and came up with an exciting article that appeared in *Fashionista* just a month ago on August 5, 2015. It was a report on *Vanity Fair's* 2015 International Best-Dressed List, and you guessed it, my guy's name is on it! Here is the list of the top ten men now:

1. Bill Nighy—Occupation: Actor.
2. Stavros Niarchos III—Occupation: Financier.
3. Iké Udé—Occupation: Artist, portraitist.
4. William Ivey Long—Occupation: Costume designer.
5. Jonathan Ive—Occupation: Designer.
6. H.R.H. Prince Carl Philip of Sweden—Occupation: Major in the Swedish Amphibious Corps, licensed racecar driver, third in line to the Swedish throne.
7. Jonathan Tisch—Occupation: Chairman, Loews Hotels & Resorts; co-chairman of the board, Loews Corporation.
8. H.R.H. Prince Harry—Occupation: Patron of multiple charities; fifth in line to the British throne.
9. Russell Wilson—Occupation: Quarterback for the NFL's Seattle Seahawks.
10. Robert Couturier—Occupation: Architect, decorator.

When I mentioned this to Vera today, her response was very interesting. "You do know," she said, "that many men who are named on these best-dressed lists are gay?"

"Nope. Didn't know that," I replied. "I'll have to forward the whole list to you so you can see the ten men on it."

"But we're only interested in one man on the list. Don't you agree?"

"Yes, of course," I said. "Just my Bill."

"Have you had any inkling that he is gay in all that you have read about him?"

"I think he's straight. There is an often-quoted statement from him that he 'got briefly mistaken for someone who might be good in bed' and he said that was 'very, very good.'"

"Can't that quote swing in either direction, though?" Vera asked, scrambling my brain.

I tried again. "He is also quoted as saying he wanted to be a journalist when young because he thought it was glamorous and that he'd meet beautiful women in the rain."

"That one's better," she said. "I'll give him a couple of points for that. Has he ever been married?"

"Sort of. He was never married, but he was in a long-term relationship with Diana Quick for more than two dozen years. They have an adult child together. Since the demise of their relationship in 2008, though, the only person he has been linked with romantically has been Anna Wintour of *Vogue* magazine. But from what I can see online, he and Diana Quick have been friends with her for years, and many photos of Bill Nighy with Anna Wintour also include Diana Quick."

"So there are no women in his life?"

"It appears that way," I replied. I knew a couple other things that I failed to mention, such as the fact that he is uncomfortable with roles that find him as a romantic lead, but out of a loyalty to him I did not feel the need to offer up information that was not specifically requested. So I mentioned this instead, "In the movie, *Pride*, about gay activists in the U.K. in the 1980s, he plays a gay man; indeed, his biggest scene in the movie is when he comes out of the closet to a female friend. However, he has also played the part of a zombie in *Shaun of the Dead*, and that doesn't make him a zombie in real life, does it?"

"No, he's not a zombie; and no, he's not a gay man, not necessarily. But how would you feel about him if he were gay?" she asked.

"A part of me would like to believe that if I found the right fellow, I would discover a grand sexual passion that has been missing from my life for all sixty-three years. Another part of me thinks that's hogwash and that no such passion exists for me. Indeed, if I were 'playing' with a man and the game was called 'I'll Show You Mine if You Show Me Yours,' I would prefer to be seeing the inner workings of his heart as opposed to his naked body. Thus, a heterosexual man might not really be what I am looking for, especially if all his parts still work."

"Have you ever had a gay male friend?" she asked.

"Nope. But I know you have. What's that like?"

"It's stereotyping gay men to say that they like to shop, however, it is very true that they do. And they have a great sense of style, as *Vanity Fair* has already declared worldwide regarding your guy. But anyway, since you and he are not competing for the same lover, a relationship with a gay man is non-competitive, so he will help you look snappy too."

"Snappy—does that mean I will soon be wearing designer clothes to fingerpaint with the grandkids at Marmel School on Mondays?"

"No, it means that while you always look terrific, you would always look terrific in a slightly more trendy way. I bet even you could learn to like shopping in high-end stores, given a little encouragement, which you would get from a gay man. You would also get the security of knowing you have a date to all events requiring one and you'd get a lot of harmless flirting with no need to 'pay up' at evening's end. And if that's not enough, these guys are really funny, so a lot of laughter would come your way."

"Hmm," I said, "I bet even I could learn to like that."

She laughed for a moment before getting serious again. "You didn't really answer the question. How would you feel about Bill Nighy if he were gay?"

"He is who he is. I like the man just the way he is. His sexual orientation changes nothing. So, what do you think are the chances?"

"Of him being gay?"

"No! Of me figuring out a way to be in a relationship with him!" I took one look at her stricken face—or was it an exasperated face?—and answered for her, "Still zero to none, right? Darn!"

FRIDAY, SEPTEMBER 4, 2015

Dear Diary,

I'm safe and sound in St. Louis, though I don't actually know how I managed to get here. Somewhere around Terre Haute, my mind started to wander, and the next thing I knew, three hours had passed and I was in Missouri. It all started when I heard the little bing-bong that indicates I have a text message on my phone. Waiting to be at a rest area to actually read it, I started to wonder who would be texting me. Could it have been at that exact moment that my Sirius Radio channel, '60s on 6, started to play "Lay Lady Lay"? I don't know many of Bob Dylan's songs, but of course I know that one. Doesn't everyone?

- So that reminded me of Bob Dylan's number one fan, beloved Bill
- Which reminded me of my last road trip and the fact that when my fantasy left off, I had just given him my card
- Which reminded me that the card had four ways (4 ways!) to get in touch with me
- Which reminded me that one of those ways was my cell phone number
- Which reminded me that a text message from my man was possible
- At least in my dream world
- So off my brain went, spinning the sweet cotton candy of fantasy
- One hundred and eighty miles later, I found myself in St. Louis
- Oh, by the way, it was Vera texting to wish me a safe trip

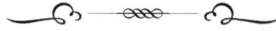

Text Messages:

Unknown phone number to Lorie—Perhaps Gina and Lawrence can meet again? How about tomorrow? Same time, same place, same ice cream flavors?

Lorie to Bill Nighy (!!)—That's a delicious plan. Yes!

BN to Lorie—I am eager to know you better.

Lorie to BN—Speaking of such, any chance you received a second letter from me in recent days?

BN to Lorie—I wish so, but no. The little fan mail I receive usually finds its way to me in London, but I'm not there. What did you say?

Lorie to BN—The specifics are unimportant; the overall message being, "Please, oh please, oh please, can I flirt with you a little more?"

BN to Lorie—Ah then, we can handle that request tomorrow.

A Bit of Fantasy—The Male

Okay, I have tried on every outfit in my closet and I find that absolutely nothing works! My first inclination is to dress in a navy blue suit as he does. Should I also wear a light blue button-down shirt? I don't own one. Should I buy one? That's insane!

One of my long-ago Google searches paired him romantically with Anna Wintour. She is the English editor-in-chief of American *Vogue* and has held that position since 1988. I have looked at hundreds of images of her and I cannot come close to her brand of chic. No way. No how. No one has ever accused me of being chic. Ever! And then there is his ex-"wife," Diana Quick, who—according to my Google gods—was once hailed the world's most beautiful woman. I can't compete on that front, so I'm not going to try to dress like her either! There is also that description in Miranda Sawyer's 2006 interview with him in *The Guardian* about how he likes women to dress: a Chanel suit, nine-inch heels, very little makeup, great hair, and no handbag, as he likes to see women with their hands free. Surely Chanel is not going to happen for this T.J. Maxx girl. As for nine-inch heels, is that a typo? I never heard of such a thing, and besides, since turning sixty I can only walk in flats. In heels, I galumph. Regarding very little makeup, I'm good to go! Regarding great hair, mine was created by God. Can't get any better than that! As for the handbag, I need one! Can't give it up even for the man I love.

So okay, it's not Halloween. I guess I better go dressed like myself. I put on a pair of Not Your Daughter's Jeans. They go all the way up to my waist, so I will have no muffin top today! I love their tummy-tuck panel as well. I buy the straight-leg style, not the slim, not the skinny, not the legging. I may be thin, but I'm sixty-three years old for God's sake; tight pants are not my thing. I will pair my denim jeans with a white, long-sleeve T-shirt and one of my colorful cotton cardigans, a white background with blue and black splotches, new this season from Lands' End. And as a concession to him, I'll carry a cross-body bag so my hands will be free. Looking exactly like me — ugh! — I leave for Graeter's.

"You're early," he said when I walked in the door, a smile filling his face.

"You too."

"I didn't want to miss you," he confessed.

"Me too you," I said with a nervous and hopeful smile.

"It was dreamy being with you the other day."

"Oh my, I agree. It couldn't have been any more wonderful if I dreamed it up on my own. In some ways, I feel as if I did."

"Well, you caused it to happen, our meeting each other. And you caused it to happen that I have a new addiction — Graeter's ice cream! Shall I go order our favorite flavors?"

"I can dig it," I said, laughing with sheer joy and with the knowledge that my kids would plotz if they heard me utter that phrase. But I have read many a Bill Nighy quote that has contained that anachronism. If he likes the term, so do I! No, no, what I mean is, if he *fancies* the term, so do I. The same goes for groovy, cool, and dreamy.

"You encouraged me last time to ask you a question," he said when he returned to the table with our cold licks. "I squandered that opportunity by speaking to Gina instead of Lorie. May I ask Lorie a question today?"

"Lorie would love it."

"I have read the letter you sent me many times," he said giving me full eye contact when he could have chosen to look at his ice cream instead. "Do you remember what you wrote, or should I quote it?"

I laughed out loud. "You're kidding, right?"

"No," he said very seriously and then began to recite, "You wrote, 'I loved you in *Love Actually*. I loved you in *About Time*. I loved you in all three Johnny Worricker films, and in both Marigold Hotels.' Shall I go on?"

"Oh gosh, I see you have lots of experience learning your lines," I replied, a bit shaken.

"No, that's not it. Something in your letter resonated in me. But I wondered about something in it as well. You are a sixty-three-year-old woman with a crush on this not-so-famous actor, but you did not say if there is a husband who is chagrined over this crush."

I teared up a little at his question. "No, there is not. I am long divorced, twenty-one years! But there was a man who I dated for the last ten years. He passed away a year ago. He added a lot of drama to my life. I think in allowing myself to be a giddy fan, in allowing myself to write you, I was trying to get some of that drama back."

"I am so sorry for your loss but happy you are allowing yourself to live again."

I nodded a thank you and then brought us to a happier note by saying, "I have a question for you too, about your letter to me. Do you remember what you wrote, or should I quote it?" We both laughed. I continued, courageously, "You signed your name with an X beside it and then you put two more X's on the front of the note card. Quite frankly, those X's had me reeling. No, I take that back. They still have me reeling. I Googled your signature and see that you often add these X's, so I wonder if there is a rating system I should know about. In the same manner that I would give *The Girl in the Café* a five-star rating for a great movie, what does a three-X rating mean for my letter, and what does it take to get five?"

He laughed and then answered, "The significant thing is the fact that I posted a letter to you. I don't ordinarily do that—find a card, find a pen, find a stamp, find a letter box. But I felt compelled to respond to you. Regarding the X's, I ran out of room to add more X's with my signature, so I added a couple to the front of the card."

"Really? You actually remember writing me?"

"Your letter was lovely," he replied. "I saved it."

Holy smokes is what I thought, but what I said was, "Groovy."

SUNDAY, SEPTEMBER 6, 2015

Dear Diary,

I am still in St. Louis. It's been a lovely visit so far. There is still brunch with Cousin Kenny tomorrow before heading home. When I first hit town on Friday, I headed directly to Beth Hamedrosh Hagodol Cemetery to visit Mom and Dad as is my habit. I visited lots of other family graves there as well, which is very fitting since this is the family reunion weekend. Dad's sisters and their husbands are all buried there, as are several first cousins. I always come prepared with a bag full of decorative rocks to place on the headstones, as is the custom. I was tickled to find that all of the graves I visited had golf balls commemorating someone else's visit as well. It was adorable. I am sure Dad and Uncle Ruby in particular are loving the gesture from the great beyond.

At the reunion last night, I told everyone about those golf balls, and Kenny is the one who confessed to doing the deed. We proceeded to have a fabulous conversation and have a date to continue it over brunch in the morning. What is so odd and wonderful about this is the fact that while I have known this first cousin all my life, I don't think I have ever bothered to sit down and talk to him. Yes, he is fifteen years my senior, but even so, at some point long ago, we were both adults on a level playing field.

What caused me to have a real conversation with Kenny last night is the fact that I am trying to engage more with people these days. In the last year or so, whenever I went to Shabbat services at Temple, I timed things so I arrived just as the service started and then I rushed right out to my car after its conclusion. Lately, I try to chit chat with fellow congregants, and frankly, I am enjoying it. I have a note taped to the dashboard of my car reminding me about this brand of fun. It says "Be less aloof," and it sure worked for me with Kenny.

Roberta was delighted for me when I told her all of this during our conversation tonight, and a little bewildered as well. "You tape notes to your dashboard?" she asked skeptically.

"Only of things I want to remember," I said as we laughed.

"Now I understand how you get so much done. Who else did you have great conversations with?"

"Lots of people, really. Like Aunt Betty's granddaughter-in-law? She has a shop on Etsy. Should I ever really open one, she is ready to offer advice."

"And how was Aunt Betty?"

"Not great, but I think she loved seeing everyone. All of her kids and their spouses and their children attended. Even her great grand-child was there—coming all the way from California. And you know how she has knitted dolls and teddy bears for my grandkids through the years? Well, we brought all those Betty Dolls and Betty Teddies to the reunion and had them on display. I bet there were two dozen. It was wonderful."

"I would have loved to have seen that. What a tribute to her!"

"You would have liked the party, Bird, it was fun. I wish you had come. What have you been up to this long holiday weekend?"

"You know me. I worked yesterday and today to get tons of reports written up. But tomorrow Flo and I are going to the movies to see the new Robert Redford film, *A Walk in the Woods*. Have you seen it yet?"

"No, not yet. It's on Vera's list, so we should see it soon. Text me and let me know how you guys like it. But speaking of getting lots of reports written, I forgot to tell you I finished writing The Book of Irv before coming to St. Louis."

"Great news! How do you feel about it?"

"All I can say is that something in me absolutely had to write the last chapter before leaving town."

"I like the symbolism," Roberta said. "You're finished with all that. You're not going to start a new chapter when you go home; you're going to start a new book."

"Roberta, I know you were busy acting in high school musicals when we were kids, but you really should have been on the cheerleading squad. You're great at it!"

———— ✥ ————

So okay, dear Diary,

So much to be grateful for today with Roberta right there on the top of the list.

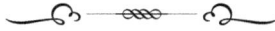

Text Messages:
Beloved Bill to Lorie—XXXXX

Lorie to Beloved Bill—Swoon!

BB to L—Rigorous filming schedule for the next few days and then I depart Cincinnati. Will be sure to see you before leaving if that is okay?

L to BB—It is okay to see each other, not so okay that you are leaving.

BB to L—5X

A Bit of Fantasy—The Male

The text message came a couple days ago asking me if I could meet him at "our place" today at two. Of course my answer was yes. One should never give up the opportunity to eat chocolate chip ice cream at Graeter's, right? And of course, a date with Bill Nighy is also worthy of rearranging anything else—at all—that might be on the calendar.

Dressing like me worked out so well the last two times that I am going with another iteration of myself today. I was in blue denim jeans on our previous date, and today I switch to black denim. Instead of a T-shirt and cardigan, I will go with a T-shirt and an infinity scarf. Such a scarf puts a little bounce on my chest where boobs would be had God chosen to give me that particular amenity. The scarf is a soft cotton knit in two shades of gray. Not too fussy at all. I will look fine sitting next to him in his navy suit. Wouldn't it be crazy if he came dressed as *Love Actually's* Billy Mack with a big, flowing, colorful print shirt on? And let's not forget the thick gold chain at his neck or the jeans. We'd have to hope that tutti frutti is on the menu as the flavor of the month.

Of course we both arrived in a timely fashion. So sure was he that this would be the case, he already had our ice cream ordered up, scooped, and waiting. It was quite a sight. "I've gotten bold today," he said. "I ordered one scoop of every chocolate chip flavor for us to taste."

Since Graeter's has eight or nine different chocolate chip flavors at all times, quite a bowl awaited me. "I notice, though, that it's only one bowl with two spoons," I said. "That's very romantic. Did dating teenagers in Great Britain drink one Coke with two straws like we did here, foreheads pressed together and all that?"

"I was too shy to date as a teenager, so I wouldn't know," he replied.

"I read that about you in some interview online. Other articles I've read seem to indicate you are still too shy to date as a sixty-five-year-old man."

"Guilty as charged," he answered. "Good thing we're just eating ice cream together and not dating. That fact causes a problem, though."

"How so?"

"I'm leaving town tomorrow—not just town, country as well. It will be hard to meet for ice cream when I am back in London."

"If continuing on in a relationship is unpalatable to a mere ice cream eater," I said, "perhaps we could explore the possibility of a friendship. I am sure you have many friends already—David Hare, Richard Curtis, Michael Gambon, Diana Quick, and Judi Dench to name a few—but can anyone ever have too many friends? I am thinking of a story I often tell about my beloved father. He was the youngest of four children, but his siblings were twelve, ten, and eight years older than he and they loved him completely as if they were an extra set of parents. Thus, he had his parents and these three siblings to love him. I have often said he was 'over-loved,' but of course this was not the case. No one can ever have too much love—or loving friends in their life. Right?"

"I like that story and I especially like that you had a 'beloved father,' as I had one of those too."

"I may have read that about you somewhere online too," I interjected. "I've been a little obsessed with the topic of you." I said this with a pathetic little smile, but with full eye contact, thinking all the while that his eyes are gorgeous.

"I'm flattered. And pleased. Those people you mentioned, my... friends? Well yes, of course, they are my friends, but probably not in the way you mean it."

"So is it…maybe…kind of lonely at the top? Wait, wait, I know you must not think you are at the top, but surely you know you are getting close, right?"

"My career is a great success. My personal life has not kept pace." He looked down at the ice cream, and I missed his eyes on mine. But before I knew it, his left hand stroked my cheek and we reestablished eye contact and smiled at each other with huge grins. Then he rotated that hand from cheek to chin and tipped my head up a bit. He dropped his mouth open in silent instruction. I copied his move, which allowed him to pick up a spoon with his right hand and start to feed me ice cream. "Can't let this melt, can we?" he said.

A full orchestral version of "Isn't it Romantic?" played suddenly in my head. Richard Rodgers may have written the melody as a ballad, but my heart thumped along with it as if it were a march or a polka. What he did next did nothing to bring me back to a normal sinus rhythm.

"Now that I think about it, ice cream eating is not enough," he said as he shook his head "no" until I followed suit and shook mine too. "Friendship is not enough," he added as we shook our heads together one more time. "I want more," he said. The tear that slipped from my right eye seemed to seal the deal, or maybe it was his lips—tenderly on mine—that did it.

<u>TUESDAY, SEPTEMBER 8, 2015</u>

Dear Diary,

The customary expression is "to get something off one's chest," but in my case, I seem to have gotten all that Big Irv stuff "out of my brain," leaving lots of empty space for other things to fill it. Thus, more Big Bill Nighy stuff rolled out of my head as I drove home yesterday. I keep running the three episodes of the Graeter's ice cream parlor fantasy through my head, enjoying every moment of our blossoming love story. I think I should send it off to Richard Curtis to produce. Not only is he a Bill Nighy buddy, but he wrote the screenplay for *Bridget Jones' Diary*. Maybe he'd be interested in Lorie Kleiner Eckert's. Or maybe Edgar Wright and Simon Pegg would like to work on it as a big, daft, stupid comedy: *The Graeter's Ice Cream Trilogy*. Ha! Now that's a fantasy on steroids.

Obviously it continues to be fun to think about BN, Google him, and fantasize about him, so I am thinking I will send another letter his way. Why not? It will buy me several more weeks of excitedly looking in my mailbox, several more weeks of peeking out onto the front porch in search of roses. Speaking of such, though I have never confessed to Vera that I am on the lookout for roses, she sent me flowers today! I was not here when they arrived, so the delivery guy left them on my porch and I saw them when I peeked out the window! Did all my wishful thinking cause this to happen? Who knows? The universe works in mysterious ways. Whatever the case, her card was adorable: "Welcome home from your trip. Just want you to know that the scale of zero to none does not work for rating our friendship. We're a solid ten out of ten. Love you! Vera"

Is it any doubt I love that woman? Sweet as she is, though, it's a toss-up whether or not I will tell her about letter number three. But even if I do, I won't tell her I plan to include a photo of myself this time. While I nixed that idea with the second letter, I just have to resurrect the plan now. I remember well the dating years before meeting Big Irv when I placed personal ads in *Cincinnati Magazine*. I never asked the respondents to send me a photo, as I did not want to appear shallow. Of course I know a handsome face can hide a horrible heart. But even so, as I made plans to meet those men sight unseen, it was unsettling. Every unkempt, disheveled, long-haired, morbidly obese, wild-eyed guy I passed on the street could be the one I was meeting for coffee later that day. There is a reason why the expression "a picture is worth a thousand words" is so overused—it's so true! And so I plan to send Bill Nighy a photo. I will send the one Bird snapped of me at the theater in New York—when I was standing in front of the billboard advertising *Skylight*—and I will add a comment on the back: "Us together in New York." Oh, wait a minute; the idea of an "us" might be as presumptuous and off-putting to him as was that phrase "after we're married." Hmmm… Okay, this is better: "Here I am 'with you' in New York." I hope he will find it cute, though creepy is also a possibility. However, everything I have written to him has been equal parts him and equal parts me, so the same will be true for the photo.

I need to write this fan letter and get it in the mail so my ordinary life can resume. Yikes! It's a busy week ahead. Rosh Hashanah is Sunday, so I literally need to get cooking on that. I also have a column due this week and it is not yet started. However, it's going to be about Dad again. After a weekend with family reminiscing over many Morrie Stories, how can it not be?

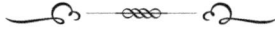

September 8, 2015

Dear Bill Nighy,

Three things about you. Three things about me.

YOU: 1) In 2014, you gave an interview in which you listed ten BN movies you recommended. *Pride* was on the list. 2) Recently *Vanity Fair* named you a best-dressed man of 2015. *Fashionista* reported on it, noting additionally your fine coiffure. 3) Taking these items together, I saw you in *Pride* as a very pleasant-looking fellow, where in full BN dress and hair you are a dashing and handsome man. But I wonder, isn't it a heavy burden to have to be BN every day? Do you know that bn is equally terrific?

ME: 1) For the better part of the last decade, I was in a relationship with a man who passed away fourteen months ago. 2) I am a very organized person, and as his executrix, I took care of business, not realizing as I shuffled papers how much of me had died with him. 3) In my crush on you, I find myself coming back to life. I have found laughter again with my friends and I have even found some joy— especially in viewing your films. I have my own version of Saturday Night at the Movies here, complete with Cornetto ice cream bars. Neat, huh?

Fond regards,

Lorie

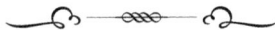

SEPTEMBER 11, 2015

A Slice of Life: A Monthly Column

BECOMING MY DAD

Recently I came across an old journal of mine. I had written in it during the years of 2010-2012, the two years immediately following my dad's death. To give full disclosure here, I should state that this was a "guided journal" within a book called *Mourning & Mitzvah* by Anne Brener. The book contains "over sixty guided exercises…for walking the mourner's path through grief to healing." Good girl that I am, I did all of the exercises offered at that time, plus I wrote copious comments in the margins and on blank pages throughout the book. In reading it all over from the vantage point of today, I was amazed I had worked on that journal for two solid years. When I mentioned this to my son, however, he was not surprised by the length of my mourning at all. "It's *Grandpa*," he explained to me, stressing the "G" word. "We're all still mourning him today."

There is some truth to my son's comment. All of my children speak fondly of him frequently. I can't talk to my brother or sister-in-law without them waxing poetic about the man. My nephews, too, have loving Morrie Stories to tell—always. Indeed, we all seem to have holes in our hearts where Dad used to be. At the same time, our hearts are filled to capacity with thoughts of him, and love for him.

Certainly there is a lesson for me here. It's a given that I long to be the central figure in my adult children's lives like I used to be when they were little kids. And it is a given that those days are over. But I wonder, wouldn't it be nice to have a central spot in their hearts—like Dad has—and isn't that what I should be working toward consciously? So I ponder the charm of Dad:

- He was honest and trustworthy.
- He did not exaggerate.
- He did everything in moderation—give the guy a pound box of chocolates, he would eat one a day until they were gone, never finding an excuse for seconds.
- He took care of himself—after suffering a heart attack in his fifties, he started to eat right and to exercise regularly via walking. He walked four days a week into his eighties. Even when confined to an assisted living facility at age ninety-one, this amazing man took his walker on little strolls around the grounds until he physically lost the ability to stand.
- He never asked "Why me?" For a dozen years, he was dependent on blood transfusions due to a bone marrow disorder. His response to this malady was to say, "Everyone has something. This is mine."
- He was "blue" from time to time, but he managed it.
- He was like a Timex watch. He took a licking and kept on ticking.
- He believed in the mottos "Do your best" and "If you can't say something nice, don't say anything at all."
- He loved to read and he lulled himself to sleep every single night with a book.
- He loved to listen to music and he kept a baton handy to help conduct the orchestra when he listened to his favorite classical music radio station.
- And most of all, he loved to watch baseball games. Even when his beloved St. Louis Cardinals were not playing on TV, he watched whatever game was on and pretended to be the umpire, calling the balls and strikes.
- He was a marshmallow and he wore his heart on his sleeve. He cried at bar mitzvahs and weddings and graduations. Just

the opening bars of "Pomp and Circumstance" brought him to tears. A daughter or granddaughter in a wedding gown? Oh my!

- He had the darling idiosyncrasy of taking little cat naps sitting up in his easy chair, with four fingertips tucked neatly into the waistband of his pants. He had no problem with being teased about it. He loved that we found him so adorable.
- He did volunteer work post-retirement in elementary schools, where each year he was assigned a student with whom to work one-on-one in order to enhance the child's reading skills.
- He liked people in general. He was a devoted friend. He was a loving relative.
- He was a quiet man and a good listener. He never copied a Ken-L Ration commercial to tell anyone, "My dog's bigger than your dog."
- He was not judgmental.
- He did not speak negatively of others and never ever gossiped.
- He uttered a cuss word exactly once in his life, when he finished painting a living room wall late in the evening only to have soot from a heat exchange shower down on his work. He said, "Damn!"
- He understood that if he sat back quietly, others would come to him, particularly little kids.
- He said "I love you" by giving out "love squeezes," and his grandchildren lined up for the loving.

My dad was very successful at being loved, cherished, and even adored. It makes perfect sense to me, therefore, to try walking in his footsteps to have a similar outcome. And so as I try to figure out LIFE AT AGE SIXTY-THREE, my new thought process will be WWDD — what would Dad do? And then I will behave accordingly.

Oh, come let them adore me.

Amen.

Dear Diary,

Almost two dozen people are coming here for dinner tomorrow night, so I have been occupied this week cooking the traditional Rosh Hashanah feast. I still had the mashed potatoes and matzo ball soup to prepare, so that kept me busy all day today. As things bubbled away on the stovetop, I passed the time by reading about beloved Bill online, and of course my reward for completing all recipes will be my movie date with him tonight.

Regarding today's search, I Googled "Bill Nighy quotes" and came up with four different websites with loads of quotes attributed to my guy. When he said these things, to whom he said them, and if he still agrees with what he once said are all unknowns. With those caveats in place, here are the sources: IMDb, Billnighy.info, Brainyquote.com, and Likesuccess.com. And here are some quotes related to acting:

- "When I do a play, it's like agreeing to be ill for a couple of months." (Brainyquote.com)
- "When you are in something that you're proud of and it's funny and it's a good night out and all of those things, there's nothing quite like it. The rewards are proportionate to the amount of alarm and distress it causes you." (Likesuccess.com)
- "When people warned me there would be long periods out of work if I became an actor, I couldn't keep a straight face, because that was exactly what I had in mind." (Likesuccess.com)
- "All actors who have been around for a long time, which I have, and have been skint for long periods, which I have, find it difficult to turn down jobs. If I turn anything down, my stomach turns over. I feel sick. It feels like gambling." (Brainyquote.com)
- "I'm not famous for my back-story investigations; I'm lucky that I work with good writers and it's usually in the script." (Brainyquote.com)

- "Actors always talk about taking their work home and I always think: 'What are you on? You just turn it off. You are at work and then you go home.'" (Brainyquote.com)
- "I'm not mad about the action part of things. You know, if you show me a stunt, I want to lie down and go to sleep. I have zero interest in fighting, zero interest in horse riding. I like the bits where they talk, and where the story is told. And fortunately, I have a brilliant man called Paul Shapcott who takes over when it gets physical. He looks extraordinarily like me—so I get to go and lie down in my trailer." (Billnighy.info)
- "There was a time when you were supposed to question everything the director said, to create some kind of conflict, out of which creativity would be born. But I love it when they tell you what to do, you know: 'Start there, walk over there, say the line and I'll shout: Cut!' I think it's groovy. When we were filming with Stephen Poliakoff, his first note to me—he prefaced it with: 'That was marvelous,' which is always a good start—anyway, his note was: 'Don't wiggle your eyes about so much,' and you know, my heart leapt. Because I know that. I know how to not make my eyes wiggle about." (IMDb)
- "If you're in a play and you have the same jokes to deliver, eight times a week, it's endlessly fascinating, just trying to hit it each time, and maybe a little bit quicker, a little bit later, trying to feel the air in which you're about to place it. To have 400 people laugh at the same time, you would go to your grave trying to get it right. And it's also very glamorous when it's on film, because you're not there. I love it when a producer phones up and says: 'It played very well in France. They were laughing.' In France." (IMDb)

Beyond these comments on acting, here are some quotes about BN as a writer, a rock star, a post-modern jive talker, and a dad:

- "I am a world-class procrastinator. I'm only an actor because I've been putting off being a writer for thirty-five years." (IMDb)
- "The fact that [my hobby of playing the air guitar is] so deeply uncool encourages me even more. I can even tune my air guitar, which not a lot of people can do." (Billnighy.info)
- "A phrase I use far too often…'You groove me out,' in almost any context. I can say it instead of goodbye, or if people say 'I'll meet you on the corner.' It's post-modern, ironic jive talk." (Billnighy.info)
- "To be serious, the things you really want to relive are things like bedtime with your daughter when she becomes incredibly entertaining 'cause she doesn't want to go to sleep. They're at their most enchanting 'cause they just want to put it off, so they do a cabaret for you. You sit there thinking, 'Please don't let this end.'" (Likesuccess.com)

Ah, dear Diary, I'm sorry to let the Bill Nighy quotes end but thrilled to have finished all that cooking, and now from mashed potatoes to couch potato I go.

Saturday Night at the Movies

I Capture the Castle
DIRECTOR: Tim Fywell
WRITERS: Dodie Smith (novel), Heidi Thomas (screenplay)
RELEASE DATE: 2003
RUNNING TIME: 1 Hour, 53 Minutes
ALSO FEATURING: Romola Garai, Rose Byrne, Tara Fitzgerald, Henry Thomas, and Marc Blucas.
FRIENDLY CONNECTIONS: Romola Garai and Bill Nighy went on to play father and daughter again in *Glorious 39* in 2009.

I Capture the Castle tells the story of the Mortmain family and is set in the 1930s in England. James Mortmain is played by Bill Nighy, and his daughters, Rose and Cassandra, are played by Rose Byrne and Romola Garai respectively. The girls have a stepmother named Topaz, played by Tara Fitzgerald. James is a writer whose first book was a big hit but who has suffered writer's block since its release a decade or so ago. Each year the income from his book decreases, and so as the movie opens, the family is on the verge of bankruptcy. They live in a decrepit castle and they are selling off the furniture to buy food.

The family is eccentric or exotic or some other brand of odd. James has angry outbursts and is possibly insane, or maybe just drunk. Part of his history includes having attacked his first wife with a kitchen knife, a crime for which he spent four years in prison. Meanwhile, his second wife, Topaz, is an artist herself. An equally strange bird, she finds release in communing with nature in the buff. As for the daughters, Rose is twenty-one years old and is very angry with her father for being such a poor provider. She wants money to live and enjoy life and she is bound and determined to get it! Meanwhile, Cassandra is seventeen years old and she is content to sit back and watch all the drama in her family. A budding writer herself, she is the first-person narrator of the movie as she "captures" all that happens at the castle in her journal.

Eventually two men, Simon and Neil Cotton (Henry Thomas and Marc Blucas respectively), enter the picture. They are American brothers, and Simon, the elder of the two, has just inherited the castle. This means he is the Mortmains' new landlord. Both Rose and Cassandra are intrigued by the unmarried brothers. Though Rose is more smitten with Neil, she goes after Simon because of his greater wealth. She is intent on marrying him both to escape her poverty and to help her family do the same. Unfortunately, Cassandra is likewise attracted to Simon. Though various romantic combinations of brothers and sisters get played out before the movie ends, Rose manages to win a proposal from one of the guys.

Rose then goes away to London to purchase her wedding trousseau with Simon and Neil's mother and with Topaz. While they are all away, Cassandra manages to imprison her father in a medieval tower near the castle, keeping him there under lock and key until he produces fifty pages of a new novel.

Thus, the movie ends with the Mortmains' future doubly secured, once by Rose's marriage and then by James Mortmain's release from his writer's block. However, it is not a completely happy ending due to Cassandra's unrequited love.

This movie and I got off to a slow start, in a similar manner as I did with *The Boat That Rocked*. I watched it for thirty minutes, then I gave myself some time off for good behavior, then I came back to it, and finally got into it. My overall feel is that it was very British. No, I don't really know what that means except it was slow and dreamy and just didn't look like it came out of Hollywood. Which of course it didn't.

My main reason (only reason?) for liking the film was Bill Nighy's part in it, and I am happy to report that his role was substantial enough to please me. Of particular note was a segment in which he portrayed great anger. My mind immediately juxtaposed that scene with his angry scene in *Notes on a Scandal*. Both were terrific, but they were totally different because of the time periods in which they were set. *Notes on a Scandal* was a modern-day tale and *I Capture the Castle* took place in the 1930s. I think that people were more genteel or sedate back then; even in the way they expressed anger. "Going ballistic" was not an option.

Though I wasn't smitten with the movie, there are a few things that tickled me about it:

1. Bill Nighy's daughter from *Glorious 39*, Romola Garai, is again his daughter in this movie. Whereas he "imprisoned" her in *Glorious 39*, she "imprisons" him in *I Capture the Castle*. I have to confess, though, that I am not so tickled by the fact that in both movies she has top billing and is the star of the show.

2. I am glad the Los Angeles Film Critics Association gave Bill Nighy the LAFCA Award for Best Supporting Actor for this movie—and for his work in *Lawless Heart*, *AKA*, and for *Love Actually*—in 2004.

3. I was interested to learn that the movie was based on a book of the same name written by Dodie Smith, whose greatest claim to fame is that she also wrote *The Hundred and One Dalmatians*.

4. Finally, it is fun to realize that the actor who played the part of Simon Cotton was Henry Thomas, who as a child starred in *E.T. the Extra-Terrestrial* in 1982.

In the unauthorized biography, Bill Nighy says he never read Dodie Smith's book even though many fans told him it was one of their very favorite books. Trying to do justice to a well-loved novel made him nervous, as did the fact that James Mortmain was described as a brooding and charismatic man, traits with which Bill Nighy does not identify. But in the end, it worked out. As BN says, "I've met several people since who are devotees of the book, who have seen the film, and none of them have hit me!"

Devotees of the book? His expression is so intriguing I looked up the book on Goodreads.com, where a reader named Martine labeled it a quintessential English coming-of-age story, adding, "A summary would make it sound slight, trite, and predictable, all of which it is, and would not reflect the fact that it's also funny as hell, charismatic, deliciously eccentric, Austenesque, and so utterly charming that I quite literally had sore cheeks after reading it because I couldn't stop smiling at the delightful nonsense the incomparable Cassandra Mortmain spilled out on the pages."

My goodness! No wonder I didn't love the movie. I had the wrong mind-set while watching it. I thought I was seeing the story of the Mortmain family starring an ensemble cast while instead I was viewing Cassandra's coming of age and her reportage of it. I wonder if I should watch it a second time? Nah. Or maybe I should read the book? Nah. Since Bill Nighy hasn't, I probably won't either. It's not that I am swamped with other things to do; it's just that I have spent quite enough time trying to capture this particular castle.

In that the LAFCA gave Bill Nighy an award for this movie and in that this movie was not among my favorites, I have to wonder about my taste in films. Trying to compare myself to the general public, I did a little test. Here are the four movies I watched during my most recent Saturday Nights at the Movies: *Hot Fuzz, Punch-Drunk Love, Glorious 39,* and *I Capture the Castle.* According to my ranking of the films, the two comedies, *Hot Fuzz* and *Punch-Drunk Love*, are definitely at the bottom of the heap, proving, I'm sure, that I have no sense of humor. Of the other two, the dramas, *Glorious 39* was much more enjoyable than *I Capture the Castle*, especially since it had a bit of history to teach. I laugh as I compare my opinion to the audiences surveyed by Rotten Tomatoes. They awarded these approval ratings instead:

Glorious 39—43 percent

I Capture the Castle—77 percent

Punch-Drunk Love—77 percent

Hot Fuzz—89 percent

Dear Diary,

It's been two days in a row without walking. Yesterday I was at services all morning for Rosh Hashana and this morning it rained. Missing back-to-back days of exercise is not good for my psyche—which is in need of endorphins—so I forced myself onto the treadmill this afternoon. I usually hate that contraption, but today some channel on my DirecTV had an interesting movie in progress. It caught my attention, making the treadmill palatable. The film starred Jennifer Aniston and Aaron Eckhart and was called *Love Happens*. Aaron Eckhart's character, Burke, holds a Ph.D. and is the author of a book that gives advice about dealing with the loss of a loved one. Perhaps I should have changed the station right then, but I didn't. Instead, I watched Burke speak to a conference room full of people as he tried to help them progress with their grieving. The only thing was, he was not moving forward with his own. His beloved wife was killed in a car wreck. So unfinished was his grief work that he couldn't make himself attend the funeral. Anyway, he has a breakdown—or breakthrough—at the conference. In a very emotional scene, he confesses that he was the one who was at the wheel the night of the accident. As it turns out, his father-in-law is in the audience, and as Burke takes the blame for the death, the father-in-law stands up and publicly proclaims, "It's not your fault. It was an accident. We don't blame you."

As fast as those words were uttered on the screen, I was sobbing. Somehow managing to get myself away from that TV set, I tripped the trigger on the safety cord that connected me to the treadmill, causing it to turn off immediately. My tears were not so quick to stop. When they did, I found myself on the basement sofa, a snotty mess. More tears threatened as these words played in my head: *It's not my fault. Big Irv died of a multitude of illnesses. No one blames me.*

As I rested on the sofa hoping and praying those words were true, I reflected on my own grief work in The Book of Irv. In so doing, I recalled the starting point of our relationship when Big Irv reupholstered my desk chair. I remembered him telling me in his very soft voice that even if he had hurt himself while removing that staple from the seat cushion, he would not have told me about it. He would have braved the injury on his own. And so it occurred to me that had the man been well enough to get out of bed, and had he been well enough to drive his truck, he would have taken himself off into the woods, where he would have laid himself down and died. But he couldn't drive, so he drove me away instead, and then in his own style, with his own dignity, he died in his own home. No retirement community for him. No hospital or hospice. And certainly no IV line stuck into his arm. He did it his way, true to himself one hundred percent.

Respect for him—perhaps a grudging one—opened in my soul and with it a speck of forgiveness for both of us.

WEDNESDAY, SEPTEMBER 16, 2015

Dear Diary,

When I walked with Robin this morning, I told her about the movie I saw yesterday, the crying fit it engendered, and the fact that I have only cried like that a handful of times in my life—the last time being after Mom died. I'll be darned if I didn't get a little teary just talking about it. Seeing that, she advised me to take it easy today. So, in my best goofing-off mode, I played some Sudoku and FreeCell. When I got bored with that, I switched to my other favorite pastime, Bill Nighy.

Over the months of my adoration, I have printed out or written down a bunch of BN quotes from interviews I have read or watched. All of these quotes astound me in that beloved Bill cannot say an unkind word about anyone with whom he has worked. Having time on my hands today, I assemble all my snippets here for review.

1. In the Behind the Scenes Featurette at the end of *The Girl in the Café,* he praises the script and the writer by saying, "As you'd expect from Richard Curtis—who is world-class—it's extremely funny."

2. He also said of his co-star in the movie, Kelly Macdonald, "Kelly is deeply gifted and dreamy to work with."

3. In an article from *The Sydney Morning Herald* on October 12, 2013, he said more about Richard Curtis: "He is an extremely nice man, a wonderful man and a very good director; it gives me confidence, the fact he's asked me four times (to work together)."

4. In the bonus material on the *Pride* DVD, he says: "It's certainly one of the best scripts I'd read in years and years and years. I was beyond keen to be a part of it."

5. In an interview with HeyUGuys called "Bill Nighy Interview *Pride,*" Bill Nighy says this about Imelda Staunton, who

performs in the movie with him: "I love working with Imelda. Working with Imelda is heavenly. It's sort of actually dreamy. She is a great woman, and I say it quite seriously. And she's a wonderful artist. She's completely overburdened—almost— with talent. She's also just incredibly easy and dreamy to be around."

6. In a Charlie Rose interview dated March 27, 2015, Bill Nighy said, "Michael Gambon is touched with genius." (Bill Nighy and Michael Gambon worked together in *Page Eight*, which is part of the Johnny Worricker trilogy, and both men played the part of Tom Sergeant in *Skylight* at some point in their careers.)

7. In a Charlie Rose interview dated May 15, 2012, in which they discussed *The Best Exotic Marigold Hotel*, Bill Nighy said, "Dame Maggie Smith has what they call timing from God."

8. In the Behind the Scenes clips at the end of the *Notes on a Scandal* DVD, he praises Cate Blanchett, saying, "She is supremely gifted. There's a very few rare individuals like Cate Blanchett, and between her and Judi (Dench), you have two of the finest performers currently operating."

9. In the bonus material at the end of the *Glorious* 39 DVD, BN says this about writer and director Stephen Poliakoff: "I would happily work with Stephen all the time…I always know it will be original and powerful and beautiful and unlike anybody's else's work…[Poliakoff] has an incredible body of work. There is a queue of people that would love to work with him."

10. In the interview he did with *Movies Ireland* about *Pirate Radio*, he says, "Joanna Johnson who did the costumes gave me some of the coolest outfits I've ever had in my professional life."

11. In an interview with John Balfe of entertainment.ie that is dated April 27, 2009, Bill Nighy praises the entire ensemble cast and

the director/writer of *Pirate Radio* when he says, "There was a complete absence of careerism and there was no elbowing each other out of the way to get to the camera. They're classy guys and they're very, very good. They're comic assassins. And Richard also creates an atmosphere which doesn't really include any kind of static-full behavior...he's an extraordinary and gifted writer."

Really, is it any wonder I love Bill Nighy? These many quotes prove him to be—like his cohorts in the *Pirate Radio* film—a classy man.

Thursday, September 17, 2015

Dear Diary,

Vera and I saw Robert Redford and Nick Nolte in A *Walk in the Woods* today. I didn't love it.

"I read the book years ago. Bill Bryson's tale was laugh-out-loud funny," I said to Vera.

"Well, they didn't capture that in the movie," she replied.

"That's for sure," I agreed. "And, as you know, I have taken day hikes on the Appalachian Trail. They were challenging, to say the least. But Redford and Nolte were supposedly hiking all 2,200 miles of the trail from Georgia to Maine. I don't think those two old coots could manage day hikes, much less through hiking."

"Old coots? They aren't much older than your buddy Bill Nighy," she argued.

"No, no, no, no!" I protested, pulling out my smartphone on the spot and Googling the guys. "I know Bill Nighy's birth date is December 12, 1949. As for Robert Redford, he was born...August 18, 1936 and Nick Nolte was born...February 8, 1941. There you have it: one young guy and two old coots! Sorry for Googling at the table. You do know, don't you, that when I hiked on the AT, my trail name was 'Google'?"

"I may have to call you that myself. Which reminds me, what's new about your young man Bill?"

"Oh God, Vera, he is just the nicest guy. I love reading about him. He is always caught in the act of saying nice things about his costars, directors, costume designers, etc. You name the person; he's got something lovely to say about them. He reminds me of that song from old Westerns, 'Home on the Range.'" When she looked at me weirdly, I broke into song so she would catch my drift. In my best nasal twang—and doing my best to sound like a dog howling—I sang:

"Home, home on the range,
Where the deer and the antelope play;
Where seldom is heard a discouraging word
And the skies are not cloudy all day."

"And your point is?" she said through her laughter.

"Bill Nighy never has a discouraging or disparaging word for anyone. Meanwhile, I am a woman who has survived men who had the audacity to think I did not put forks in the dishwasher the right way or mail in the mailbox the right way. Bill Nighy is a perennially positive person—a 3P guy. I think I'd like to spend some time around him. It would do wonders for my self-esteem, and besides that, the skies wouldn't be cloudy all day."

SATURDAY, SEPTEMBER 19, 2015

Dear Diary,

God is great. God is good. And I thank Him for this…soccer schedule? Having finished The Book of Irv, I was wondering how I would fill my Saturdays. I was delighted, therefore, when my daughter informed me that two of my grandgirls are playing soccer this season! All games are on Saturday from now until the end of October. Woo hoo! I will admit that it is odd to be excited about a sports season. I sure did NOT love it when I was the mom and my kids were the athletes. My calendar did not need any more events, much less one practice and one game per child per week! It put my schlepping way over the top and was its own brand of hell. How funny it is that now it seems like a little bit of heaven. Today's games were outstanding. I don't really know who won, but the schmooze-fest with other parents and grandparents was a blast, and our little family group even went out for lunch after the last whistle blew. Which takes me back to where I started: God is great. God is good…

Also in the good news department, there was something interesting in the mail this week. No, no, not a letter from beloved Bill, but something lovely just the same—my tickets for this year's Broadway Series. There are six shows over the next nine months and the adult kids take turns going with me, filling the seat that was once Big Irv's. A fancy-pants dinner beforehand is also part of our custom. So there is a lot to look forward to in the weeks ahead. Whew! What a relief!

As for tonight, Bill Nighy is the loved one I turn to for fun. There are three of his projects that I am dying to see, but the library does not have copies of them so I hunted for them online and was able to purchase two of them from Amazon, *Still Crazy* and *Gideon's Daughter*. The third title, *The Men's Room*, is a five-part miniseries produced by the BBC in 1991. Thus far, I am not able to find it in a format that can be watched on DVD players in the U.S. Darn! It sounds like the most sexual part he has played. *The Men's Room* tells the story of an affair between two academics played by Bill Nighy and Harriet Walter. According to Radio Times, Bill Nighy's character "is energetically unfaithful, a serial womanizer." It goes on to describe their affair this way: "Their sex is frequent, passionate, and sometimes violent; their feelings for each other consuming and volatile." Sounds like must-see TV to me, but unfortunately, I can't! I will have to content myself with the other two movies. So, okay, I will! *Still Crazy* is my pick for tonight.

Saturday Night at the Movies

Still Crazy
DIRECTOR: Brian Gibson
WRITERS: Dick Clement and Ian La Frenais
RELEASE DATE: 1998
RUNNING TIME: 1 Hour, 35 Minutes
ALSO FEATURING: Stephen Rea, Jimmy Nail, Timothy Spall, Bruce Robinson, Billy Connolly, and Juliet Aubrey.

Still Crazy tells the story of a fictitious band called Strange Fruit. They disbanded in the 1970s and are reunited twenty years later, which is the starting point of the movie. Originally the band had five members: Keith was the vocalist, Tony was the keyboardist, Les was the bassist, Beano was the drummer, and Brian was the guitarist. Evidently Keith died of a drug overdose back in the Seventies and was replaced by Ray Simms, who is played by Bill Nighy.

As the movie opens, all the band members are shown in their current lives. Ray is still in the music business, working unsuccessfully as a solo artist, though he is successful at sobriety after years of drug and alcohol abuse. Tony is a salesman. Les is a roofer. Beano is doing gardening work at a nursery. And Brian is presumed dead. Tony is the one who is trying to reunite the band, and he enlists the aid of Karen, the band's original runaround-girl who now becomes its manager. One other person joins in on the fun as Hughie comes back on board as their roadie. He is also the narrator of the tale and opens the movie with these words, "History teaches us that men behave wisely...once they've exhausted all other alternatives. For most rock bands, the pursuit of wisdom's a low priority compared to fame, fortune, and fornication. Such a band was Strange Fruit."

Though twenty years have passed for the band members, it looks like egos and differing opinions will continue to cause problems for these guys, and even though they have some success in reuniting, the film closes with these words from Hughie: "And how will the Fruits conspire to bollocks things up this time around? We wait with baited breath!"

While Hughie's words feel prophetic and we are pretty sure the guys will be unsuccessful together in the long haul, that is not the case for the movie itself. Its success is evident in the fact that it was nominated for two Golden Globe awards in 1999. It was nominated for Best Motion Picture-Comedy/Musical and it was nominated for Best Original Song-Motion Picture for the song "The Flame Still Burns." Unfortunately, it lost out to the movie *Shakespeare in Love* and to the song "The Prayer," from the movie *Quest for Camelot.* Also, Bill Nighy won the Peter Sellers Award for Comedy for his role in the film. Beyond his obvious comedic success, it should be noted that all his vocal performances in the film feature his real voice and that the soundtrack from the movie is still available.

It was fun to see Bill Nighy in this role. I have never seen him in more flamboyant attire. I especially loved seeing him in a full-length, green, furry coat with aviator glasses to complete the look. The fact that several buttons of his shirt were often undone likewise was a hoot. His makeup was rock-star gorgeous and over the top. The man looks great in purple eye shadow, and his teased hair takes him to...uh...new heights.

Beyond all this fun visual stuff, I loved the vulnerability of his character, as evidenced in several scenes.

- In one, he is giving himself a pep talk in front of the mirror and shouts, "You are the man!" But as he punctuates the sentiment with a little jab of the arm, he throws something out in his back.

- Then there is the scene in which Ray's fiftieth birthday is upon him. This fact does not please him, nor does the cake he is given with that number emblazoned upon it. Indeed, he slams the cake against the wall as if that can stop the aging process.
- Another such scene has him primping for the stage only to have his hairdryer stop working when only half his hairdo is in place.
- And oh my, while he is on the road with the band, he seeks out a twelve-step meeting to help him through all the trials and tribulations of his life, only to realize he is at a meeting for overeaters anonymous instead of AA.
- But all of these pales by comparison to the time he is asked for his signature. Thinking he is dealing with an autograph seeker, he is all puffed up, only to be deflated when he realizes he is dealing with the pizza delivery man and that his signature is needed on the tab.

While these minor things are vexing, there is also the underlying problem that Ray was not an original band member, but instead a replacement for the much-beloved person who OD'ed. It is clear that some of Ray's fellow band members will never forgive him for that. Thus, Ray had a lot of issues to deal with, making him a very sympathetic character.

According to Bill Nighy, Ray Simms was also a very important character for his career. In the unauthorized biography, he explains that Ray Simms was a *principal role* and that in order to get a principal role, one needs to have had a principal role in the past. Thus, it's a Catch-22 for an actor wanting bigger and better roles. When director Brian Gibson cast him in such a role, it set a precedent. It was a big turning point in Bill Nighy's career.

Bottom line:

- *Still Crazy* was a fun and funny movie.

- Bill Nighy's wardrobe and makeup in it were a visual delight.
- His acting was fabulous and award-worthy.
- The film was a major landmark in his career.
- It is a must-see film for his fans.

Dear Diary,

It was a tough day today: Yom Kippur. Along with a twenty-four-hour fast, I was at Temple all day moving through the lengthy liturgy for this Day of Atonement. The largest part of the holiday is to seek forgiveness for all wrongdoings of the past year, but a memorial service, Yizkor, is also a part of the day. I am not the only one in the congregation who is emotional wreckage during Yizkor. Like a funeral, it comes with a permission slip to cry as we remember all of our loved ones who are now deceased.

In my personal list of wrongdoings is the fact that according to Jewish custom, I have failed Big Irv. I should have had a grave marker in place by the first anniversary of his death, but I have not accomplished that. Had I buried him in a Jewish cemetery, I would have had a stone dedication ceremony as well. I cried guilty tears over these issues today, even though I wonder if these rules pertain since his sendoff was Catholic. I don't know. What I do know is this: We are taught that by the end of Yom Kippur, God has forgiven us for our sins. We are also taught to forgive ourselves for these sins. If we don't, it means we are holding ourselves to a higher standard than God does. I like this rationale and I am thrilled to get the grave marker off my conscience and onto my to-do list. I will take care of it this week!

Cried out, I left Temple and went to Shana's house for the break-the-fast meal. It was wonderful to be with the whole family and to watch the antics of eight grandkids after such a serious day.

Friday, September 25, 2015

Dear Diary,

I ordered the cemetery marker for Big Irv today. As teary as I have been as of late, it was a surprisingly unemotional experience. Perhaps because the process itself was so interesting? The cemetery representative and I merely sat down with his computer, its design-a-tombstone program, and a big screen upon which to view the marker as we created it. It was neat, like creating a greeting card on Shutterfly.

Before meeting with this man, I visited Big Irv's burial site and photographed the grave markers of his family members so his would fit in with the rest of the gang. With the style thus chosen, it was a simple matter of adding the specifics of Big Irv's life. Besides listing his name and dates of birth and death, the cemetery required that I add at least one religious symbol. There were tons to choose from: angels, praying hands, rosaries, crosses, and the like. I chose the most basic cross and placed it between his dates of birth and death where a dash might otherwise appear. There was also a place where I could add a Bible verse, or other words, if I was so inclined. I was in such a fine frame of mind that I toyed with the idea of honoring all the fun Big Irv and I had shared by saying, "For a Good Time, Call Big Irv," but that sounded so much like bathroom graffiti that I chose something else instead. The cemetery rep typed it in, and just that quickly, the mock-up of the finished product was up on the big screen for me to see. I loved it! I wrote out a check and placed my order. It will arrive in four to eight weeks.

Instead of scratching more things off my to-do list for the day, I decided to go home and watch that other Bill Nighy movie I bought on Amazon. It's not exactly in character for me to do this, but why not? For a good time, trust Tootser?

Friday Afternoon at the Movies

Gideon's Daughter
DIRECTOR: Stephen Poliakoff
WRITER: Stephen Poliakoff
RELEASE DATE: 2005
RUNNING TIME: 1 Hour, 45 Minutes
ALSO FEATURING: Miranda Richardson, Emily Blunt, Robert Lindsay, Ronni Ancona, and Tom Hardy
FRIENDLY CONNECTIONS: Bill Nighy and Miranda Richardson worked together in another Stephen Poliakoff project, *The Lost Prince*, in 2003. They went on to work together in *Harry Potter and the Deathly Hallows Part I* in 2010, and they both provided voices for the animated movie *A Fox's Tale* in 2008. Bill Nighy and Emily Blunt went on to work together in *Wild Target* in 2010. Other Bill Nighy/Stephen Poliakoff connections were listed previously.

AN UPFRONT APOLOGY: There are all sorts of political things happening in this movie, as is Stephen Poliakoff's style. Per Wikipedia, the film "is set against the backdrop of New Labour's rise to power, the death of Princess Diana, and the ill-advised development of the Millennium Dome." As is my style, all of this went over my head. What I focused on instead was a beautiful story about love, loss, and parenthood.

Gideon's Daughter is the story of public relations guru Gideon Warner (Bill Nighy). Though wildly successful when we first meet him, he is a man of humble beginnings. His father was a chauffeur, and often in his childhood he rode in the father's car as they drove by and peeked into windows to see how the other half lived. Gideon's early days in the business found him as an ordinary PR guy promoting washed-up comedians. But then somehow, almost magically, the high and mighty—plus every manner of celebrity—start coming to him for advice. Not even he knows how or why that has happened.

Unfortunately, Gideon's personal life is not quite as successful as his career. He is a widower who has played around plenty to the dismay of his only child, Natasha (Emily Blunt). For years, Natasha has held a grudge against him because he left the hospital room at the crucial time when her mother/his wife died of cancer. Does she know he was on the phone with his girlfriend for those minutes? And does it matter or does his disappearance alone damn him in her eyes? For whatever reason—maybe because he is too busy at work—he does not endeavor to fix this breach in their relationship, and though they continue to live under the same (exquisite) roof, they are estranged. As the movie starts, Natasha is on the verge of high school graduation and about to go off to college. This unhinges him, as he fears she is leaving him forever.

At this point, Gideon meets Stella (Miranda Richardson), a woman whose young son was killed when he was hit by a car while riding his bike. Stella is nothing like the starlets and society women with whom Gideon usually associates. Indeed her lopsided haircut could be construed as an attempt at self-mutilation, and her wildly colored wardrobe is possibly a glaring effort to come back from the darkness in which she has found herself. A woman like Stella would not even make it into a focus group Gideon might assemble professionally. However, she understands his feeling of loss over his child, and so they bond.

When Natasha goes off to university and continuously neglects to answer the phone when Gideon calls, he gets crazed with fear. Has someone harmed her? Or has she split from him forever due to their original rift? Either option is horrendous. In the end, he finds her but has a catatonic breakdown in the process. Stella comes to the rescue with a plan that will save them all—or so the viewer hopes—because they are all very sympathetic characters who are deserving of a happy ending.

There are many things I liked about this movie:

1. It was great to see Bill Nighy in the role of a sexually magnetic man. We are told his love life has been prolific through the years, and by movie's end, we have seen him in bed with two different women. Woo hoo! Lucky for Gideon Warner, but lucky for Bill Nighy fans as well, as we actually get to see his naked back and arms. At any rate, when we first meet him, he is in a relationship with Barbara (Ronni Ancona), and by movie's end he is with Stella.

2. It was also fun to ponder the concept of gurus after watching this film. There were two things in the movie that were pulling Gideon away from his work: his impending emotional breakdown and his growing interest in spending time with Stella. Interestingly, the less he listens to clients, the more successful he becomes. The Gideon Warner mystique carries the day even when he is not emotionally present and when he has stopped performing. This reminded me of the character Chauncey Gardiner—aka Chance the Gardener—in Jerzy Kosinski's book and movie of the same name, *Being There*. Both cases remind us to be careful in following gurus.

3. And speaking of gurus, due to Gideon's fame and status as a PR genius, his friend, William Sneath (Robert Lindsay), is writing a book about him. Indeed, Sneath is the narrator of this movie and we all listen in as he dictates the manuscript to his secretary. In telling Gideon's story, he spits out some interesting parent/child observations that hit close to home for me:

4. He notes "the power a child has over a parent."

5. He asks about our children, "Do they ever really forgive us?"

6. And he comments that "When they go to university, it's like a little death."

7. As a woman who is still affected by empty-nest syndrome even as my children move through their thirties, I was delighted by the validation this movie gives to such a loss. Not only is Gideon Warner bereft, he is catatonic. It is also wonderful to note that the "out-of-control parent" here is not some hysterical female, but instead a high-powered male. And finally, even though the viewer is firmly reminded that Gideon's loss pales by comparison to Stella's, Gideon's loss is still treated as worthy of sympathy, even by Stella.

8. Further validation comes from the fact that film critics loved the storyline, as evidenced by the many awards this movie won. Both Bill Nighy and Emily Blunt won Golden Globe Awards for their performances, and the production itself won a Peabody Award.

9. Speaking of Emily Blunt, the DVD has bonus materials at the end, including an interview with her. In it, she said this about my man: "Bill Nighy is a wonderful, wonderful man and friend. He's a true gentleman of the business and he's effortless to be around and work with. And I laughed so much with him. He's great."

10. The final thing I loved about this movie is that when Stella and Gideon first meet, she gives him her business card, which he ultimately uses to track her down. Yes, yes, I know that she loaned him a camera and he needed to return it to her, but just the same, I was thrilled to see that Bill Nighy has some experience with the concept of using a business card to get in touch with another human being. Have I mentioned that when I sent him mine, I gave him four ways (4 ways!) to contact me?

Sunday, September 27, 2015

Dear Diary,

I just talked to Roberta and told her all about Dylan's second birthday party last night.

"His mommy created a Star Wars party for him," I said, "complete with Jabba the Hot Dogs, Princess Lay's Potato Chips, Yoda Soda, and the like. It was adorable."

"Your kids come up with some great party ideas," she agreed.

"I can't argue with you about that. But wait until you hear this part. Dylan's grandpa showed up in a Darth Vader costume that scared the daylights out of the birthday boy. He literally jumped into my arms when Darth Vader entered the room! But then when the grandpa took off the helmet to reveal his true self, Dylan resumed his normal life, only to jump right back into my arms when the grandpa put the helmet on again! Except that the poor kid was so distressed, it was really funny," I said, laughing at the memory.

"That sounds great and so do you," she said.

"I love getting to hold that little guy under any circumstance."

"And you love being with all your kids under any circumstance."

"You got that one right," I agreed. "Plus, it's great when I have something to do on a Saturday night. Hey! Here's something else that's great: I'm sleeping a little bit better these days. I can fall asleep at night; I just can't stay asleep. But it's a start."

"Indeed it is. In fact, it sounds like it's time for Roberta's Recovery Plan Part II…"

"Uh-oh, I'm getting nervous. Now what?"

"I see a sewing machine in your future," Roberta said. "How about you?"

"Nice try, Bird, but I have been thinking of travel instead. It's been so much fun being in the Bill Nighy version of Fantasyland that I think I want to try out Disney's brand next. You're welcome to join me…"

"Thanks for the offer. I would maybe do *Lion King* on Broadway with you, but you're on your own for Orlando. However, you love Disney World, so it's a great plan. But why don't you drop your sewing machine off for a tuneup before you leave town, and that way it will be ready to go when you are."

October

Thursday, October 1, 2015

Dear Diary,

There were no movies we cared to see today, so we just went out to lunch. Sue was with us and she likes burgers, so I suggested a few places nearby and thus Paxton's was chosen. It was one of Big Irv's favorite places for a sandwich. He ate the Big Paxton there—no relation—with its ten ounces of beef and with its bacon and two kinds of cheese all on a Kaiser roll. While Big Irv and I used to eat there several times a month, I haven't been back there without him. It's changed a little. There is now an enclosure around the outside patio to keep out the elements. I'm not sure I like it, but change is inevitable. I've probably added a protective outer shell, too, over these many months.

Another difference—a big one—was that some other couple was sitting at our table, the high-top by the front window, second table out from the interior wall. Their clasped hands were on the table top as they awaited their food just as our clasped hands used to be. I didn't see it if he likewise rotated the back of her hand up to his lips for a kiss. That would have been weird if he did that. And weird if I saw it. Thank you, God, for keeping me safe from that trauma. Watching them chat away easily at our table was painful enough.

I miss talking to Big Irv. I miss having him take my side in every dispute I have with a third party. If I was annoyed with someone, he was annoyed with them too. And if someone dared to hurt my feelings or make me sad, he was downright angry, calling that person a motherfucker or a piece of shit. As much as I have taught my children—and my grandchildren—not to talk like that (!), I kind of liked it when it was him speaking out in defense of me. And all of those conversations ended with him telling me, "You're a good Tootser," his way of applying a salve to my soul.

I know I am very fortunate to have lots of close friends. Roberta! Vera! Robin! How could I live without them? But as close as I am with each of those wonderful women, my relationship with Big Irv was different because he lived each installment of my life with me. It's like watching an entire television series with someone as compared to giving that person a *TV Guide*-like synopsis of the season. Since I walk with Robin five days a week, she comes closest to getting all the nuances of the stories of my life. But it doesn't compare to what Big Irv and I had. And I miss that and I miss him. And while I'm on this topic, why does the house make so many strange sounds in the night now that he's gone?

It was a sound that brought me out of my lunchtime reverie today, the sound of our waitress's voice as she asked to take our order. Vera had the veggie wrap. Sue had the burger. Very unlike Big Irv, she ordered the regular fries instead of the sweet potato fries. What was she thinking? It goes without saying that I had the Mandarin chicken salad. Meal choices out of the way, Vera told us the latest escapades of Avalon, the teenage granddaughter whom she is raising. And we heard all about the latest man Sue met—and did not click with—through match.com. And of course our meals came, and we ate them, and then we were done. At that time, I looked over to Big Irv's and my table and that couple was gone! It was confusing and incomprehensible to me! It took my breath away! And it still makes me sad now. Gone. That couple was gone.

FRIDAY, OCTOBER 2, 2015

Dear Diary,

I have been eating nonstop since my emotional experience at Paxton's. As I sat at the kitchen table self-medicating today, I Googled my guy and read an interesting article about *his* food obsession, Marmite. The source is movieroomreviews.com dated February 27, 2015, and the headline is this: "Bill Nighy 'got busted' smuggling Marmite." Evidently, when he was traveling to India to film *The Second Best Exotic Marigold Hotel,* he packed a jar of Marmite that was too large to go through security. An airport employee came to his rescue by finding thirty tiny jars into which the Marmite could be subdivided, and in this manner my man made it to India food fetish in hand.

I went on to read about Marmite at its website, marmite.co.uk, where I learned there is a great schism between its lovers and haters. At wikihow.com I learned how to eat it: spread it on toast *very* sparingly, mix it with butter to dilute its taste, take small bites, take big drinks with each bite, and try not to smell it before eating it. I am thinking it sounds so awful that I won't be dabbing it on his cheek and licking it off any time soon—even in my dreams.

Speaking of such, off to bed I go, hoping for a better day tomorrow. Thank goodness for soccer games and Saturday Night at the Movies.

Saturday Night at the Movies

Lawless Heart
DIRECTORS: Tom Hunsinger and Neil Hunter
WRITERS: Tom Hunsinger and Neil Hunter
RELEASE DATE: 2001
RUNNING TIME: 1 Hour, 40 Minutes
ALSO FEATURING: Douglas Henshall, Tom Hollander, and as the two women in Bill Nighy's life, Ellie Haddington (as his wife) and Clémentine Célarié (as his love interest)
FRIENDLY CONNECTIONS: Bill Nighy and Tom Hollander have worked together many times as detailed in my review of *About Time.*

This movie opens with the death of a thirty-eight-year-old man named Stuart Marsh. We later learn that he died accidentally in a boating accident, but this is significant only because the death was unexpected and took everyone by surprise. The funeral quickly segues to the reception, where we meet the three main characters: Nick, who was Stuart's lover; Dan, who was his brother-in-law; and Tim, who was his childhood friend, though the two had not seen each other in eight years. Tom Hollander plays the part of Nick; Bill Nighy is Dan; and Douglas Henshall is Tim. Stuart's unexpected death causes each of these men to act out in some manner, as they remember Stuart's philosophy, to "seize life by the horns." As the title of the movie suggests, all cases of acting out have to do with matters of the heart, as the three men find themselves subject to unsettling desires after the funeral. Nick, while gay, manages to find comfort in the arms of a woman named Charlie, whom he meets at a party. Dan contemplates an affair with Corinne, the local florist, after chatting with her at the funeral reception. And Tim, who is a footloose fellow, falls madly in love with Leah.

It is very interesting the way these stories unfold. Writers Neil Hunter and Tom Hunsinger present the three stories one at a time. We start out at the funeral reception, watch Dan and Corinne interact; see what happens to them in the days following the funeral, and then magically, we are transported back to the funeral reception again. This time we see what was happening to Nick at the event, and then we follow Nick for the few days following the funeral. And then we repeat the process one more time to learn all that happened to Tim there and to see things from his point of view. Of course "in reality" these three stories are happening simultaneously, but this format allows the viewer more insight with each retelling. As *TV Guide's* Maitland McDonagh explains in his review, "The film's three-thread structure is deftly handled; in each succeeding section, stories from the previous one are expanded on and/or shown in a different light. Apparently inexplicable bits of dialogue and behavior are explained, motivations come into focus, relationships are clarified, and ironies reveal themselves."

Of the three characters and their story lines, I liked Tim and his tale the least. As a childhood friend of the deceased, he must have been in his late thirties too, yet he acted like an irresponsible teenager. Beyond the fact that he was broke and homeless, when Nick showed compassion and gave him lodging, Tim repaid the favor by throwing a wild party. When Nick threw him out, Tim tried to borrow money from Dan, and when Dan refused him, Tim tried extortion. Not a nice guy.

As for Nick, I liked him a lot and I felt great sympathy for him. The confusion he felt at the loss of his lover, Stuart, was palpable, and the writers made it crystal clear how he could find comfort in the arms of the girl named Charlie, though the friendship caused him problems not only with his sexual identity, but also with Stuart's sister, Judy, the person who would decide if Nick inherited money from Stuart or not.

While I did not personally identify with either of these stories, the story of Dan, Bill Nighy's character, spoke to me greatly. Nick is married to Judy and therefore the brother-in-law of the deceased. He is rattled by the funeral, or is it by life in general? When we meet him, he is chain smoking—and seems very skilled and adept at that endeavor—and a bit disheveled, with a collar standing up at attention instead of lying down next to his tie. At the funeral reception, Corinne, the florist, approaches him and tries to converse with him, but this is an endeavor at which he is not very skilled or adept.

"Are you family?" she asks.

"No. Well, yes," he replied.

"You look tired," she tried next.

"I didn't sleep well," he said.

"Because of the funeral?" she offered.

"No, I never sleep well," he said, shutting things down again.

"Perhaps you're anxious?" she tried again.

"I don't think so."

"Depressed?" she tried still again.

"How would I know?"

"How would you know?" she said, throwing it back at him.

"I've often wondered if I'm depressed," he offered, using six whole words!

"Because you've never been happy?" she asked.

"What do people mean by the word?" he replied.

"Happy?" she queried.

"No, depressed, but happy too."

From this inauspicious starting point, the two characters finally break into a meaningful conversation. Throughout it, Dan seems to be studying Corinne and hanging on her every word as if he is trying to figure out not only his diagnosis, but the cure for his life. Their conversation lasts about five minutes and includes several meaty tidbits:

1. Dan says that when one is young, "life is like a boulevard. It is wide and full of possibility and everything opens to you." She finishes up his thought by suggesting that "life has become narrow."

2. His next analogy about his stage in life is to say that "it's like the whodunit when you've worked out who did it and there's still fifty pages left to go."

3. Her next volley is, "The question is, the life you have, is it the life you want?" She also reminds him that it takes courage to get the life you want.

These questions about life are right up my alley, so of course I identified with Dan's character and loved the section of the movie that focused on him. Since it was the first of the three stories told and this entire conversation happened within the first seven and a half minutes of the movie, the scene was easy to find, watch, rewind, find, watch, rewind, etc. And I liked that very much, just like when the same thing happened in *Hot Fuzz*. As I watched and re-watched this part, I came up with Dan's diagnosis—he's suffering from the human condition—but I am clueless as to the cure. Darn!

You will need to see the film to know whether Dan had an affair with Corinne. But I am wondering if his actual choice makes a difference. Yes, of course there would be ramifications to his choice—to fling or not to fling?—but in either case, a meaningful life could be found. That's odd to say, but I think it is true. Odder still is the fact that both choices require courage.

In the unauthorized biography, Bill Nighy speaks of the making of this film. He says the writers called the actors together and explained the bare bones of the story, the characters, and their relationships. They then asked the actors to help improvise from there. Sitting around a table—with lots of coffee—they all built the scenes and characters. This model was successful, because the movie won the British Independent Film Award for Best Screenplay. It was also nominated for four other awards: Best British Independent Film, Best Director, Best Technical Achievement, and Best Actor—for Bill Nighy.

Knowing Bill Nighy helped create some of the dialog gives me pause. As a woman who is trying to dream up a relationship with this man—who I hope is emotionally responsive—how do I reconcile that with Dan/Bill Nighy's line, "I suppose I have emotions, but I don't make a meal of them"? I guess I will just have to pray that someone else imagined and wrote the line even if he did deliver it in Best Actor fashion, 100 percent believably.

SUNDAY, OCTOBER 4, 2015

Dear Diary,

As a result of last night's movie, I have a couple confessions to make. The first one is that in spite of the fact that I have watched scads of Bill Nighy movies, I still have a little lots of difficulty deciphering his British accent. This causes me to worry that my future relationship with him will be exactly like my past relationship with Big Irv—we will literally have trouble speaking English to each other. Isn't that crazy? The way I have assuaged the issue with the DVDs I have watched at home is to seek out the main menu on the disc and look for the bonus materials. I then choose "Subtitles" from the options offered, turn them on, and voilà, printed English words accompany the British voices! I have been ever so proud of my ingenuity in this regard. The system has failed me twice. The first time was when I recorded the Johnny Worricker trilogy off my local PBS station and had no bonus materials from which to choose. The second time was during last night's viewing of *Lawless Heart*. Yes, it had subtitles. Yes, I could turn them on. But what accompanied the British voices on the screen were Spanish words instead of English. ¡Ay, caramba!

My other confession is more serious. I am reluctant to even speak it aloud. I don't want to say anything negative about this man I adore, nor do I want to put any bad ideas out into the universe. But this troubles me, so here it is, dear Diary. I am worried about Bill Nighy's health after his years of smoking. I have known that beloved Bill is an ex-smoker, but last night's movie was jarring. The ease and agility with which he flipped around a cigarette was visually captivating and did more than just hint at experience. That he puffed away on three different cigarettes in the seven minutes of screen time—telescoped though that time may have been—was also disconcerting. But still, that was just a movie, so I Googled "Bill Nighy Smoking" to get the real scoop.

Various articles online set the year of his smoking cessation at 2003. *The Guardian*, for instance, said on September 13, 2003: "It is now 142 days since he stopped smoking." Doing the math, he was smoke-free starting April 25, 2003. The same article tells us more about his addicted days when it quotes him saying, "There just weren't enough hours in the day to drink and smoke enough, and all the time your brain's working up some bullshit to persuade yourself you're doing the right thing, that you're in control." But of course he was not in control, as he explains in this interview with Inquirer.net dated September 27, 2014: "I smoked for England, Ireland, Scotland, and Wales. I smoked passionately, like a slave, a fool."

So that is Bill Nighy's reality, and now here is mine: Mom gave up smoking in 1983 and died of lung cancer in 2002. Big Irv gave up smoking sometime before meeting me in 2005 and died of lung cancer in 2014. This smoking thing is more than a nasty habit; it's a killer. How many loved ones can I lose to the dreaded disease it brings?

Forgive me for being so morbid, dear Diary. I am working on my October column on how to survive the death of a friend, and I guess it has me down.

Dear Diary,

Two things worked together to make me look awful today. The first was that there was so little time between my workout and when Vera picked me up for the movie that I was unable to put on makeup. The second was all that crying I did on the way home from the gym. Really, can you believe that my '60s on 6 radio station played Sammy Davis Jr.'s "The Shelter of Your Arms" and followed it up with Roy Orbison's "Crying"?

When I explained the genesis of my looks to Vera, she asked very gently, "Does Big Irv come to you in your dreams?"

"Does he come to me in my dreams?" I repeated and then shook my head "no."

"Mort comes to me," she replied, referring to a man she had long ago dated and loved. They had stayed in touch through the years, and she told me all about him when he died about a year ago.

"What does that mean? How does he come to you?" I asked her.

"It's always the same kind of dream. I come upon him in some location where he's not aware that I'm seeing him, and then I watch him do something mundane. In the last dream, he was putting on his tie as I had watched him do dozens of times in life. He stood there at the mirror with his crisply starched dress shirt buttoned all the way up to the neck, his collar turned up, and his necktie in place. He had the skinny end of the tie in his left hand and the fat end in his right. He then tugged on those ends, pulling the tie back and forth, back and forth, back and forth across his collar until he got it exactly where he wanted it, and then he quickly and adeptly made the Windsor knot. And then after getting the knot finished and the collar folded down, he pivoted away from the mirror. As he turned around, he saw me and he smiled. Somehow he went from just being in shirtsleeves as he put the tie on to having his suit coat on too. And it's not like the dream had been in black and white and that it suddenly went to color, it's just that I hadn't been aware of color until he turned around, and there it was, a bright red hanky in his breast pocket. You know that dream from college days when you are going to class, but you don't have your homework and your heart is pounding—thump, thump, thumping in your chest? Mort dreams are the antithesis of that. I wake up in bed awash in warmth and calmness."

"Was Bob Marley playing in your head—every little thing's gonna be all right?" I asked in all seriousness.

"No, but that sure seems to be the message."

"Is it the exact dream each time?"

"No, it changes. Each time I come in on him doing something different, but it's always something mundane and always something I've seen him do before. What remains the same, though, is the vividness of the dream, the fact that I can remember it long after I wake up, and of course that wonderful sense of calm."

"How many of these dreams have you had?"

"A total of three," she said. "He was at his desk once. Another time, I saw his back as he talked to a group of men across a room."

"Has he ever spoken to you in one of these dreams?"

"No," she replied, "except for the message that is so clear that even you picked it up." It was a good thing we were at a stop sign then, because we just looked each other in the eye for a good long time.

"That's really neat, Vera," I said. "I wish Big Irv would come to me in the night." She loves me, so I know she wishes that for me too. Unable to provide that specific gift, she gave me a different one; she got me to the movie theater, thus helping me keep my mind off '60s on 6.

Today's movie was *Grandma*, starring Lily Tomlin as Elle, a lesbian poet who is recovering from the recent death of her long-term partner. Elle's eighteen-year-old granddaughter, Sage, arrives on the scene, pregnant and in need of cash for an abortion. Elle is broke but tries various avenues to come up with the cash. As a last resort, she turns to her ex-husband, Karl, for help. By the way, Karl is not Sage's grandfather. Elle has not seen Karl in years but is willing to do anything to help her grandchild. Ultimately he turns Elle down, and his reason for doing so reveals a huge and meaty plot point—but no spoiler here, no way, no how. Eventually the women find a solution to their problem and we hope they live happily ever after.

Since I started the day fretting over messages from the universe via radio waves, I am surprised I was not more affected by Elle's status as a grieving "widow." Didn't the universe likewise bring me that message to ponder? I don't know. I just know I did not identify with Elle, perhaps because I am not a lesbian poet? There was, however, something about the movie that did affect me. Indeed, it felt like a cosmic zinger. The actor who played Karl was Sam Elliott, and the last time Vera and I saw him he was in a movie with Blythe Danner. That movie was called *I'll See You in My Dreams*. I hear *The Twilight Zone* theme song in my head. Did someone turn on '60s on 6?

OCTOBER 9, 2015

A Slice of Life: A Monthly Column
CHANGE IS

Twenty some years ago, I made a quilt with words pieced into the design. It said, CHANGE IS. To illustrate the concept, I surrounded my words with a pattern called ocean waves because waves roll in and roll out constantly changing, creating the shifting sand of metaphor. At that point in time, I was going through divorce and feeling guilt over the fact that I had changed, so in the caption that accompanied the quilt I wrote, "Change is. It exists. It cannot be denied. It is not good or bad. It just is—end of sentence; period. Do the trees feel guilty for changing? Do the clouds? Do the waves? Then why do I?"

Now here I am, two decades later, stunned by the concept that even change changes. Back then I struggled with the fact that I had changed, and now I struggle with the reality that the world around me keeps changing. I ache specifically over the recent loss of a loved one, my friend of almost ten years, Big Irv, the first close friend I have lost to death.

Beyond the void created by losing this specific significant person, Big Irv's death drives home two facts to me. In that my contemporaries and I are in our sixties, this is going to happen again with other friends, and it's also going to happen to me. For now I choose to ~~bury~~ hide my head in the sand and ignore thoughts of my own demise to focus instead on the question: How do I rebound after losing a loved one?

I am fortunate that my Jewish heritage has a response to this question. Jewish mourning practices contain three specific stages, each with decreasing intensity. The first stage lasts for seven days, the second stage lasts for the remainder of the first month, and the third stage lasts for just shy of the first year. However—and this is BIG—one only enters that third stage if mourning for a parent. With all other loss, one is to return to a normal life after thirty days with these caveats: Jews remember the anniversary (yartzeit) of a loved one's death annually, and there are four Jewish holidays each year at which a memorial service (yizkor) is included. With both yartzeit and yizkor, candles are lit, names are read, and a special prayer is said. In effect, one is given permission to cry. For millennia it has been thought that this prescription allowed for a full—but not excessive—expression of grief. Who am I to question it now?

As boldly as I make this pronouncement, I confess that I am tardy in following this course after losing Big Irv. It's been fifteen months since his death, and I often still sob on the sofa. But the point is not just getting over Big Irv; it's preparing myself to do this again (and again and again) in the future as more loss surely comes my way. While I am certain that there is a learning curve and that I'll get better at it after each experience of loss, this is hardly comforting. But then on the other hand, it *is* comforting because there is a bigger point here: As my days become fewer, they become more significant and I have to find a way not to lose too many of them to this particular brand of sorrow.

This is where my religion's mourning practices continue to come in handy. They not only instruct me to move past the loss, they give me a clue how to go about it. Whether one is mourning for the thirty-day period or for eleven months, a special prayer (kaddish) is said daily and the prayer is supposed to be said *in community*, with one's congregation, not in the privacy of one's home. One could call this a stricture, but in reality it opens a door by getting the mourner at least away from sobbing on the sofa, if not away from his or her Kleenex box. Being in community, one just might make a new friend or two, which comes in handy after just having lost one. This road to new friendships is a "social security" worthy of embrace.

Though I ask forgiveness for such ~~grave~~ somber thoughts today, the truth is that I have always been a serious student of life, so the contemplation of death is not new to me. As my friends laughed and sang "When I'm Sixty-Four" along with the Beatles in 1967, I felt a little chill as I realized death—or at least old age—was playing peek-a-boo with me. Even more jarring for me was Simon and Garfunkel's song "Old Friends," which came out in 1968. It spoke of old men sharing not only a park bench but sharing the same fear. That the word "fear" was in the singular rattled me to the core. Now that I am sixty-three and two-thirds years old and now that I have experienced the loss of Big Irv, I'm wondering if peek-a-boo is over and if it is now time for hide-and-seek instead. I think that is the case, though I will hope not to be "it" any time soon.

But even if I am, I need to equally embrace my religion's basic belief that death is not a tragedy but instead a natural process, a part of life. It's like those trees, clouds, and ocean waves I mentioned earlier. They keep on changing and changing and changing because CHANGE IS. It exists. It cannot be denied. It is not good or bad. It just is—end of sentence, period. I sure hope to convince myself of this soon.

Happier days ahead? Stay tuned...

SATURDAY, OCTOBER 10, 2015

Dear Diary,

I just wrote my column on the topic of change. It was a personal triumph for me that I did not mention my empty-nest issue as one of the ways the world has changed around me. My poor friends listen as I continue to beat that dead horse, but I don't want to make my readers suffer as well. For your ears only, here's the latest on that front: It seems that at the ages of seven, seven and a half, and nine, my three oldest grandgirls have gotten iPads and have the capability to send text messages. And so they do…often to me! Additionally, nine-year-old Tillie likes to cook and she has been coming into the kitchen on family dinner nights to see what she can do to help. "Just hang out and talk to me!" I want to shout as I give her veggies to arrange on a platter. Somehow I failed to realize that my eight little grand-kids—who are such distractions to adult conversation—would grow into conversationalists of their own.

This change is wonderful, but as I now understand things, it is bound to change. These older grandchildren will turn into teenagers and turn their backs on all of us adults. But then, the littler grandkids will move into place as people with whom to text and talk. And when that group moves on to teen years as well, well…their parents will be facing their own empty nests and might be looking for someone to hang out with, and I might just be the one they pick. Ah, the passage of time. It's really kind of funny how this is working out.

I see change in more than just the family situation. Borrowing from Bill Nighy's hit song in *Love Actually,* "Change is all around me… it's everywhere I go." It's even in a place that I thought was quite unchangeable—Bill Nighy's wardrobe. After Googling images of the man for months, I have found a new source for them on Pinterest, which is a photo-sharing website. One goes to the Pinterest website, types in some words to perform a search, and then watches as scads of photos come up to illustrate that search. As for me, I have created a bunch of pinboards. I am collecting photos of gorgeous quilts. I am collecting toddler craft ideas for Marmel School. I am collecting easy recipes for Thursday night family dinners. And of course, I am collecting photos of Bill Nighy. I waste far too much time on this website. Indeed I hear Big Irv chastising me that I have too much time on my hands. Be that as it may, I am noticing something major about beloved Bill: His wardrobe is changing, and many photos find him in jeans! After all I have read about his bespoke suits, and about the fact that if you want him at his best you better put him in a lounge suit, this is pretty shocking.

On Pinterest one can "visit" the site from which a photograph originated, and so on one of the jean-clad photos I did. This picture showed BN crossing what appeared to be a busy street and says it was saved from the U.K. version of *Esquire*. Visiting that website, I found an article in the style and fashion section of the magazine called "How to Wear It/No Brain Smart Casual." It starts by asking the question, "Stuck for what to wear on a smart casual day? Take some tips from the ever-dapper Bill Nighy and keep it simple." Four items of his look are then mentioned:

- A light blue dress shirt by Uniqlo, £20
- A dark blue blazer from Mr Porter, £625
- Dark denim jeans from My-Wardrobe, £120
- Brown loafers from Mr Porter, £340

The key to BN's look, *Esquire* says, is that his blazer and shirt fit perfectly, that the dark brown shoes compliment the outfit without overpowering it, and that the straight jeans bring the whole outfit down to earth. Converting the cost of the outfit from British pounds to U.S. dollars, this down-to-earth look costs about $1,500.

272 · Lorie Kleiner Eckert

I am rattled, not by the price, but by this departure in his look and have no idea when the seismic shift took place. The *Esquire* article is dated September 4, 2012. Not even a year earlier, on November 15, 2011, *Mister Porter The Journal* had an article about BN called "The Look: Mr. Bill Nighy." In this article, writer Mansel Fletcher says, "Discovering that the revered British actor Mr. Nighy is a man of stylistic principles comes as no great surprise. When asked what exactly enticed him to do a shoot for *Mister Porter*, he simply states: 'It was the idea—a meditation on the navy blue suit. I found that concept intriguing.' No wonder, because it turns out he only wears blue suits. I don't mean that when he wears suits he only wears blue ones, but that he only, ever, wears blue suits—even on the ski slopes."

I wonder what this writer from *Mister Porter The Journal* would think about Bill Nighy's smart casual look? I wonder what he would think of other pictures I have found on Pinterest showing BN doing his work for Oxfam? Oxfam is the international confederation of organizations working worldwide to find solutions to poverty and injustice. Linking to Oxfam's website, I found photos of beloved Bill's visit to Malawi, Africa, in November 2012. In these images, BN not only has on jeans, but he wears no jacket and his shirt is not tucked in. While I am sure this is the manner in which he has "rolled up his sleeves" and gotten down to work, and while I find this work extremely admirable, it is still very surprising to see him dressed in this manner.

I can't let go of this topic until I address one more thing: the brown loafers that are a part of his dapper look. Just a few pages ago, I listed many quotes from brainyquote.com but left out this one: "Never go anywhere you have to wear brown shoes." Whoa, mama! These revisions to his personal code astound me.

Of a much smaller magnitude on the Richter scale, I have one more change to write about: Saturday Night at the Movies is again canceled tonight. My plans for the evening are NOT with beloved Bill Nighy but instead with beloved son Scott. It is his turn to be my date to the Broadway Series. We are seeing *Motown the Musical* and dining beforehand at Via Vite. That's a change too, this "beforehand" at Via Vite. That was one of Big Irv's favorite places to go on theater nights, but of course he wanted to dine after the theater instead of before.

Changes large and small:
with my nest
with Bill Nighy's wardrobe
with my Saturday night routine
with my theater-going habit
Changes and more changes.
What can I say?
I feel it in my fingers, I feel it in my toes…change is.

This is a Python library for creating beautiful command-line interfaces.

Sunday, October 11, 2015

Dear Diary,

I am perhaps a little jealous of a journalist named Ariel Leve. She has interviewed Bill Nighy twice for *The Sunday Times Magazine*. One of the interviews, dated January 18, 2009, was the cover story. Photos abound, including the one on the cover, a full-page shot of beloved Bill with eyeglasses askew. Both interviews are extensive and indicate lots of time spent in each other's company. For the 2009 story, they are together at a west London gastropub and also at a restaurant at Fortnum & Mason, an upmarket department store. The earlier interview, in 2007, found them in New York City having tea together at his hotel. When that venue got noisy, they continued their conversation in the back of a car as they headed to the Morgan Library for a Bob Dylan exhibition. In both interviews, they communicate via text messages and voice mail messages as well. If this isn't enough to provoke jealousy, he provided a blurb for the jacket of a book she wrote in 2009. Argh!

But okay, jealousy aside, they are wonderful and informative interviews. I had read the 2007 interview before. In it he speaks about the world being divided into two parts, those who love Bob Dylan and those who don't. As I recall, his mom fell on the wrong side of the divide. As for BN, he listens to BD daily. He says that BD is the most important artist in his life, explaining it this way: "If I'm in trouble, I go to Bob Dylan. And if I'm feeling really good, I go to Bob Dylan. I don't know where I'd be without him, really. I'm never tired of listening to any of it."

Beyond explaining why Bob Dylan's music is alluring to beloved Bill, the interview also explains why the profession of acting is alluring to him. It was in his teens that the reality of working for a living hit Bill Nighy. He couldn't imagine having to get up every day and do something he didn't particularly like. When he heard that as an actor he might have stretches of unemployment, he was thrilled. In his words, "the idea that you could legitimately loaf was glamorous for me." An additional perk of acting is the fact of being on tour. Other actors may hate it, but not BN. He likes going places. Where? He doesn't care, though he prefers going to new places he's never seen before. (Oh! I love his thought process, dear Diary! Maybe that aborted fan letter inviting him to Ohio wasn't so crazy after all.)

As for the 2009 interview, two things are particularly compelling. The first is BN's Howard Hughes statement. Though beloved Bill admits he is a solitary man, one who feels "slightly disarmed" in a social situation, one who has "difficulty persuading [himself] that [he's] on a guest list," and one who prefers the company of books and music, he still does not like being compared to the famous recluse Howard Hughes. "Oh come on!" he says, "I bite my nails. I can't be Howard Hughes!" The second thing that was compelling in the article was Bill Nighy's confession that he has "a tendency to accentuate the negative." He goes on to say, "You have to be discreet about it, otherwise it alarms people. I try not to feature it in conversation too much. It's like being undercover." The Howard Hughes topic has me aching for him and the going-undercover topic has me aching for myself, as I identify with him.

What I recognize here is that I, too, have a topic I need to stop "featuring" in conversation: the empty-nest thing. In my case, I don't think I alarm people, I just bore them to tears. But here's the thing, if continuing to talk about it is so ridiculous that I need to go undercover with it, isn't continuing to have feelings about it likewise ridiculous? What a shocking sentiment! And like all shocking sentiments in my life, I discussed it with Roberta in our Sunday night debriefing, telling her about the Ariel Leve/Bill Nighy interviews as well.

"On the one hand, I feel a little embarrassed about all the years I have spent moaning and complaining about this, Bird, and on the other hand, I am not quite sure I'm finished."

"Well, recognizing that you're stuck is the first step to getting unstuck, isn't it? And as far as embarrassment goes, perhaps it's a good emotion as a catalyst for change."

"That may be true, but I'm just so embarrassed. I even wrote a column about it a couple of months ago," I said matter-of-factly. But then I got a little crazy when I added dramatically, "It has been my obsession!" I said this to make Roberta laugh, as that word triggers one of our fond memories. We were in New York together, walking through Bloomingdale's cosmetic department, when an employee stepped into our path trying to give us a fragrance sample. "Obsession?" she said, to which Roberta replied, "No thank you. I have my own."

"That's the perfect answer here," Roberta said, laughing. "We all have our own obsessions. No need to feel embarrassed over yours. But changing the subject here, Bill Nighy and that female interviewer went to the Morgan Library together? That's something to be jealous of! Do you remember that I took you there too?"

"I do! But I don't remember what exhibit we saw. I just remember a lovely lunch there in their café. Do you remember the show?"

"Actually I think it was only lunch that day before you hopped a plane back to Ohio. We'll have to go back there again sometime. I was there recently and saw an Alice in Wonderland exhibit in honor of the story's 150th anniversary. The original manuscript was on loan from the British Library and there were original drawings as well. It was wonderful."

"I sure wish you could figure out a way to live in New York. Museums. Theater. Concerts. You love it all."

"Truer words were never spoken. It is my obsession," she said.

We laughed, and I felt better as I often do after talking to Bird. I also felt grateful, not just for the clarity she helps me find but for the fact that she would never chide me about my other obsession here, Bill Nighy.

October 12, 2015

Dear Bill Nighy,

I have a confession to make: I have been flirting with you. Indeed, like Tom Sergeant trying to get noticed by Alice, I have been wooing you with roses. Oh, you already knew that? Darn! And here I thought I was being so subtle. Well since the secret is out, I may as well be blatant and bold, therefore:

> You are cordially invited to explore friendship
> With a lovely/lonely lady in **OHIO**!
> Yes, she understands that you are a big star
> But she, in her own way, has quite a twinkle.
> She certainly has gall/balls/courage/chutzpah
> To suggest such a venture.
> Meanwhile, a whole large ocean of separation
> Provides a modicum of protection
> Should you choose to peruse the enclosed business card
> And use one of the four ways mentioned (4 ways!) to
> contact her.

Kind sir, I have read a variety of interviews in which you have said you never wanted a job in which you would know today where you would be in twenty-five years. Because of this sentiment, you threw a suitcase out the window at age fifteen and courageously hit the road! That road now offers you a very odd—but interesting—twist. Why not give it a try?

Very sincerely yours,

Lorie

TUESDAY, OCTOBER 13, 2015

Dear Diary,

Last week I got a great deal on a ten-pack of Crayola paints for kids! So focused was I on the low, low bargain price that I neglected to think about the huge, huge mess they would make when used by four kids under the age of five. Suffice it to say we will never paint again and that I threw out all remaining product to assure that outcome. The only remnant to be seen is the stains in the wool rug that sits under the kitchen/craft table. What was I thinking?

At the close of Marmel School, I texted Robin for some sympathy. She confessed to having a stressful day too and suggested we go have a glass of wine together to unwind. And so we did. In fact we each had two glasses. In fact we laughed all the way home from the restaurant. I don't remember what about. Usually when I am buzzy from alcohol, I get drowsy and go right to sleep upon returning home. Last night I was giddy and ALIVE, and I decided to write a letter to Bill Nighy instead. What was I thinking? Right into the trash can it goes, along with those Crayola paints!

SATURDAY, OCTOBER 17, 2015

Dear Diary,

Not counting the letter I trashed Monday, it's been five and a half weeks since I last wrote to beloved Bill. My post office told me it could take up to two weeks to get a letter to the U.K., and I suppose it would take an equal amount of time to get a letter back to the U.S. Given that fan mail has to go first to his agent and then on to him, I will throw in another couple of weeks for good measure. When I add it all up, the magic number is six weeks; thus, a letter could arrive momentarily and so I am excited again when I go to my mailbox each day and peeking out onto the porch for roses is back on the agenda. It's kind of like my coffee habit; it's wonderful to find joy in such a small thing. Imagine my disappointment, therefore, when two oddball missives turned up in my mailbox today instead of a letter from my man.

- The first was a letter *to* a man. It was an invitation addressed to Big Irv from the University of Cincinnati Neuroscience Institute, inviting him to a patient symposium on the "Effects of Cancer and Cancer Treatment on Memory and Thinking." The first item on the agenda is "Sleep and cognitive function," a topic we definitely needed to explore two years ago when he was alive and sleeping. Argh!

- The second was a letter *from* a man, just not from the right man. It was from long-ago love Jimmy Jet, looking to resume friendship after twelve years apart. I know the universe works in mysterious ways, but this is ridiculous. I want to shout, "Listen to my words, Universe! It's Bill Nighy I want a letter from, not his doppelganger!" This letter from Jimmy Jet really puts a damper on things. Now a ding-dong at my door could just as easily be him dropping by as it could be the florist with my roses. Argh!

Lucky for me, I have power over some things. Tonight is movie night, so since I want Bill Nighy, I shall have Bill Nighy. *Wild Target*, a film from 2010, is duly checked out from the library and waiting to play. I believe he is the leading man in the movie, so I am thrilled to see it. Speaking of such, I listened to an interview BN did with Dave Davies on the NPR radio show *Fresh Air* on November 2, 2011. The interview was in conjunction with the premiere of *Page Eight*, the first of the Johnny Worricker films. In the interview, Dave Davies comments that after a career as a character actor, *Page Eight* is one of the first films in which Bill Nighy plays the lead. Beloved Bill comments that beyond the fact that he was in every scene and never got ten minutes off, the experience was exhausting because of the considerable responsibility he felt to the project in general and to all of the supporting cast. "The pressure is greater," he said, "because in the end, it's going to depend on whether people can stand looking at you for that length of time." Rest assured, Bill Nighy, I'll have no problem with that.

Saturday Night at the Movies

Wild Target

DIRECTOR: Jonathan Lynn

WRITERS: Lucinda Coxon (screenplay), Pierre Salvadori (film *"Cible Emouvante"*)

RELEASE DATE: 2010

RUNNING TIME: 1 Hour, 38 Minutes

ALSO FEATURING: Emily Blunt, Rupert Grint, Rupert Everett, Gregor Fisher, Martin Freeman, and Eileen Atkins.

FRIENDLY CONNECTIONS: In this movie Bill Nighy, Gregor Fisher, and Martin Freeman are competitors in the assassination business. Previously, Gregor Fisher was Bill Nighy's agent in *Love Actually*. He does bumbling murderer—and bumbling agent—well. As for Martin Freeman, he has various professional connections to Bill Nighy. Previously the two men were in all of the Cornetto Trilogy movies together. And both were in *Love Actually* as well. (Martin Freeman was the naked man in all those pornography scenes!) They also worked together in 2005 in *The Hitchhiker's Guide to the Galaxy*. Finally, five years before *Wild Target*, Emily Blunt and Bill Nighy starred together in *Gideon's Daughter*.

Today's movie is *Wild Target*. It is based on a French comedy from 1993 called *Cible Emouvante*. In this movie, Bill Nighy is the leading man and also the romantic lead—thrilling facts for this BN fan because it means he is in almost every scene. Bill Nighy's character is Victor Maynard, and he is a professional hit man. Indeed, it seems that being a hit man is the family business. Victor's father—and mother—worked in this capacity. The father is deceased while the cold, hard mother (Eileen Atkins) is still living.

The story starts with Victor pulling off a couple of murders without breaking stride, showing the viewer what an expert and effective assassin he is. We are also introduced to a woman named Rose, played by Emily Blunt. She is a thief who steals things as easily as Victor murders. Her latest thievery involves selling a fake Rembrandt painting for one million pounds to a man named Ferguson, played by Rupert Everett. For this reason, Ferguson hires Victor to murder Rose, which proves to be very difficult due to Victor's easily won admiration for Rose. As he follows her through a busy marketplace — gun in hand — he sees her steal a scarf and a tote bag and a bunch of flowers, and then a second bunch as well, and then a dress. Victor says to himself, "She's completely out of control." She goes on to steal a sweater and a glass of orange juice — right off a diner's table — and with these acts, his admiration turns to attraction. Kind of…

Ultimately Ferguson realizes Victor has let him down and sends two new assassins to kill Rose. Meanwhile, Rose hires Victor to protect her from them. She tells Victor, "I feel safe with you. You're wise and calm and steady like a mighty, ancient oak." In the process of protecting Rose, however, Victor's gun gets knocked away as he tussles with one of the new assassins. Things look bad for Rose and Victor until a stranger turns up at the scene, picks up one of the guns that has been dropped in the scuffle, and saves the day for Rose and Victor. The stranger is Tony, played by Rupert Grint, and his skill with the gun impresses Victor. Before we know it, Tony is Victor's new protégé.

A little glitch in the romance between Rose and Victor is that Victor is not sure if he is gay or straight. Indeed he may never have pondered the question except that his mother ponders it for him early in the movie. And even more than that, he may never have thought about himself and the word *love* in the same sentence, for he is a lonely and isolated sort of guy. He is focused on one thing and one thing alone: murder. However, after a bath tub scene in which Victor sees Tony naked, Victor decides that he is straight, and a relationship with Rose begins. And screwball love story that this may be, they seemingly live happily ever after and even produce a next generation of professional killer.

Some interesting things about this movie are:

1. When this film was made, Bill Nighy was sixty years old while Emily Blunt was twenty-seven. This age difference probably did make him seem ancient to her. But in the fantasy of filmdom, such real issues are meaningless.

2. And speaking of being ancient, the subtitles for this film were called, "English for the Deaf and Hard of Hearing." Well gee, thanks a lot. In retrospect, that makes the Spanish subtitles in *Lawless Heart* so much more appealing.

3. And while the appeal of this movie to me is Bill Nighy's leading role, others like the film because it features Rupert Grint, an actor I did not previously know. Evidently he is famous for his work as Ron Weasley, one of the three main characters in the Harry Potter films. There is an entire interview with Bill Nighy regarding his take on working with such a famous fellow. The interview is posted online as Vulture Chat Room, *Bill Nighy Sizes up Rupert Grint's Sex Appeal.* It was written by Kyle Buchanan and appeared October 27, 2010. BN is asked about the bathtub scene with Rupert Grint. His response is, "Life is cruel! There are many young women all over the world — and perhaps young men, too — who really would yearn to be in my situation and see Rupert naked in a bath full of milk. That it should fall to me is kind of cruel, isn't it? But yeah, [Rupert] was very cool to work with."

4. Also cool in this movie is the mustache Bill Nighy sports. It is homegrown, not added on by the makeup department.

286 · *Lorie Kleiner Eckert*

5. Lovers of Bill Nighy will also be interested in his take on the film's subject matter. He says, "I guess part of the hit-man appeal is the solitude. Everybody is lured to the idea of the solitary life." (Brainyquote.com)

6. Lovers of Bill Nighy will be dismayed to learn that while BN's name appears first in the opening credits, he gets no star treatment in the bonus materials that are part of the DVD. Emily Blunt is the only one who is featured in an interview there. I wonder, to whom may I protest?

7. Megafans also will be dismayed to watch Bill Nighy and Emily Blunt's seduction scene, which starts with him massaging her feet. No, it won't be jealousy that causes the dismay but instead disbelief that the director used a body double for BN's hands since the hands in this scene do not have Dupuytren's contracture. I was offended that someone felt Bill Nighy's hands weren't good enough to appear in the movie, leaving me to wonder again, to whom may I protest?

Protests aside, I liked this movie a lot because the Victor Maynard character was reminiscent of Lawrence Montague in *The Girl in the Café*. In an interview with *The Telegraph* dated June 22, 2010, Bill Nighy describes playing Victor—though he could just as easily be describing Lawrence—when he said, "I like stuff where people are buttoned up and nailed down and/or disabled by self-consciousness, particularly if it's supposed to be amusing." There is a scene very early in *Wild Target* in which Victor is practicing his French as he is out and about committing murder. Thus, we hear him conjugate a verb, "I feel. I felt. I have felt." This feeling stuff is all academic at the start of the film, but happily for Victor, he learns to live it instead of just conjugate it by the movie's end. The same is true for Lawrence Montague. Who knows—maybe it's true for the rest of us as well.

Isn't that the raison d'etre for all these crazy love stories? They give us hope that every pot has a lid, and they make us believe that someday we will find ours as well.

Sunday, October 18, 2015

Dear Diary,

I woke up this morning thinking about last night's movie. I still like the story a lot, but I am having some trouble with the casting, with the pairing of Bill Nighy and Emily Blunt as lovers and then as a married couple. Having seen *Gideon's Daughter*, I liked them more as father and daughter and I wonder why movie makers must perpetuate this older man/younger woman thing? It's such a cliché! And in this case, with a thirty-three-year difference between them, it borders on disturbing, doesn't it? Or am I just skittish about this issue because Big Irv and his Suzie Q at ages seventy and thirty-seven were equally ridiculous?

I Googled both of the Bill Nighy/Emily Blunt movies to see if I could find any interviews in which this age difference was discussed and found a couple that pertained. The first was a film clip of an interview after they won Golden Globe awards for *Gideon's Daughter*. In it, a reporter told BN she heard that while they filmed the movie there was an ongoing joke between him and Emily that made Emily cringe. He responded by saying, "Any reference to the fact that I may have, at any point in my life, had any kind of romantic contact with a member of the opposite sex used to render Emily almost physically nauseous." I am thinking Emily would have equal queasiness if she were the member of the opposite sex in question, right?

The second interview appeared in print in 2010. It was written by Matt Mueller under the heading "*Buzz* sneaks on [the] set of *Wild Target* and catches Emily Blunt and Bill Nighy bickering..." From the article, it appears that the two actors have been in email contact since their work together in *Gideon's Daughter*, and referring to this, EB asks BN, "What is my aim in life?" And he responds, "To humiliate and embarrass me. To make me cringe and blush. When I read the script, I thought, 'Fuck me, somebody's been reading our emails.' It's a romantic comedy. I'm old enough to be her grandfather, which puts it in a rarely visited cul-de-sac of the genre." So there you have it: Emily Blunt, Bill Nighy, and I all have problems with this casting.

With thoughts of Bill Nighy's love life firmly in mind, I continued my Googling by repeating a search I have done once—okay, a few times—in the past. Thus, I typed in "Bill Nighy and girlfriend." I came up with lots of images of him with various female co-stars such as Winona Ryder and Rachel Weisz in the Johnny Worricker series; and loads of photos with Carey Mulligan of *Skylight* fame; and several with Judi Dench in the Marigold Hotel movies, etc. Emily Blunt and he also made an appearance. There were also many photos of him with ex-"wife" Diana Quick and with purported special friend Anna Wintour. There were even a couple of him with his daughter. Having done this exact Google search before, I was a little surprised to see a new woman in the mix, a very young woman, a darling gal wearing a skirt that is eight or nine inches above the knee. When I clicked into the photo, I was given the option to visit the page from which it originally appeared, and when I did so, I found an article from www.dailymail.co.uk dated just a month ago, September 12, 2015. The headline reads "Always a joker! Bill Nighy cracks a smile as he makes his young companion giggle on a leisurely afternoon stroll." You will note, dear Diary, that she is so young that she giggles instead of laughs.

Of course I am jealous, so I won't be pinning this particular photo to my Bill Nighy Pinterest board. I sure hope she is his niece (great niece?) or his agent's assistant or his neighbor's daughter home from college for a visit. She is holding his arm, not his hand, so maybe that's the case. Yes, yes, I hope Bill Nighy finds love in his life—preferably with me—but I also hope he doesn't embarrass himself in the process.

I forwarded the link to Roberta before our evening chat. She thinks the young'un is his great niece. She says he is far too classy to be a cliché. She's right about so many things, hopefully about this issue too.

THURSDAY, OCTOBER 22, 2015

Dear Diary,

On the way to the movie theater today, I told Vera about *Wild Target* and the thirty-three-year age difference between Bill Nighy and Emily Blunt. She assured me there was no crazy casting in today's movie, *The Intern*. While Robert De Niro and Anne Hathaway star in it, they are not romantically linked in the plot. Indeed, Vera informed me, Rene Russo plays his girlfriend. It's a long drive to the Mariemont Theater, so I had a lot of time to Google all of these actors. De Niro is seventy-two, Hathaway is thirty-two, and Russo is sixty-one, making De Niro and Russo worthy of a Credible Couple Award. Hooray for today's casting director!

Now then, here's the rest of the scoop on the movie. Robert De Niro plays the part of Ben Whittaker, who is a seventy-year-old widower and a retired executive. He is suffering from all three legs of the bored-lonely-depressed triumvirate, and besides that, he has too much time on his hands. To remedy things, he applies to a senior citizen intern program and is hired by Anne Hathaway's character, Jules Ostin, who is the founder of a quickly growing e-commerce fashion startup. She is resistant to his help at first, but by movie's end, he has solved all of her problems — professional and personal. Of course he has solved all of his, as well, with a new job and a new girlfriend in the picture. They all live happily ever after. Ah, Hollywood, how easy life looks on the big screen!

"We seem to see a lot of movies about loneliness," I said to Vera as we chowed down on Graeter's ice cream after the movie. "If I were a New Age thinker, I would have to assume it's no coincidence and that the Universe is bringing me such messages intentionally."

"I don't believe that. We're exercising a lot of free will here," she replied. "We don't choose action/adventure movies. We don't choose thrillers or fantasies. We don't choose superheroes or animation. Horror and sci-fi? They're not on our list either. Human drama is our thing, and loneliness is a part of that tale."

"Of course you're right, but I still have the vague sense that SOMEONE is trying to tell me SOMETHING," I said. "But speaking of loneliness, you'll be shocked to hear that a man has offered himself up to me."

She looked at me funny and replied, "What does that mean?"

I handed her Jimmy Jet's letter, cautioning her, "No need to clutch this to your breast and scream. It's not from BN in NYC. It's from Jimmy Jet in Indiana."

"The guy you dated before Big Irv?" she asked as she took the letter and read it.

"Yes. Him. But brace yourself, Vera, I'm going to go New Age-y on you again. Since I go to the mailbox daily praying for a letter from a man—meaning beloved Bill, of course—did I cause this to happen?"

"No. You did not cause this to happen except for the fact that you are a wonderful woman and after all these years Jimmy Jet has figured that out and wants you back. Are you planning to write him?"

"No! The only thing I want to tell him is that I don't wish to be in touch, but if I write that then I am in touch, right?"

"Of course, but don't you want to know how he is?"

"Sure. But not enough to check in with him. I tried Googling his name, but he's off the grid. Hey, by the way, I'll kinda be off the grid too. I leave for Disney World tomorrow morning."

"I forgot! That's great. Just you or is Roberta joining you?" Vera asked.

"Just me. I'm a little nervous traveling alone, but I can do it!"

"Yes, you can," she replied. "It will be good practice for bigger and better travel down the road. No need to sit home and be *lonely*. A whole world awaits you!"

"There it is," I said. "The SOMEONE who is trying to tell me SOMETHING is you!"

Friday, October 23, 2015

Thank God:

1. I made it to Orlando okay and found the Disney booth that was handling my transfer from the airport to my hotel. Easy peasy. Amen.

2. On the HUGE complex that is my Disney Hotel—the Caribbean Beach Resort—I found the building that contained my room! Then I found the bus stop for the shuttle to Epcot! After Epcot, I found the bus back to the hotel and I even found my room again—this time in the dark! Hungry for a late dinner, I found the shuttle to the food court associated with the hotel! And after eating, I found my way back to my room once again! I was none too confident but I DID IT! Eureka, I found it all! Amen.

It was a good, good day. I am proud of myself. All on my own in Disney World. Is that Johnny Mathis playing in my head? "On my own, would I wander through this wonderland alone?" YES! Amen.

<u>THURSDAY, OCTOBER 29, 2015</u>

Dear Diary,

I am at the airport awaiting my flight home from Orlando. It's been a great trip, equal parts Disney and dawdling. I have always wanted to do a behind-the-scenes tour, and I managed to pull that off this week, seeing secret stuff at all four parks, Epcot, The Magic Kingdom, Animal Kingdom, and Disney's Hollywood Studios. Here are a couple of interesting things I loved learning:

- There are lots of tricks used to keep animals in the viewing area at Animal Kingdom even though they might prefer to get out of the hot Florida sun. Hence the large rocks upon which animals perch are air conditioned. As for the smaller rocks, snacks are jettisoned out of them on an intermittent schedule, keeping the animals around as they hope for treats.

- Cooler still—pardon the pun—is a whole world underneath the Magic Kingdom. It's like a tunnel system except Florida is too swampy for tunnels, so it is a ground-level "tunnel" with the park built on top in what are actually a second and third floor. This area is called the "Utilidor," a shortened version of the words "utility corridor." The food sold in restaurants and the gifts sold in shops in the park come up "magically" from this lower level without the need for delivery trucks to spoil the mood in the park. Likewise, one will never see a cowboy from Frontierland walking through the sci-fi-themed Tomorrowland to get to his job. He arrives at his station via the Utilidor, allowing the magic of both lands to remain intact.

I could go on, dear Diary, but the life lesson for all of this is the more important thing to write down and remember: Magic doesn't happen magically—a lot of planning, problem-solving, and hard work are involved.

Another lesson from this tour is that there are a lot of rabid Disney fans out there. The park has many behind-the-scenes tours available; one can even swim with over 6,000 sea animals in the saltwater aquarium at Epcot that holds almost six million gallons. I was astounded to learn that many of the people on my behind-the-scenes tour had the habit of spending ALL their vacations at the park, and they were meticulously ticking off all such experiences from their bucket list. As for our tour director, his love of Disney has him on a quest to eat at all 346 restaurants in the Florida Disney parks and resorts complex. This includes "character dining," dinner shows, food trucks, pool bars, lounges, and so forth. I looked down my nose at all these crazy people and wanted to tell them to get a life! They certainly seemed over the top to me. But then, I found myself the next day on a ride in Epcot called Spaceship Earth, which is the huge silver ball at the front of the park. During the fifteen-minute ride, a narrator tells about advancements in human communications throughout history. The most astonishing thing about this tale was that I recognized the voice of the narrator telling it—it was Bill Nighy's buddy, Judi Dench. When I got off the ride, I Googled it in order to doublecheck my hearing. Thus, I learned that four people have narrated the attraction since it opened in 1982: Lawrence Dobkin, Walter Cronkite, Jeremy Irons, and now, since 2008, Dame Judi Dench. That I had voice recognition for Bill Nighy's co-star unsettled me. Rabid fans indeed!

An additional BN tie-in from my trip is that during my time away from the parks, I read a wonderful book that made me think of him. The book was *A God in Ruins* by Kate Atkinson. It is a companion book to her earlier, and fabulous, novel, *Life After Life*. Both books tell of an English family by the name of Todd. Both books take place between and after the two world wars with a heavy focus on World War II itself. The main character in *A God in Ruins* is Teddy, who is a bomber for the RAF. Though the reader "knows" from the get-go that Teddy survives the war, the author did such a superb job of depicting the harrowing nature of Teddy's final battle that when his plane got shot down into the sea, I cried an ocean's worth of tears for this most dear and beloved character. "Seeing" war so up close and personal, I was very grateful that the U.S. has never had a world war fought on its shores, and I regret that I looked down my nose at the policy of appeasement I learned about in *Glorious 39*. Clearly I proved I know nothing about the realities of war. Clearly it makes sense to want to avoid war at any cost. One other thing is clear after having read this book: I love to read! I haven't had the patience to read in recent months, so I have turned on my DVD player instead. I will need to remedy that upon my return home.

Speaking of home, I just checked for voice mail on my landline and discovered two messages there. The first was from the cemetery telling me Big Irv's grave marker has arrived and is installed. The second was from Dr. Popa's office reminding me of my upcoming appointment. I can't believe three months have passed since I saw him. I can't believe I am feeling so well. Indeed, sleeping has been so easy these days that not even a hotel bed has impacted my slumbers. Whew! He'll be so happy to hear this. Roberta too!

Before I board the plane, here is a beautiful quote from *A God in Ruins*. In it, Teddy is remembering his grandmother, "who led a gloomy drawing room life...with heavy cotton nets drawn to prevent the light entering the house. Or perhaps to stop the dark escaping." What a beautiful life lesson, Kate Atkinson: Lightening up is a two-step process. It's time to head home and open the drapes!

THE BOOK OF IRV

MY LETTER TO HIM

Well, here I am, writing in The Book of Irv again. I thought I was done with this particular endeavor—finished too—but I guess not. It's interesting how much has happened since I last entered my thoughts in this journal. I have traveled to St. Louis for the fabulous family reunion. I have survived the introspection of the Jewish High Holiday season. I have seen scads of movies in theaters with Vera, on my DVD at home, and even on my treadmill. I have traveled to Orlando for a wonderful dose of vacation therapy. I have spent loads of time with Robin, Vera, and Roberta. I have served up lots of craft projects to Marmel School students and an equal number of hot meals to those beloved little kids and their beloved parents. And let's not forget, I have eaten loads of ice cream in these days, weeks, and months. Hmmm, funny that I just wrote those words, because I think that is the point: Time has passed. And so I find myself feeling kindly toward a man named Irv, and I want to do better than close this journal with vitriol.

It seems that as of late I have written many letters to my fantasy love, Bill Nighy. Today I will try my hand at writing one to Big Irv. I will visit the cemetery soon to see his grave marker. Perhaps I will read my letter to him while I am there, as a eulogy of sorts. His Catholic funeral—rendered by a priest who had never met him—was less than personal. He deserves more than that.

OCTOBER 30, 2015

Dear Big Irv,

I apologize for the many ways I hurt you and failed you in the years of your illness, and I hope that in your heart of hearts you would say the same thing to me. I particularly apologize for and regret those months you spent in that hellhole hotel, but that was your choice, though I forced your hand. So okay, we made mistakes, right, Big Irv? And some of them were enormous. But let's forgive them and let's forgive each other and let's remember the good instead. I give you a standing Irvation for all the wonderful times, and I think I hear you whisper in response, "You're a good Tootser."

Beyond apology, I also have a confession to make. In spite of the fact that all of your sleeping made me crazy, not to mention that it drove a stake through our relationship, I have to admit that you were right. You said that when you are sick, you need to sleep until you feel better. While all that sleeping did not cure your cancer, it did buy you lots of time. Your original prognosis was that you would live for two years after the diagnosis. You lived for three and a half years instead. That's wonderful, Big Irv. Way to go!

From apologies and confessions, I now turn to memories. Reform Jews are taught that the deceased live on in the memory of those who loved them. In honor of that concept and in honor of those many, many good times we shared, I will say:

When I see that Cirque du Soleil is coming to town, I will think of you.

When I hear Toby Keith on the radio, I will think of you.

When I read about the opening of the Ohio State Fair, I will think of you.

When I sit down in our seats at the Broadway Series, I will think of you.

When I hear NASCAR news, I will think of you.

When I order something expensive on the menu, I will think of you.

When I pick at an appetizer or eat the last three bites of a dessert, I will think of you.

When I go to a restaurant whose name starts with an X, Y, or Z, I will think of you.

When I see a couple holding hands at all those restaurants, I will think of you.

When I buy up all the tins at a flea market, I will think of you.

When I hear the jingle-jangle of my dumbbells, I will think of you.

When someone pushes back from the table and says they are done, I will think of you.

When I hear Sinatra sing "My Way," I will think of you.

In all of these small ways that made up our grand life, Big Irv, I will think of you.

I will think of you and remember the love.

N.F.D.

Your Tootser

November

SUNDAY, NOVEMBER 1, 2015

Dear Diary,

It feels good to be home after my vacation, especially now that I have all the accumulated laundry, email, and snail mail handled. I even managed to write an epilogue in The Book of Irv since coming home. A strong compulsion came over me as soon as I heard that Big Irv's grave marker had been installed, and it wouldn't leave me alone until I addressed it. I will take myself to the cemetery soon, but it didn't happen today. I only had free time in the morning and I was too lethargic then to get up and go. Could it be all the candy I ate last night as I visited all the grandkids and helped them with their Halloween haul? By the way, Josh wins the prize for most adorable costume. Completely consumed with trains at age almost-five, he dressed up as a railroad crossing sign.

Lolling in bed this morning with iPad in hand, I spent some time on Pinterest hunting for photos of my guy Bill. Whew! No new photos of him with that young woman, but then again, not much in the way of new photos at all. Wanting to add something—anything—to my BN Pinterest collection, I added a photo of Marmite. But then I managed to find a nice picture of him that had a twenty-minute interview with DP/30 as its source. When I tuned into the video, I realized I had seen it before too. In the couple of minutes I watched, though, I caught a great quote. Bill Nighy said that his "process" when it comes to acting is this: "Don't panic and show up." Short and sweet, it says a lot. In my head, I thanked him for a nice life lesson and then bid him adieu as I turned to a different Pinterest search: quilts with words pieced into the design. It can't hurt to check out the competition in that field, can it? Not to mention the fact that doing so will make Roberta happy.

Eventually I blasted myself out of bed but only because I had theater tickets with Margot for the afternoon. Though she lives right next door, it's been a while since we have hung out together. I always enjoy her company. Her kids are a dozen years older than mine, so the stories she tells about them are like previews of coming attractions for me. Additionally, since she is a widow, I thought she might be available for an outing when I read about an intriguing play in the newspaper. The Ensemble Theater had the regional premiere of a play called *Buyer and Cellar*, which is an entirely fictional work about Barbra Streisand. Since I have been known to write entirely fictional stories about a certain celebrity myself, the concept appealed to me. The play tells the story of the "mall" Streisand has in the basement of her home that houses all the memorabilia from her career. The story is told from the point of view of an unemployed actor who is hired to oversee the collection. In that this is a one-man show, this young guy plays himself and Streisand. As the playbill tells us, soon the job "begins to take a toll on his patience, his love life, and his view of people (who need people)." It was adorable. Margot and I loved it. Dinner and ice cream afterward weren't bad either.

I can't wait to tell Roberta all about the play when we talk tonight. She was headed to New York for the weekend so we can swap tales of our theater experiences. Wanting her to be as happy as I am, I hope she saw a musical. Borrowing from Streisand and Stephen Sondheim—and even Bill Nighy—music is her brand of "Being Alive."

TUESDAY, NOVEMBER 3, 2015

Dear Diary,

It was an absolutely gorgeous Indian summer day today. Big Irv would have loved it. He was always bound and determined to wear shorts through the month of November no matter what the thermometer reading, and today such action was actually warranted. I took advantage of the day to visit him at the cemetery and to see the new grave marker. What can I say? It's marvelous; in fact, the words on it are as perfect as was the day. I had every intention of reading my "eulogy" aloud, but that didn't happen. I stood there instead looking at his name as one thought led to another.

- It all started with a helicopter flying overhead, which reminded me of the helicopter ride we took at the Ohio State Fair—only $60 per person. "Of course we should do it," he said.
- Which reminded me of the aerial tramway we rode in Gatlinburg en route to Dollywood.
- Which reminded me of holding hands and giggling our way through the Bourbon Trail in Kentucky on our way home.
- Which reminded me of the embarrassed laughter we shared as we took dancing lessons before Lisa's wedding.
- Which reminded me there was a time I entertained the notion of marrying the man—at least to the extent that I picked music for our big day.
- Which reminded me that one of the songs was indeed by Roy Orbison. But it wasn't "Crying." It was "You've Got It" instead.
- Which reminded me I could Google that song even standing in the cemetery, and so I did. And I sang along.
- And then I Googled the other song I had chosen for the wedding, the Pointer Sisters' signature song, "I'm So Excited." And as I played that one next, I not only sang but joyously danced as well.

To be sure, it was quite a sight for the cemetery. It reminded me of the time I bought tampons, M&M's, and a hacksaw at Target. Both times I was surprised the authorities didn't carry me away and lock me up.

- I laughed at that thought, as I had laughed at so many things during the good old days with Big Irv.
- Which brought me back to his name on the cemetery marker and the perfect verse beside it. How odd life is: I once hurled these words at him in anger and now I read them with heartfelt respect and admiration, grinning from ear to ear.

BIG IRV
I FACED IT ALL. AND I STOOD TALL.
AND DID IT MY WAY.
JULY 8, 1942 ✝ JULY 16, 2014

THURSDAY, NOVEMBER 5, 2015

Dear Diary,
Over lunch today at Steak 'N Shake, I told Vera about my singing and dancing debut at the Gate of Heaven Cemetery. I am sure she was glad I did not reprise my act.

"I'm really surprised to hear that you were singing and dancing instead of crying," Vera said. I shook my head in agreement as she continued, "And I am shocked to hear that you ever considered marrying the man. Did he know that?"

"Oh God, no," I responded. "I don't think I even told Roberta."

"What made you imagine such a thing?" she asked.

"I think I was intoxicated, certainly by all the cocktails but even more so by all the fun we had. I can be such a serious person and I can live so much of my life inside of my own head—not to mention inside of my house—but that wasn't Big Irv's M.O. It was amazing to be with a guy who knew how to go out and have fun. Did you know we ate dessert at Dairy Queen so often that the teenage clerks not only knew our order but began to prepare it when they saw us walking across the parking lot toward their door? If that's not fun, what is?" Fellow ice cream lover that she is, she conceded the point as I continued. "Seriously, though, I think I was dizzy or giddy or something bubbly like that from all of our comings and goings."

"Well then," she responded, "prepare yourself for more carbonation." With that, she pulled a newspaper article from her purse and gave it to me. "We're moving into Oscar season, so many big films are opening soon. We may have to double up and see two movies a week to fit them all in. We're seeing Matt Damon in *The Martian* today so we can soon scratch that one from the list, and we have both turned thumbs down on DiCaprio in *The Revenant*, but here are all the others."

And so, dear Diary, I faithfully reproduce the list for you now, printing the titles in the order of their release:

Already opened in October:
- *Bridge of Spies* starring Tom Hanks
- *Steve Jobs* starring Michael Fassbender
- *Suffragette* starring Bill Nighy's buddy Carey Mulligan

In November:
- *Brooklyn* with Saoirse Ronan
- *Trumbo* with Bryan Cranston

In December:
- *The Big Short* starring Christian Bale, Steve Carell, Ryan Gosling, and Brad Pitt
- *Carol* starring Bill Nighy's buddy Cate Blanchett
- *45 Years* starring Charlotte Rampling
- *The Danish Girl* starring Bill Nighy's buddy Eddie Redmayne

In early 2016:
- *Spotlight* with Michael Keaton
- *Joy* with Jennifer Lawrence
- *Room* with Brie Larson

One would think that this daunting list was enough of a challenge for the two of us movie partners, but Vera is made of tougher stuff, so she had still another newspaper clipping in her bag of tricks...I mean in her purse. It was a listing of the 2015-2016 Bolshoi Ballet Cinema Season. Evidently ballets are broadcast direct from Moscow to select cinemas across the U.S. and our local Regal Theater is a participant. Three ballets will be shown in Cincinnati: *Jewels* on November 15, *The Lady of the Camellias* on December 6, and *The Taming of the Shrew* on January 24.

"Do you like ballet?" she asked.

"I have no idea," I replied honestly, "but I like you, so if you're in, I'm in."

"Great. Put those dates on your calendar," she instructed me.

"Will do," I replied.

She touched my arm so I would look at her, and she said, "There's a lot to look forward to. You got it?"

"Are you quoting Roy Orbison?" I asked her, but she wouldn't let me get away with a joke.

"You got it?" she repeated.

"Yes. I got it." She smiled at me, and so I dared to continue, "I'm so excited!"

FRIDAY, NOVEMBER 6, 2015

Dear Diary,

Usually when "the check is in the mail," that's a good thing, right? Well, not when it's a reality check. I got mine today. It came in the form of a *Vanity Fair* magazine. The address label congratulated me for being a new subscriber, which was news to me. A call to the magazine helped me understand that my recent purchase at Travelsmith.com came with a free subscription. Who knew?

In looking over the magazine, I noticed two things. First, of course, were all those amazing clothing ads for items that more closely resembled works of modern art than wardrobe pieces that would be found in my closet. The second thing I noticed was that the magazine's list of editors, contributing editors, publishers, associate publishers, etc., goes on for two solid pages. I still don't know exactly why I focused on those masthead pages; neither do I know how my eye picked up the last name mentioned on that second page of names, but it did. The name given was Anna Wintour. She is listed as the magazine's artistic director.

I was confused. I thought she was the British editor-in-chief of American *Vogue*—not to mention being a possible love interest of Bill Nighy's. I had no choice but to Google her.

Wikipedia explained that in 2013, Condé Nast announced she was taking on the position of artistic director for the company's magazines (plural) while remaining at *Vogue*. Wikipedia also mentioned that in 2005—when she was *only* the editor at *Vogue*—her salary was reported to be two million dollars per year, plus additional perks such as a chauffeured Mercedes and an annual $200,000 clothing allowance. Two hundred thousand dollars for clothes! In my humble opinion, that's a college education, not a clothing budget.

All this information slaps at my consciousness. Beloved Bill is a gorgeous guy and is always impeccably dressed, but does the fact that he was named a best-dressed man for 2015 in *Vanity Fair*, one of Anna Wintour's magazines, hint at who nominated him? Does it validate the rumors of a relationship? And what about the fact that they both wear designer clothes right out of the pages of this magazine? I always assumed he had a healthy income, but does he find cash as expendable as does she? If they are not a pair, are they two peas in a pod? And what am I by comparison—a garbanzo bean?

This reality check leaves me rather nauseous, as does the fact that this reminder of my other-ness will come to me monthly. It will certainly take some of the joy out of the heretofore exciting experience of going to my mailbox.

SATURDAY, NOVEMBER 7, 2015

Dear Diary,

It was a great day today. Even reading the newspaper over my morning coffee was special thanks to my horoscope. It echoed lessons learned at the Disney complex when it said, "Often the changes that seem magical and miraculous are merely a matter of consistent, daily effort made over a long period of time." Since the Universe has chosen to bring this message to me twice, I guess I should listen. The "consistent, daily effort" I have in mind is the one taped to my car's dashboard: Be Less Aloof. It worked with Cousin Kenny and with neighbor Margot. Could it work again today?

Checking the hypothesis, I called my friend Kim. We have a lot in common. Both of us try not to complain on yachts, and both of us are quilt makers. We always yak, yak, yak like crazy when we are together, talking non-stop about quilts. It has often occurred to me that we should get together more often, so I called her today. As it turns out, Kim's husband is out of town so she was free, and by early afternoon we were headed up to Waynesville, the antiquey town thirty minutes north of home. While Big Irv and I frequented the little shops there as we hunted up tins for my collection, the real attraction in Waynesville is Fabric Shack, a huge store chock-full of 100 percent cotton fabrics, the stuff of quilts. It is an understatement to say we enjoyed the day. We bought lots of stuff and left only when forced to — the store closed at 5.

Of course, all that shopping makes a girl hungry. Lucky for us there's a gem of a restaurant up the street from the fabric store, and that's where we headed next. Kim had never been to the Cobblestone Café, but she loved it. I do too. I am usually there solo — at least since Big Irv's death — so it was a treat to have her company. When we got back home, closing in on eight, we agreed on two things: It was a perfect day and we need to repeat it in the future. Woo hoo! So much for insufferable Saturdays.

As I sit here in bed writing to you, dear Diary, my fabric purchases are spread out on the bedroom floor. They are yummy; they are the colors of rainbow sherbet. I think they will look great in the quilt that has started percolating in my head. After buying fabrics, my next step in the quilt-making process is to see how they look together in different types of light. Thus far, they are great in artificial light, but I knew that from the fabric store. I hope the same will be true for natural light—both morning and afternoon. I can't wait for tomorrow!

Sunday, November 8, 2015

Dear Diary,

"You're going to be so proud of me," I almost shouted as Roberta picked up the phone tonight. "I bought fabric for a quilt!" Of course she was extremely pleased and of course she asked me to tell her all about it. And so of course I did, mentioning in the process that my next column is coming due Friday and that I plan to turn my quilt idea into a Slice of Life Column, as well. I love double dipping—in ice cream and in life.

"You were out of town this weekend, weren't you?" I finally asked her when I calmed down from my news.

"Yes. Flo and I went to Ten Chimneys."

"Good for you! I know you've wanted to do that for a long time," I replied, "but I forget why. What's at Ten Chimneys?"

"It was the estate of theater greats Lynn Fontanne and Alfred Lunt. Do you know anything about them?" she asked me.

"I have exactly one factoid on that topic. In the bonus materials for the Bill Nighy movie *Gideon's Daughter*, his co-star Miranda Richardson is interviewed. In it, she says that since the two of them have worked together several times before, they joke about being the Lunts."

"As you can imagine," Roberta replied in a deadpan fashion, "the docent didn't mention that on our tour." She then went on to tell me about the Lunts, who are purported to be the greatest acting couple in theater history. And she told me all about their sixty-acre estate, which does indeed have ten chimneys: six in the main house, three in the cottage, and one in the studio. And she told me about all the programming that goes on there if you manage to plan a trip at the right time. Unfortunately, only the estate tour was available this past weekend.

"Where is this place, Bird?"

"It is neatly tucked away in Wisconsin," she told me. We flew to Milwaukee, rented a car, and then drove thirty miles to reach it in a town called Genesee Depot. Though we were unlucky at catching activities at the estate, we were able to see a bit of fall foliage during our ride. It was beautiful."

"My dad loved trees dressed in autumn color, which of course means I do too," I told her. "I've always drooled over travel brochures depicting the New England states in October."

"Me too," Roberta said. "You know what…let's go!"

"Huh? What? Are you serious? When?"

"I'm two years away from retirement," she replied.

"So you want to take this trip then? In two years? The fall of 2017?"

"Oh no," she answered, "when I retire, I'm taking a *huge* trip. But this one will do for a year from now."

"OK, I'm in for autumn 2016. But where are you going after that?"

"Why don't you come too?" she said.

"Sure. Why not? Where is it that we're going, though?"

"New Zealand, Australia, and Bora Bora," she said, all proud of herself. Actually, I was proud of her too.

"That's astounding, Roberta!" I said through a bit of stunned laughter. "You have worked so hard for so long. A big blowout of a celebration upon retirement is exactly what you deserve."

"Would you really consider going along?" she asked me.

"I have every bit of confidence that I can travel the world alone, but at the same time I know I was a nervous Nellie on my own in Orlando. I'd be a fool to say no to an amazing trip that comes complete with a handy-dandy travel companion, especially when she is my oldest and dearest friend."

"Wow!" Roberta said.

"Wow!" I echoed.

And then there was another echo, too, when she said, "There's a lot to look forward to!"

TUESDAY, NOVEMBER 10, 2015

Dear Diary,

It was a rainy day today, so I took myself to the mall for my morning walk. While there, I happened to pass through the ladies' clothing department at Dillard's and discovered a couple of brands I have never noticed before. They were a little pricey—but really cute—so I tried on a few outfits. Yowza! I liked what I saw in the mirror! My first thought was that if I ever really finagle a date with Bill Nighy, this is where I would come to buy the perfect ensemble. I further reasoned with myself that in that dream situation, I'd even pay full price to look and feel so good. That's quite a concession for this inveterate bargain shopper!

The glow of the dressing room experience remained with me as I drove home. *When was the last time I felt pretty,* I wondered? The answer that came to me was when Big Irv and I went to a wedding in…I don't know, maybe 2009? Certainly it was before he was ill. Whatever the date, I wore a semiformal dress with a halter top, a fitted waist, a big full skirt, and a wide sash tied in a bow. The dress was black, but the bodice was lined in a hot pink that peeked out just a smidge every time I moved. Big Irv told me I hit a home run when I bought the dress and I agreed. On the night of the wedding, as Big Irv and I walked from the parking lot to the party venue, a stranger we passed on the street likewise complimented my dress. I was pleased but not 100 percent surprised, I felt gorgeous in that dress!

Speaking of feeling pretty in clothes, I am excited to report that I made a purchase in that Dillard's department today. Yes, yes, of course it was on the sale rack, but it is totally adorable just the same. It is a multicolored print blouse with huge sleeves created in a very drape-y fabric. It will look great with jeans. It reminds me of things I wore in college during my pseudo-hippie days, but more than that, it reminds me of the shirt Bill Nighy wore in the opening scenes of *Love Actually*, when he was in a recording studio singing "Christmas Is All Around." I'm not exactly sure why, but somehow having a reminder of him when I wear the blouse seems fitting.

WEDNESDAY, NOVEMBER 11, 2015

Dear Diary,

I have good news and bad news. The bad news is that still another reality check came to me today, this time via my computer. Have I mentioned that there is a Facebook group for Bill Nighy fans? And have I mentioned that it has over 300 rabid fans, most of them/us women? Today, one of the ladies posted a photo of herself with BN with this comment: "I am sharing my birthday fantasy for tomorrow, the 12th. When this photo was taken last May, outside the John Golden Theatre, where Bill and Carey Mulligan were starring in *Skylight,* I gave him my business card. It'd be so neat if sometime tomorrow he went through his pockets, found the card, and gave a call. I'd invite him to visit my little ole hometown whenever he is able to make it."

Upon reading her post, my first thought was this, *What kind of fool in small-town USA thinks she has a chance with Bill Nighy?* I had a second thought too: *I wonder if her business card gave him four ways (4 ways!) to get in touch with her.* Ouch! I am so embarrassed.

Lucky for me there is some good news in all of this, and here it is: If I never have a date with Bill Nighy, I will never be tempted to buy an outfit at full retail price at Dillard's!

———

P.S., dear Diary: To assuage the *tiny* bit of jealousy I felt today over the possibility of this woman's fantasy coming true, I checked in with dalje.com whose column from January 19, 2009, is titled "Bill Nighy Has a Dry Cleaning Fetish." It reminded me of BN's motto, "If it stands still long enough, dry clean it." This proves, I think, that her business card is long gone. Ha!

A Slice of Life: A Monthly Column
I ACCEPT WHAT IS

PLEASE DON'T RUN when I tell you that today's column is about how to design a quilt. Instead, be assured that whether I am writing this column, making a quilt, or just sitting at my kitchen table drinking coffee and reading the newspaper, I am always hunting for life lessons to share. In the quilt design process, I promise to tell you a few. Here's one now: When life gives you scraps, make a quilt. Sew far, sew good? Then come on along!

Let's start by talking about my kind of quilts. First, they are wall hangings, not bed covers. But more important is the fact that they have words pieced into the design and the words are spelled out in capital letters, five inches tall. When one uses all caps in email, it is considered shouting, and maybe I am shouting here, but the person I am shouting at is myself. It is said that we teach best that which we most need to learn, so the words on my quilts are all lessons aimed at me.

Today's quilt starts with the fact that I have struggled with the death of my friend, Big Irv, for months. Had I been the one to die first, I know exactly how Big Irv would have dealt with my death. He would have explained the unexplainable to himself by saying, "It is as it is," and then he would have moved on. I like these words. They are similar to an expression from a book called *The Tao of Pooh* by Benjamin Hoff. Hoff uses Winnie the Pooh to explain the basic principles of Taoism. Thus Pooh says, "A fly can't bird, but a bird can fly…Things Are as They Are." Liking this general idea, it occurred to me that I could use Big Irv's expression or Benjamin Hoff's expression on a quilt. I was all cranked over that idea for a couple of days until I realized it was too benign. Knowing that "things are as they are" is one thing, but accepting that "things are as they are" is quite another. Thus, I arrived at more powerful words for the quilt: I ACCEPT WHAT IS.

Often in a quilt, I use words to frame the design, and if I divided the four words in this statement in half, and then repeated the statement twice (because the concept bears repeating), that gave me four border sections with which I could surround my design. The words "I Accept" would be the top and bottom frames, and the words "What Is" would frame the right and left sides of the quilt.

Okay, so I had the word frame for my quilt, but what design could illustrate the words? With the work of M.C. Escher in mind, I decided to find quilt blocks that tessellate. Since tessellations are shapes that fit together without overlapping or leaving gaps, they are ideal for my message: Things are as they are; they fit together perfectly. I chose a star pattern called Milky Way for the center of the quilt and a second tessellating block called Snail's Tail for an outer border. The finished quilt will be fifty-six inches square.

I was pleased with myself and with my quilt design, and off I trotted to the quilt shop to buy fabric for my project. I bought gorgeous yard goods in the colors of rainbow sherbet—orange, lime, and raspberry. Once I had the material at home, I spread it out on the floor around my bed so I could see it in all sorts of light and was thrilled when I loved the fabrics morning, noon, and night. But a couple of days into this love affair, I had misgivings about the new-ness of the fabric because it wasn't in keeping with the message of the quilt. Like most quilters, I have a vast supply of fabric in my stash, and it suddenly occurred to me that for this topic I needed to make the most of what I already had on hand. Isn't that accepting what is? I need to take what

I already have and figure out a way to make it work. I have to make the discordant harmonic.

It is scary to do a quilt this way. My stash has lots of fabrics but mostly leftovers from other projects, not big chunks of material. Thus, this wall hanging will be a scrap quilt using lots of different fabrics, and it looks like yellow will be the background color solely because I need a lot of background fabric and I own so many yellows. It's intimidating to make design choices in this manner. The many fabrics I have pulled out have a carnival feel, but is it a happy carnival or chaotic one? I don't know. And I'm afraid. Like that bell ringer game at a carnival, I wonder if I am up to the task.

As I look for encouragement to cheer me on, I am reminded of the great quote from spiritual leader Emmet Fox, who said, "Do it trembling if you must, but do it." I am also reminded of the great quote from a favorite film star of mine, Bill Nighy, who said, "Don't panic and show up." And of course there are always the wise words of my high school swim teacher, Mr. Stricker, who said, "Close your eyes, pinch your nose, and jump!"

Are you convinced by any of this? Me neither. So here's my plan: I think I am just going to start sewing. I'll take one of those yellow fabrics and sew it to a green one—my favorite color—and see what happens. And sew on and sew forth, one decision will lead to another until I have a quilt. And with some perseverance—not luck—I plan to hear the *ding!* as I win the bell ringer game of life.

Saturday, November 14, 2015

Dear Diary,

I just sobbed through the ending of *All the Bright Places* by Jennifer Niven. It is a story about love, loss, and moving on. What can I say? I loved this book—and I hated it.

- I loved the love story of Violet Markey and Theodore Finch.
- I hated that this teenaged couple met out on a ledge as each considered suicide.
- I loved Theo's pet name for Violet, Ultraviolet Remarkey-able.
- I hated the bipolar disorder that plagued Theo.
- I hated his family's inability to get him help.
- I loved the fact that in the process of telling this story, the author takes us on field trips to all the bright—and quirky—places in Indiana, such as a field of retired book mobiles and the "Shoe Trees" of Milltown, Indiana, population 815.
- I loved the fact that a YA book such as this can be such a great read for adults. But why not? The topics of love, loss, and moving on impact people of all ages.

There was a time before meeting Big Irv when I spent Saturdays reading. Back then, the best book was one that could be read in a day, especially if it made me laugh and cry. Today's book filled that bill. And speaking of Bill, I think I am going to forsake BN tonight in favor of B&N. Translation: Instead of Saturday Night at the Movies, I am headed to Barnes & Noble to see what other books are available by this author. Hey! I can pass a Graeter's ice cream parlor on the way home as well. Sweet!

Thursday, November 19, 2015

Dear Diary,

Vera and I saw *Heist* today. It stars Robert De Niro and Jeffrey Dean Morgan and it is about a casino robbery that does not go as planned, causing the thieves to hijack a city bus to get away. This turns the movie into a shoot 'em up adventure. Obviously this is not our normal kind of movie, but we saw it because Vera has a crush on Jeffrey Dean Morgan due to his work in *The Good Wife* and in *Grey's Anatomy*. He was a complete unknown to me, but I could easily see his appeal.

"Your boyfriend, Jeffrey, is a cutie pie," I said as we enjoyed lunch at Mitchell's Fish Market after our movie. "He's right up there with Rick Springfield and Sam Elliott."

"If you could have one of them," she said, "which one would you take?"

"Which one would I take?" I repeated, a bit baffled by such a question. She nodded her head yes, so I played along. "I'll take Sam Elliott."

"With that scratchy mustache?" she said—with some distaste. "You want all that hair touching you?"

"Yuh!" I said. "I like facial hair."

"He'd look ten years younger if he shaved," she rebutted.

"But not as VI-RILE," I said, making both of those "I's" long vowels.

"There's a man with a big mustache over there. You want him too?" With a tic-like motion, she used her eyebrows to point at a man at a table nearby.

"Nope," I answered after sneaking a peak at the man. "Great mustache, but the rest is not so fine."

"So which man here do you want?" she asked.

"You go first," I said.

"I'll take that one over there by himself. He's not working on a laptop or playing with his phone. He's just sitting there calmly. He's the kind of guy who would have time to talk with me. Your turn."

"What is the point of this?" I asked.

"No stalling, just take your turn."

"Okay, I'll take that one to my left," I said, using the same eyebrow maneuver to point him out. "The one who is talking so animatedly as his friends smile and listen."

"You're going for the extrovert? That doesn't make sense. You're a quiet person. Maybe you better rethink that."

"You're right, you're right, you're right," I agreed. "I am often attracted to extroverts, but over time I get crazed being with them. It's like that Sixties song, 'You Talk Too Much.'"

"So then pick one of his listeners," she suggested.

"Okay! Good plan! Thanks for the tip! I'll go with the one with the green tie. It's my favorite color, plus he's kinda cute."

"Good choice, she said. "And good job of looking around, which by the way, is the point. It's time for you to start doing that again. Here in Ohio. Not overseas."

"Ah, now I get it," I replied. "But here's what I have been thinking… I spent the first twenty-one years of my life with my mom and dad, the next twenty-one years in my marriage, and the next twenty-one years in relationships with Jimmy Jet and Big Irv. With age sixty-four coming down the pike, maybe these next twenty-one years are for me to be on my own."

Vera looked at me like I had squirted too much lemon in her iced tea, and then she responded, "Maybe you better rethink that one too."

I smiled at my dear friend as '60s on 6 began to play in my head, "I Get by With a Little Help from My Friends." What would I do without her?

<u>Friday, November 20, 2015</u>

Dear Diary,
How odd is this?
There are only two pages left in this journal and I went from
"Nothing But Heartaches"
to
"Dancing in the Street"
in the space of its 300+ pages.
"God Only Knows"
how I pulled off such a feat, but it's wonderful to
"Let the Sunshine In"
and to realize anew
"What a Wonderful World"
it is. Clearly I could go on and on in this vein,
but I want to save the last page of this journal
to draft a final letter to that guy who helped
"Light My Fire."
I hope he will be happy to know
"I Feel Good!"

This Viewer's Choice Award is given to the phenomenal Bill Nighy
on November 20, 2015.
It is for your many outstanding portrayals
such as these very favorite roles:

1. Lawrence Montague in *The Girl in the Café*
2. Billy Mack in *Love Actually*
3. Gideon Warner in *Gideon's Daughter*

But the most significant roles played—
at least in the view of this fan—
were the roles of crush and crutch
through a difficult time in my life.
Yea, though I walked through the valley of the shadow of death
your films and your interviews comforted me.

Simply put: Your work has been important in my life
and I thank you.

Very fondly yours,
Lorie Kleiner Eckert

P.S. Happy upcoming birthday!
Merry Christmas!
Happy and healthy New Year!
Happy life!
Over and out…LKE.

www.ingramcontent.com/pod-product-compliance
Lightning Source LLC
Chambersburg PA
CBHW070327090426
42733CB00012B/2390